Also by David Roberts

A Newer World: Kit Carson, John C. Frémont, and the Claiming of the American West

The Lost Explorer: Finding Mallory on Mount Everest *(with Conrad Anker)*

Escape Routes: Further Adventure Writings of David Roberts

In Search of the Old Ones: Exploring the Anasazi World of the Southwest

Once They Moved Like the Wind: Cochise, Geronimo, and the Apache Wars

Mt. McKinley: The Conquest of Denali *(with Bradford Washburn)*

Iceland: Land of the Sagas *(with Jon Krakauer)*

Jean Stafford: A Biography

Moments of Doubt: And Other Mountaineering Writings

Great Exploration Hoaxes

Deborah: A Wilderness Narrative

The Mountain of My Fear

TRUE SUMMIT

*What Really Happened
on the Legendary Ascent
of Annapurna*

DAVID ROBERTS

*A Touchstone Book
Published by Simon & Schuster
New York   London   Toronto   Sydney   Singapore*

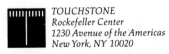 TOUCHSTONE
Rockefeller Center
1230 Avenue of the Americas
New York, NY 10020

First Touchstone Edition 2002
TOUCHSTONE and colophon are
registered trademarks of Simon & Schuster, Inc.
For information about special discounts for bulk purchases,
please contact Simon & Schuster Special Sales:
1-800-456-6798 or business@simonandschuster.com
Designed by Edith Fowler
Map by Jeffrey L. Ward
Manufactured in the United States of America

10 9 8 7 6 5 4 3 2 1

The Library of Congress has cataloged the Simon & Schuster edition as follows:

Roberts, David, date.
  True summit : what really happened on the
legendary ascent of Annapurna / David Roberts.
      p.   cm.
  Includes index.
  1. Mountaineering—Nepal—Annapurna.
  2. Annapurna (Nepal)—Description and travel.
  3. Herzog, Maurice, 1919– 4. Lachenal, Louis,
  1921–1955.   5. Mountaineers—France—
Biography.   I. Title.
  GV199.44.N462 A5664 2000
  796.52'2'095496—dc21   00-027140
  ISBN 0-684-86757-5
      0-7432-0327-5 (Pbk)

PHOTO CREDITS
Galen Rowell/Mountain Light: p. 13
Dauphiné Libéré: p. 28
Collection Rébuffat: pp. 45, 70, 135, 192
Collection Ecole Nationale de Ski et d'Alpinisme:
    pp. 95, 158
Collection Lachenal: pp. 119, 212

In memory of
Gaston Rébuffat
Lionel Terray
Louis Lachenal

Contents

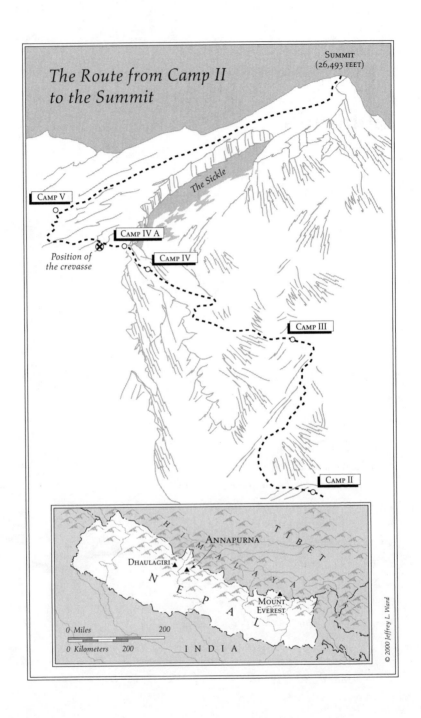

The Route from Camp II
to the Summit

SUMMIT
(26,493 FEET)

The Sickle

CAMP V

CAMP IV A

Position of
the crevasse

CAMP IV

CAMP III

CAMP II

HIMALAYA

ANNAPURNA

TIBET

DHAULAGIRI

N E P A L

MOUNT
EVEREST

0 Miles   200

0 Kilometers   200

I N D I A

© 2000 Jeffrey L. Ward

True Summit

ONE

June 3

IN THE FIRST LIGHT OF DAWN, at 6:00 A.M., the two men left their tent at 24,600 feet and headed up the broad, glaciated slope, their crampons biting crisply into the hard snow underfoot. The summit of Annapurna gleamed in the morning sun, only 1,900 feet above them. The wind that had raged all night had died with the dawn, leaving a piercing cold to rule the stillness.

For Louis Lachenal, a brilliant, impetuous mountaineer of twenty-eight, and Maurice Herzog, three years older and the expedition leader, it had required a long struggle that morning simply to jam their feet into frozen boots. Herzog had managed to lace up the gaiters that covered his ankles, but Lachenal had given up trying to fasten his. Neither man had slept a minute through the terrible night, as the gale threatened to rip the tent from the pitons and ice axes that anchored it to the 40 degree slope and send the men hurtling down the mountain. Through long hours in the darkness, they had clung to the tent poles, in Herzog's words, "as a drowning man clings to a plank," just to keep the fragile shelter from being torn apart by the wind.

The evening before, Herzog and Lachenal had brewed a few cups of tea for dinner, but they had been too nauseated by the altitude to eat. In the morning, even making tea proved too arduous a task. At the last minute, Herzog stuffed a tube of condensed milk, some nougat, and a spare pair of socks into his pack.

It was June 3, 1950, and the monsoon would arrive any day, smothering the high Himalaya in a seamless blanket of mist and falling snow, prohibiting human trespass. For the past two months, the French expedition had wandered up one valley after another, simply trying to find Annapurna. The maps were all wrong because no Westerners had ever before approached the slopes of the tenth-highest mountain in the world.

At last, in late May, with less than two weeks left before the monsoon, the team had discovered the deep gorge formed by the torrential current of the Miristi Khola. Having breached its defenses, they had emerged beneath the north face of Annapurna. Racing up glacier-hung corridors, menaced at every hand by massive avalanches that thundered over the cliffs, the team placed four camps in a leftward crescent that followed a cunning line up the mountain. On June 2, Lachenal and Herzog, aided by Sherpas Ang-Tharkey and Sarki, slipped through a notch in the ice cliff the team had named the Sickle and crossed a steep, dangerous slope to pitch Camp V beside a broken rock band. Herzog offered a place in the summit team to Ang-Tharkey, the sirdar or head Sherpa, but the man, frightened by the cold that had already numbed his feet, declined. The two Sherpas headed back to Camp IVA, leaving Lachenal and Herzog to their windy ordeal.

Now the two men clumped slowly up the interminable slope,

shrouded in silence. Wrote Herzog later, "Each of us lived in a closed and private world of his own. I was suspicious of my mental processes; my mind was working very slowly and I was perfectly aware of the low state of my intelligence."

It did not take long for both men's feet to go numb. Abruptly Lachenal halted, took off a boot, and tried to rub his stockinged foot back into feeling. "I don't want to be like Lambert," he muttered. The great Swiss climber Raymond Lambert—a friend of Lachenal's—had lost all the toes on both feet to frostbite after being trapped in winter on a traverse of the Aiguilles du Diable, near Chamonix, France.

The climbers emerged from the mountain's shadow into the sunlight, yet the iron cold persisted. Again Lachenal stopped to take off a boot. "I can't feel anything," he groaned. "I think I'm beginning to get frostbite."

Herzog too was worried about his feet, but he convinced himself that wriggling his toes as he walked would ward off frostbite. "I could not feel them," he would write, "but that was nothing new in the mountains."

The men marched on, at a pitifully slow pace. Herzog's dreamy isolation reclaimed him: "Lachenal appeared to me as a sort of specter—he was alone in his world, I in mine."

Suddenly Lachenal grabbed his companion. "If I go back, what will you do?" he blurted out.

Unbidden, images of the party's two months of struggle flashed through Herzog's mind: lowland trudges in the jungle heat, fierce rock-and-ice pitches climbed, loads painfully hauled to higher camps. "Must we give up?" he asked himself. "Impossible! My whole being revolted against the idea. I had made up my mind, irrevocably. Today we were consecrating an ideal, and no sacrifice was too great."

To Lachenal, he said, "I should go on by myself."

Without hesitating, Lachenal responded, "Then I'll follow you."

Herzog lapsed back into his private trance. "An astonishing happiness welled up in me, but I could not define it," he would later write. "Everything was so new, so utterly unprecedented. . . . We were braving an interdict, overstepping a boundary, and yet we had no fear as we continued upward."

THERE ARE FOURTEEN MOUNTAINS in the world higher than 8,000 meters (about 26,240 feet)—all of them in the Himalaya. The first attempt to climb one came in 1895, when Alfred Mummery, the finest British climber of his day, attacked Nanga Parbat. Radically underestimating the size and difficulty of the mountain, Mummery and two Gurkha porters vanished during a reconnaissance of the west face. Their bodies were never found.

By 1950, twenty-two different expeditions had tackled various 8,000-meter peaks, yet not one had succeeded. The boldest efforts during the 1920s and 1930s, on Everest, K2, Kanchenjunga, and Nanga Parbat, had been launched by British, American, and German teams. Although France counted among its climbers some of the leading alpinists of those decades, the country had made no great showing in the Himalaya, with only a single expedition to Gasherbrum I to its credit. For fourteen years, the highest summit reached anywhere in the world had remained that of 25,645-foot Nanda Devi in India, climbed by an Anglo-American team in 1936. The Second World War had interrupted the Himalayan campaigns, and it was not until 1949 that Europeans again turned their attention toward the highest mountains in the world.

Despite the fact that only one member—cinematographer Marcel Ichac, a veteran of Gasherbrum I—had ever been to the Himalaya before, the 1950 Annapurna expedition comprised as strong a party as had ever been put in the field in Asia. Herzog himself was an accomplished mountaineer, with a number of daring climbs in the Alps under his belt. The two junior members, Marcel Schatz and Jean Couzy, showed great promise (Couzy would go on to rack up a roster of first ascents equaled by only a handful of his contemporaries).

But the heart of the Annapurna expedition—its core of competence so assured as to verge on genius—lay in Lachenal and his two fellow Chamonix guides, Lionel Terray and Gaston Rébuffat.

Throughout the 1940s, even during wartime, these men had pulled off one blazing ascent in the Alps after another. By 1950, they were unquestionably the three finest mountaineers in France, rivaled in the rest of the world only by a handful of German, Italian, and Austrian peers (no American or Briton was even in their league).

Yet through most of April and May 1950, as the team wandered aimlessly trying to sort out the topography and find its way toward 26,493-foot Annapurna, the expedition threatened to collapse into utter fiasco. With the solving of the Miristi Khola, all the expertise embodied in the team's six principal climbers came to the fore. The choice of which pair would make the summit bid had seemed to depend as much as anything on the luck of who happened to reach the right camp on the right day. That luck put Lachenal and Herzog in Camp V on the morning of June 3.

Now, well above 25,000 feet, sometime after noon, the pair traversed toward the right beneath a final rock band that blocked the way to the summit. Suddenly Herzog pointed, uttering a single word: "Couloir!"

"What luck!" rejoined Lachenal. In front of the men, a steep snow gully angled up through the rock band.

"Let's go, then!" Herzog urged, and Lachenal signaled agreement. "I had lost all track of time," Herzog later recalled. Facing the couloir, he felt a moment of doubt: "Should we have enough strength left to overcome this final obstacle?" Kicking steps in the hard snow, their crampon points biting well, the men trudged upward.

Herzog later described those climactic moments:

> A slight detour to the left, a few more steps—the summit ridge came gradually nearer—a few rocks to avoid. We dragged ourselves up. Could we possibly be there? . . .
> Yes! A fierce and savage wind tore at us.
> We were on top of Annapurna! 8,075 meters. . . .
> Our hearts overflowed with an unspeakable happiness.
> "If only the others could know . . ."
> If only everyone could know!

As he stood on the summit, Herzog was awash in a mystical ecstasy:

> How wonderful life would now become! What an inconceivable experience it is to attain one's ideal and, at the very same moment, to fulfill oneself. I was stirred to the depths of my being. Never had I felt such happiness like this—so intense and yet so pure.

Lachenal, however, was in an entirely different state of mind. He shook Herzog, pleading, "Well, what about going down?"

His companion's impatience puzzled Herzog. "Did he simply think he had finished another climb, as in the Alps?" he wondered. "Did he think one could just go down again like that, with nothing more to it?"

"One minute," Herzog spoke, "I must take some photographs."

"Hurry up!"

Herzog fumbled through his pack, retrieving his camera and several flags. For long minutes, he posed with one pennant after another attached to his ice axe, as Lachenal snapped photos. Then Herzog changed from black-and-white to color film.

Lachenal exploded: "Are you mad? We haven't a minute to lose: we must go down at once."

Vaguely, Herzog sensed that his friend was right. Glancing at the horizon, he saw that the perfect day had deteriorated. A storm was moving in—perhaps the leading edge of the monsoon itself. Yet Herzog stood there, unwilling to let go of his transcendent moment, lost in a whirl of emotions and memories.

"We must go down!" Lachenal cried once more, then hoisted his pack and started off. Still Herzog lingered, drinking a bit of condensed milk, taking a reading with his altimeter. At last he put on his own pack and followed Lachenal.

Of all the qualities that had made Lachenal such a matchless climber, it was his speed on difficult terrain that was paramount. Now Herzog watched his friend dash down the couloir, then hurry along the traverse beneath the rock band. Stumping downward far more carefully, Herzog saw the gap between him and Lachenal grow.

At the base of the rock band, Herzog stopped to catch his breath. He took off his pack and opened it, then could not remember what he was about to do. Suddenly he cried out, "My gloves!"

To open his pack, Herzog had laid his gloves on the snow. As he watched, dumbfounded, they slid, then rolled toward the void below. "The movement of those gloves was engraved in my sight," he later wrote, "as something irredeemable, against which I was powerless. The consequences might be most serious. What was I to do?"

Thus the first conquest of an 8,000-meter peak began to take its toll on the victors. In his trance, Herzog forgot all about the spare pair of socks in his pack, which he could have used as gloves: instead, he descended barehanded. The two men regained Camp V only just before dark, in the middle an all-out storm that severely reduced their visibility. Lachenal had slipped and fallen past the tent before scrambling back up to the shelter. Left to their own devices, Herzog and Lachenal would probably have perished there. But during the day, Rébuffat and Terray had climbed to Camp V, hoping for their own summit push on the morrow. As Terray seized Herzog's hands to wring them in congratulation, he was struck with horror. "Maurice—your hands!" he cried out.

"There was an uneasy silence," Herzog later recalled. "I had forgotten that I had lost my gloves: my fingers were violet and white and hard as wood. The other two stared at them in dismay."

Forgoing their own chance for the summit, Terray and Rébuffat stayed up all night brewing hot drinks for their comrades and whipping Lachenal's bare toes and Herzog's toes and fingers with rope ends, in an effort to restore circulation. (Because of the damage it does to frozen tissue and cells, the treatment is now known to cause more harm than help.)

The next day, as the storm increased its fury, the four men staggered down toward Camp IVA, just above the ice cliff of the

Sickle. But in the lashing whiteout they lost their way. With dusk approaching, carrying no tent and but one sleeping bag among the four of them, the men circled helplessly looking for a familiar landmark. A night without shelter would undoubtedly prove fatal.

Then Lachenal broke through a snow bridge and plunged into a hidden crevasse. The mishap turned into salvation. Unhurt, Lachenal called out to the others to join him. The snow ledge at the bottom of the crevasse would serve for an emergency bivouac.

Huddled together for warmth, shivering against the snow that relentlessly filtered into their clothes, rubbing each other's feet to ward off further frostbite, the four men spent as miserable a night as mountaineers have ever endured in the Himalaya. After two nights in a row without sleep, Herzog and Lachenal had neared the end of their endurance. In the morning, Rébuffat was the first to poke his head out of the crevasse. Terray anxiously inquired about the weather. "Can't see a thing," Rébuffat answered. "It's blowing hard."

But after Lachenal thrashed his way to the surface, in Herzog's words, "he began to run like a madman, shrieking, 'It's fine, it's fine!' " The day before, trying to find the route down, Terray and Rébuffat had removed their goggles. Despite the storm that smothered them, at an altitude above 24,000 feet the sun's ultraviolet rays had penetrated the murk and left the two men snow-blind. Rébuffat had mistaken the gray smear of his blindness for a ceaseless storm.

The weather was windy but clear. Yet now the four men faced a cruel fate: the blind could not lead the lame down the mountain. Pitifully, Lachenal began to cry out for help. The others joined in. And then they heard an answering call. It was Marcel Schatz, who had come out from Camp IVA to look for the companions he feared he would never see again. As Schatz clasped Herzog in his arms, he murmured, "It is wonderful—what you have done."

Though the men were saved, the rest of the descent unfolded as a grim ordeal. At one point, Herzog and two Sherpas were swept 500 feet by an avalanche and partially buried. As the survivors approached Base Camp, even Terray—the sahib whose strength had made him a legend among the porters—had to be helped down the mountain like a baby, his arms around the shoulders of a pair of Sherpas who held him up and guided his steps.

Herzog and Lachenal could no longer walk. During the next month, a succession of Sherpas and porters carried the men through mile after mile of lowland ravine and forest. Jacques Oudot, the expedition doctor, gave them agonizing daily abdominal injections of novocaine in the femoral and brachial arteries. It was thought at the time that the drug could dilate the arteries and, by improving the flow of blood, forestall the ravages of frostbite; today, the procedure is known to be worthless. As their digits turned gangrenous, Oudot resorted to amputations in the field. Eventually Lachenal lost all his toes, Herzog all his toes and fingers.

The team members arrived at Orly airport in Paris on July 17, where a huge crowd hailed them as heroes. *Paris-Match*, which owned exclusive periodical rights to the story, rushed into print a special issue, with a cover photo of Herzog hoisting the Tricolor on the summit, that broke all the magazine's sales records.

As he recuperated in the American hospital at Neuilly, Herzog, who had never before written a book, dictated his account of the expedition. Published the next year by Arthaud as *Annapurna: Premier 8,000*, the book at once became a classic. The story Herzog had brought back from the mountain was a stirring saga of teamwork, self-sacrifice, and—in the two-week push to the summit—brilliant mountaineering against long odds. The descent and retreat from Annapurna figured as a tragic yet heroic coda, which Herzog narrated in a peroration saluting the highest ideals of loyalty and courage.

What moved readers beyond all else in *Annapurna*, however, was the transcendental optimism of the book. The euphoric trance that had seized Herzog on the summit persisted through all his convalescent tribulations. With only stumps left where he had once had fingers, for the rest of his life Herzog would find the simplest tasks—tying his shoelaces, buttoning his shirt—almost beyond him. Yet not a trace of bitterness or self-pity emerged in the pages of his book.

Quite the opposite. In the foreword, he wrote of his ordeal: was saved and had won my freedom. This freedom, which I shall never lose, has given me the assurance and serenity of a man who has fulfilled himself. . . . A new and splendid life has opened out before me." Of his brave teammates, he wrote, "My fervent wish is that the nine of us who were united in face of death should remain fraternally united through life." And in the book's last pages: "Annapurna, to which we had gone emptyhanded, was a treasure on which we should live the rest of our days."

The book closes with a line as resounding and memorable as any in the literature of adventure: "There are other Annapurnas in the lives of men."

Fifty years later, *Annapurna* remains one of the canonic works in exploration literature. Published in forty languages, it has sold more than 11 million copies, making it the best-selling mountaineering book of all time. Though he would never again do any serious climbing, Herzog went on to become mayor of Chamonix and Minister of Youth and Sport under Charles de Gaulle. Today, at age eighty-one, he is the only surviving climber from Annapurna 1950 (the liaison officer, Francis de Noyelle, who never got above Camp II, also survives). In France, Herzog remains a household name, one of the country's eternal heroes of sport and exploration, in a league with the late Jacques Cousteau or Jean-Claude Killy. In contrast, as one mountaineering journalist estimates, only about five to seven percent of the French public has ever heard of Rébuffat, Terray, or Lachenal.

As for Herzog, the sense that despite—even because of—his personal tragedy, a marvelous new life had thereby opened to him seems to have tided him well into old age. In 1998, he published a memoir called *L'Autre Annapurna* (*The Other Annapurna*). In its opening pages, Herzog declared that nearly half a century after his "rebirth," the sense of having discovered a new life still infused him with an "indescribable happiness." He considered it his duty to share that revelation with his readers.

FOR THIS READER, growing up in Boulder, Colorado, in the late 1950s, *Annapurna* came as a stunning revelation. Since the age of thirteen or fourteen, I had checked out of the public library a number of classic Himalayan expedition narratives—Paul Bauer on Nanga Parbat, Sir John Hunt on Everest, and the like—and devoured their sagas of brave men at altitude. But mountaineering books were for me a kind of escape literature, not unlike the Hardy Boys mystery novels or Albert Payson Terhune's fables of faithful collies, such as *Lad* and *Lassie*. It never occurred to me, reading about Nanga Parbat or K2, that I might some day go on a mountaineering expedition myself.

Annapurna hit me hard. By the time I read the book, at age sixteen, I had started hiking up some of the inimitable "talus piles" of the Colorado Rockies—shapeless lumps of scree and tundra strung along the Continental Divide, peaks such as Audubon, James, Grays, and Torreys. It took stamina to push on at 14,000 feet, and judgment to descend in the face of a July lightning storm, but I knew that what I was doing was a far cry from real mountaineering. Staring at a true precipice, such as the 2,000-foot-high east face of Longs Peak, I felt an ambivalent longing: surely it took the competence and arrogance of the gods to inch one's way, armed with ropes and pitons, up such dark landscapes of terror.

Annapurna ratcheted that uncertain longing into full-blown desire. When I put down the book—swallowed in one sitting, as I recall—I wanted more than anything else in the world to become a mountaineer.

Over the decades, Herzog's narrative has had precisely that effect on an inordinate number of adolescents of both sexes. It might seem curious that a tale fraught with near-death, with fearful trials by storm and cold, and finally with gruesome amputations of fingers and toes turned black and rotting, should encourage any reader to take up the perilous business of climbing. Yet so exalting were the ideals that Herzog lyrically sang—loyalty, teamwork, courage, and perseverance—that rational apprehension was drowned in a tide of admiration. Those Frenchmen—Herzog, Lachenal, Terray, and Rébuffat—*were* gods, or at least mythic heroes.

So I became a mountaineer, and then a writer about mountaineering. In 1980, having survived thirteen Alaskan expeditions of my own, I wrote an article for the Sierra Club's semiannual journal *Ascent,* called "Slouching Toward Everest," that tried to identify the finest mountaineering expedition books yet written, giving readers a taste of each. Summing up my roster of twenty-one classics, I concluded that *Annapurna* was the best of them all.

A decade and a half later, in February 1996, I met Michel Guérin for dinner in the French ski town of Morzine. A specialty publisher of mountaineering books based in Chamonix, Guérin and I had struck up an epistolary friendship based on many a mutual enthusiasm in the climbing world.

Our long evening's conversation took place mostly in French, for while Michel proved to be an elegant conversationalist in his native tongue, his spoken English tended to emerge in gnostic bursts of decidedly unidiomatic phraseology. Over our second Armagnac, the talk turned to *Annapurna.* Michel reminded me of my paramount ranking of Herzog's book in "Slouching Toward Everest," which he had recently read.

I nodded and said, "Don't you agree?"

It took a long moment for a wry smile to form around his cigarette; then he shook his head.

"Why not?"

I listened to the careful disquisition that spilled from Michel's lips, first in shock, then in dismay. It is a hard thing to have one's hero of forty years' standing dismantled before one's eyes.

The essence of what Michel told me was as follows. *Annapurna* was nothing more than a gilded myth, one man's romantic idealization of the campaign that had claimed the first 8,000-meter peak. What had really happened in 1950 was far darker, more complex, more nebulous than anything Herzog had written. I found myself resisting Michel's strictures: historical revisionism is an all too faddish trend of the day, especially in France.

Michel persisted. Before they had left France, the members of the expedition had been required to sign an oath of unquestioning obedience to their leader. This was not news to me, for Herzog had mentioned that pledge in his book, even recording the somewhat timid acquiescence of his teammates: "My colleagues stood up, feeling both awkward and impressed. What were they supposed to do?"

What I didn't know before that evening in Morzine was that, along with the oath of obedience, the team members had been required to sign a contract forbidding them to publish anything about the expedition for five years after their return to France. During those first five years, by prearrangement, the only version of the Annapurna story that might emerge would be Herzog's.

As soon as the moratorium expired, Lachenal had made plans to publish an autobiographical memoir, to be called *Carnets du Vertige* (*Notebooks of the Vertiginous*). The book had come out in 1956. Years ago, I had found a copy in a used book store in the States. (*Carnets* has never been translated into English.) The last quarter of the book consists of Lachenal's diary from Annapurna. As I read it, I perceived no real discrepancy between his account and Herzog's, except that Lachenal was a far more laconic, down-to-earth narrator than his vision-haunted leader.

Now Michel told me that, just as *Carnets* was going to press, Lachenal had been killed when he skied into a crevasse on the Vallée Blanche above Chamonix. I knew all about that too-early death of one of my Annapurna heroes, but nothing about what its timing signified. As soon as Lachenal had died, Herzog had taken charge of the manuscript and turned it over to his brother, Gérard, for editing. In the process, both Maurice Herzog and Lucien Devies—the president of the Club Alpin Français and the man who had devised and administered the oath of obedience to the Annapurna team—carefully combed the text. Among the three of them, they pruned Lachenal's account of every scrap of critical, sardonic, or embittered commentary the guide had penned. The published *Carnets du Vertige* was a sanitized, expurgated whitewash.

In Chamonix, Michel had befriended Lachenal's son, Jean-Claude, who for decades had held the original manuscript that his father had written. Though furious at Herzog's intercession, Jean-Claude was deeply torn in his feelings, for on Lachenal's death, Herzog had assumed the role of *tuteur* to the bereaved family—an official post mandated by French law. The same man who betrayed his father's truth took Jean-Claude and his brother on many a childhood forest walk and supervised their rocky passage through a series of schools.

After years of friendship and discussion, Michel had persuaded Jean-Claude to let him publish an unexpurgated version of the *Carnets*. The book would be out in a few months; already it was causing a stir in mountaineering circles. At the same time, journalist Yves Ballu was about to publish the first biography of Rébuffat, to be called *Gaston Rébuffat: Une Vie pour la Montagne* (*Gaston Rébuffat: A Life for the Mountains*). Ballu had received the full cooperation of Rébuffat's widow, Françoise, who had enjoined her husband not to write about Annapurna in his lifetime. In particular, Ballu would benefit from Gaston's long and acerbic letters to Françoise from the expedition, and from private notes and marginal commentaries he had jotted down in subsequent years.

The upshot of Rébuffat's and Lachenal's uncensored commentaries, Michel told me, was to paint an utterly different picture of the 1950 expedition from Herzog's. According to Lachenal and Rébuffat, the team had been frequently and rancorously divided; Herzog's leadership had been capricious and at times inept; and the whole summit effort and desperate retreat lay shrouded in a central mystery.

Herzog himself, now the father figure of French mountaineering, was about to undergo a scrutiny that would deeply trouble his old age. The grand fête of French celebration, so long anticipated, on June 3, 2000—the fiftieth anniversary of the summit—might turn instead into an *agon* of reappraisal. As the only survivor among the six principal climbers, Herzog would have every chance to get in the last word. But would his most eloquent protestations silence the posthumous oracles of Rébuffat and Lachenal?

Among the cognoscenti of French mountaineering, Michel told me, there had long been murmurs and doubts about Annapurna; but few if any of these hints had leaked abroad. Certainly before this evening I had never heard a gainsaying word about Herzog's *Annapurna*.

Listening late into the night to Michel's disquisition, I felt my shock and dismay transmute into something else. The true history of Annapurna, though far more murky and disturbing than Herzog's golden fable, might in the long run prove to be an even more interesting tale—one fraught with moral complexity, with fundamental questions about the role of "sport" in national culture, perhaps even with deep veins of heroism quite different from those Herzog had celebrated.

The revelations from the grave of Lachenal and Rébuffat, Michel suggested, might be only the tip of the iceberg. What really happened on Annapurna 1950—and everything that issued from that cardinal triumph of mountaineering—was a story that had never been told. As a narrative, it promised to bear a closer kinship to Melville's *Billy Budd* than to the Hardy Boys. As we sat stirring our coffee in Morzine, I realized that Michel had led me to a story that, no matter how hard it might be to separate the "truth" from all the layers of ambiguity in which it lay cloaked, cried out for a chronicler to grasp and tell it whole.

TWO

Resistance

WHY WAS MAURICE HERZOG THE LEADER of the 1950 Annapurna expedition? His record of ascents in the Alps was strong, but not of the very highest rank. Among French alpinists a decade or more older than Herzog, two in particular—Pierre Allain, the driving force on the first ascent of the stern north face of the Petit Dru, and the superb Chamonix guide Armand Charlet—might have seemed more qualified for leadership. Among Herzog's contemporaries, Lachenal, Terray, and Rébuffat had all made more and bolder climbs.

The reasons for the choice of Herzog as leader were several, the consequences far-reaching. By 1950, there was already an established tradition of heading up Himalayan expeditions with men whose expertise at overland travel or whose proven record of commanding others outstripped their abilities as technical climbers. In 1924, for instance, George Leigh Mallory was the sole man who had twice before attempted Everest and he was unquestionably Britain's finest mountaineer. Yet Mallory was passed over for leadership of the fateful 1924 expedition, on which, with his young partner Andrew Irvine, he would vanish into the clouds above 28,000 feet. Instead, fifty-eight-year-old General Charles Bruce, whose main qualifications were an extensive knowledge of India and long service in the army, was put in charge. Even after a malarial attack forced Bruce to abandon the expedition, another climber, Colonel E. F. Norton, was designated leader ahead of Mallory.

The choice of leader for a Himalayan expedition was usually made by some national advisory body of senior mountaineers and explorers. In Britain, that group was the Mount Everest Committee, an ad hoc assemblage recruited chiefly from the ranks of the Alpine Club. In France, the body was the Comité de l'Himalaya (or Himalayan Committee) of the Club Alpin Français (CAF), dominated by the autocratic Lucien Devies.

The rationale behind choosing a leader such as General Bruce was that logistical acumen and tactical judgment were more vital to the role than climbing ability. In addition, it was tacitly understood that a less-talented mountaineer might more readily submerge his own ambition and choose the strongest pair of teammates for the summit attempt. Herzog, however, had less experience at logistics, less mountaineering judgment than men such as Terray and Rébuffat; and on Annapurna, Herzog would prove every bit as ambitious to reach the summit as his comrades.

Another factor at play in the Annapurna expedition—all but obsolete today, but powerfully felt from the origins of mountaineering in the Alps in the 1780s all the way through 1950—was the distinction between guides and amateurs. The guide was a professional, born in the mountains where he earned his living, steeped in the nuances of weather and snow conditions. The amateur was a man who lived elsewhere, who climbed for pleasure and passion in his spare time. Even though amateurs such as Edward Whymper on the Matterhorn or Alfred Mummery on the Grépon had spearheaded the finest climbs performed in the second half of the nineteenth century, they routinely climbed with guides. Well into the twentieth century, many pundits considered it scandalous and irresponsible to undertake "guideless" climbs.

At the heart of this distinction lay a class bias. Guides were hired hands, technicians of rock and ice, closer in status to rural artisans than to the urbane milieu of the gentleman alpinist. It would never do, then, to entrust the leadership of a Himalayan expedition to a guide. Terray, Rébuffat, and Lachenal were guides. Herzog was a Parisian (born in Lyon), an executive in Kléber-Colombes, a tire manufacturing company: in short, everything that a mountaineering amateur ought to be.

Finally, and most importantly, Herzog was Devies's good friend. Both men were staunch Gaullists. Terray and Rébuffat had served as soldiers during World War II, but Herzog had been a captain, commanding a battalion of volunteers against the Nazis in several heroic campaigns. Of such stuff, the Himalayan Committee concluded, leaders were made.

This class bias is overt in the preface Devies contributed to *Annapurna:* there he characterizes the redoubtable Terray and Lachenal as "locomotives," as if all one had to do on the mountain was fire up their boilers and set them in motion. In contrast, Herzog is a saint of conquest: "Spending himself to the limit, reserving for himself the hardest tasks, deriving his authority from the example he set, always in the vanguard, he made victory possible."

With Devies pulling the strings offstage and Herzog in charge of the expedition, Annapurna was conceived as a grand nationalistic effort. Devies, one of the foremost French climbers of the 1930s, was highly sensitive to the prevailing notion that France had done next to nothing in the Himalaya. And in 1950, the whole country still lay mired in the humiliation of World War II—a once-proud nation conquered so easily by the Third Reich, liberated not so much by the Résistance as by the Allies.

Even before the war, in 1939, Devies had written an essay called "Alpinisme et Nationalités." A bizarre mélange of chauvinism and defensiveness, the piece makes for fascinating reading in the light of Annapurna. At the time Devies wrote, the two "last prizes" of the Alps had recently been plucked, with the first ascents of the Walker Spur on the Grandes Jorasses and of the north face of the Eiger, both in 1938. The former had fallen to a strong team of Italians led by the visionary Lecco cragsman Ricardo Cassin; the latter to a pair of Germans and a pair of Austrians (including Heinrich Harrer, later the author of *Seven Years in Tibet*) who had met by chance low on the wall and joined forces.

In his essay, Devies is aggrieved that these formidable walls had fallen to foreigners, for, he insists, "Today in France there are certainly climbers of the same quality as the best Germans and Italians"—adding parenthetically, "(I count the Austrians as Germans)." He enumerates the usual excuses for his countrymen: bereft, for instance, of playgrounds such as the Dolomites in which to learn their craft, the French lagged behind their rivals in the mechanics of aid-climbing with pitons. With war clouds gathering, Devies notes disdainfully that Hitler had publicly congratulated the Eiger foursome, Mussolini the victors on the Walker Spur.

Devies's polemic ends with a clarion call to French mountaineers to match the deeds of those foreigners, who would, within the year, become their literal enemies in war. Throughout his essay he contrasts French and German cultural attitudes, arguing, for example that the French have the disadvantage of being slightly more cautious "because we do not attach any mystical value to death." Instead, the best Gallic climbers, in contrast with their German and Italian peers, have "a much purer experience" in the mountains. "Their deeds are freer and more individual, they earn instead a truth that is personal and human."

Rhetoric of this sort had everything to do with the conception of the Annapurna expedition. On March 28, 1950, just before departing for Nepal, the chosen team members met with the Himalayan Committee in the offices of the Club Alpin Français in Paris. Devies gave the team a stirring pep talk, outlining the history of Himalayan exploration, reminding the men of their objectives. In *Annapurna*, Herzog quotes Devies's speech at length, then observes the "solemn air" in the "dull and dreary office in which we were meeting." All nine of the expeditioneers "devoutly longed to go to the Himalaya, which we had talked about for so many years. Lachenal put it in a nutshell: 'We'd go if we had to crawl there.' "

Then Devies abruptly announced that each member must take an oath of obedience, which he recited: "I swear upon my honor to obey the leader in everything regarding the Expedition in which he may command me." A silence followed. Comments Herzog, "Mountaineers don't care much for ceremonies."

At last Marcel Ichac, the cinematographer and sole veteran of the 1936 Gasherbrum I expedition, recited the pledge, with Terray softly murmuring in unison; then the others, one by one, pronounced the oath.

For Herzog, the ceremony was deeply moving:

> They were pledging their lives, possibly, and they knew it. They all put themselves completely in my hands. I should have liked to say a few words, but I just couldn't. . . . In that moment our team was born. It was for me to keep it alive.

Writing in 1996, Rébuffat's biographer, Yves Ballu, benefiting from Rébuffat's own notes on the occasion, put the evening's events in a very different perspective. Reading Herzog, one pictures the ceremony taking place in a small office, attended only by the Himalayan Committee and the team members. In fact, the first half of the event, featuring Devies's speech, was a press conference in the CAF's *grand salon*, with many journalists and officials present. Ballu underlines Devies's absolute tyranny over the French climbing scene: at the moment, he was simultaneously president of the CAF, president of the Fédération Française de la Montagne (FFM), and president of the Groupe de Haute Montagne (GHM). Sitting at his right hand was Herzog, secretary of the GHM.

Along with the stirring exhortations quoted by Herzog, Devies emphasized for the press that a colossal fund-raising effort bolstered by a national subscription campaign had raised 14 million francs ($350,000 in today's dollars) for the expedition. The implication became explicit: Annapurna was a campaign of national honor.

Later, in comparative privacy, Devies announced the oath of allegiance. The silence that greeted him owed less to the reticence of simple climbers, thought Rébuffat, than to sheer surprise. For Rébuffat himself, and apparently for Lachenal, the demand went beyond surprise: it was a shocking and distasteful requirement. Unquestioning obedience was not characteristic of the alpinism these two Chamonix guides had perfected over the last decade.

Against their own instincts, the men went ahead to recite the oath. They had no choice if they wanted to go to Annapurna. It was in this context—not in bland affirmation, as Herzog would have it—that Lachenal murmured (in literal translation), "On our knees, we would go!" At once Rébuffat chorused, "With joy in our hearts!"

That these two independent-minded mountaineers thus mocked the very oath they were forced to pledge emerges even more clearly in Rébuffat's notes. Rébuffat characterized Devies as a "*victoriste*" (a coinage of Rébuffat's own). Of the unpleasant charade culminating in the pledge of obedience, he jotted down: "Depersonalization. . . . A certain Nazification." In 1950, no epithet could have been more inflammatory. When Rébuffat's note was first published by Ballu, forty-six years later, the guide's sour judgment on the expedition style of Devies and Herzog reverberated throughout France.

GASTON RÉBUFFAT was born in Marseille on May 7, 1921, the son of a workaholic bank official and an overpossessive mother. No less likely background for a great mountaineer could perhaps have been imagined—although that domestic conventionality may itself have driven Gaston from the nest. From his earliest years, the boy was consumed with wanderlust. At every chance, he set out on promenades among the limestone sea cliffs near Marseille called the Calanques; and a visit when he was still very young to a cousin's farmhouse in Provence imbued him with a love of nature.

At a Catholic summer camp to which his parents sent him for the school holidays, Gaston discovered, in sports and organized hikes, the joys of comradeship. For the rest of his life, Rébuffat would sing the praises of the brotherhood of the rope as no mountaineer before him had ever done. Comradeship would center his life, and in 1950, on his greatest adventure, setting off for the Himalaya with his good friends Terray and Lachenal, he hoped to distill the elixir of shared toil and commitment.

Gaston grew up tall and lean, with a great bushy crown of dark hair brushed back from his forehead and a famously craggy face: all but concave, the jutting chin triangulating his features, the full eyebrows guarding his mountain squint, a cigarette (later a pipe) often clenched between his lips in mid-climb. On Annapurna, he was a full head taller than any of his teammates.

Not until he was fifteen, on a long hike out of Briançon, did the young wanderer discover the Mont Blanc massif. At sixteen, he quit school to take a menial job, joined the Haute-Provence section of the CAF, and befriended his first climbing partner, a modestly talented alpinist eight years his senior named Henry Moulin. With Moulin, he made his first ascents of real mountains. On top of his first major summit, during a traverse of the Ecrins, west of Briançon, he was transported. "What happiness!" he wrote later. "My dream realized. I'd done the Ecrins. Was it possible? . . . My first great summit. And now, may many others follow."

It was then, in late adolescence, that Gaston conceived as his ambition to become a member of the Compagnie des Guides de Chamonix, the most prestigious fraternity in mountaineering. That goal, as he knew, amounted to an all-but-impossible fantasy for a boy from the seashore.

The ancient village at the headwaters of the Arve, clinging to its narrow valley far beneath the soaring glaciers and aiguilles of the Mont Blanc massif, was, despite its role even in the 1930s as a world-renowned resort, one of the more xenophobic towns in France. Chamonix fiercely guarded its claim to have been the birthplace of mountaineering, from which the first ascent of Mont Blanc by Paccard and Balmat in 1786 had unfolded. The proudest office one could hold in the town was to be a mountain guide. Father passed down his expertise to son: certain families, such as the Simonds, the Charlets, the Ravanels, counted dozens of guides among their number. (In the Chamonix cemetery, the memorial to guides killed in the mountains names thirteen Simonds who lost their lives between 1866 and 1987.)

Only once before, in the case of Roger Frison-Roche (later to write the bestselling novel, *First on the Rope*), had the company of guides relaxed its vigilance and admitted an "outsider." The idea of a first-class mountaineer hailing from Marseille, however, would have seemed to most Chamoniards a rich joke.

Yet by 1940, at age nineteen, Rébuffat had indeed become a first-class climber. His hallmark was balance and grace on rock. He seemed to flow effortlessly up cliffs where others floundered; rather than seize a handhold in a death grip, he seemed to caress it with his fingertips.

By 1941, Gaston's record of climbs included a third ascent and a second ascent of two challenging routes in the western Alps. That year, as he pondered enlisting in the service of his country, he was instinctively drawn to a special division called Jeunesse et Montagne (Youth and Mountains). Since by now France had already been conquered and occupied by the Germans, all such service branches were officially civilian rather than military outfits. The rugged curriculum of the JM (as it was called)—eight months of spartan training in skiing and alpinism, with the aim of turning its graduates into instructors of other young men in the mountains— embodied a kind of French anticipation of the Outward Bound movement. JM aimed not so much at preparing men for mountain warfare as at building their characters, inculcating such virtues as manliness, industriousness, and team spirit. The service could not have been more appealing to the young Rébuffat.

On one of his first assignments, as he rode the train toward a regional climbing center, he met another partisan of the mountains, Lionel Terray, who was the same age. Gaston's first impressions were mixed. "He is nice," he wrote in his notebook, "but has an egotistical air. I spent the whole ride standing up: not for one second did he offer me his seat." Years later, Terray recorded his own first take on Rébuffat: "His narrow features were animated by two small, black, piercing eyes, and his somewhat formal manners and learned turn of phrase contrasted comically with a noticeable Marseille accent."

As soon as the two twenty-year-olds realized that they shared a consuming passion for hard routes on big mountains, a bond was formed. According to Terray, they spent the whole train ride comparing notes and talking of alpine projects. Soon they were climbing together, licensed by the JM to set off on little-traveled ridges and walls as partial fulfillment of their official duties.

With Terray in 1942, Rébuffat achieved his first new route, on the Aiguille Purtscheller. Later that year, the two men pushed a brave new line up the northeast face of the Col du Caïman, which Terray would call "my first really great climb." The somewhat obscure but very dangerous route angled up not to a summit but to a saddle between two peaks. By now the pair had agreed that Terray would lead all ice and snow pitches, Rébuffat all rock.

The Col du Caïman came close to being a debacle. A nervous Terray dropped his ice axe low on the route, after which his partner had to make do with a piton hammer. Twice, trembling on tiny nicks of footholds on steep ice, Terray started to lose his strength; twice he avoided potentially fatal falls only with desperate lunges. With the route in perpetual shade, the pair climbed in brutal cold. Night overtook them, but they climbed on by starlight. At last Terray cut his way through the cornice cresting the col and the men emerged on that lonely saddle. Wrote Terray, "We shouted our joy to the moon like a couple of madmen." For more than twenty years after this epic climb, Terray and Rébuffat's route on the Caïman went unrepeated.

Between the two men there was lively competition as well as happy camaraderie. Rébuffat was gratified to finish a particularly demanding mountain course set by the JM in first place, while Terray finished third. And in 1942, the highest honor he had ever sought was granted the twenty-one-year-old, when he was invited to join the Compagnie des Guides de Chamonix. His mentor, proffering the invitation, said, "You have great integrity, and you climb well." For Gaston, that his moral qualities were cited ahead of his technical ability formed a lasting point of pride.

All the while he was serving his alpine apprenticeship, Rébuffat was forming his own highly original aesthetic of mountaineering. After their initial spell of enthusiasm, both he and Terray grew disenchanted with Jeunesse et Montagne. By the end of his service, Terray later wrote, he was "completely disgusted with the organization." For Rébuffat, the rhetoric on which JM was founded began to seem highly distasteful. The unabashed aim of the division's architects was to form a "sportive elite . . . to exalt the finest French virtues." Climbers were to become "knights of the sky" through "the secularization of the chivalric virtues," ultimately creating "an army of true alpinists."

Ever since the first ascent of Mont Blanc, the struggle of men against the heights had been conceived of and narrated in martial terms. A team "laid siege" to a mountain; it "attacked" its objective by the likely "weaknesses" in its "defenses"; reaching the summit was inevitably a "victory," even a "conquest."

All this chest-thumping was anathema to Rébuffat. From his early years on, he had gained his remarkable proficiency on slab and serac not by battling against the natural world, but by embracing it. The mountain was not an enemy: it was a magical realm of peace and harmony, entered into in a spirit of communion, not of war.

Even though he had dropped out of school at sixteen, Rébuffat was intellectually ambitious. He wanted to write about his adventures in the mountains, and to pass on his vision of the Alps not as a battlefield but as (in the subtitle of a later book) a *"jardin féerique"*—an enchanted garden. Eventually he would become not only an author but a prize-winning photographer and cinematographer.

As he came into the prime of life after the war ended, Rébuffat grew as skilled and daring as any mountaineer in Europe. Without announcing to anyone his goal, he set about becoming the first climber to succeed on the six great classic north faces of the Alps, all first ascended in the 1930s. His initial blazing success in this campaign came in 1945, with the second ascent of the magisterial Walker Spur on the Grandes Jorasses, the "last great problem" solved by Ricardo Cassin seven years earlier. There followed the north face of the Petit Dru, the northeast face of the Piz Badile, the north face of the Matterhorn, and the north face of the Cima Grande in the Dolomites, the last two accomplished in 1949. By the time he left for Annapurna, Rébuffat lacked only the deadly Eiger-wand in Switzerland, which had killed eight of the first ten men to attempt it. In 1952 he would round out his sextet, after a life-or-death struggle on the Eiger, during which he and the Austrian Hermann Buhl—meeting by chance and joining forces, just as the first ascenders had done in 1938—led seven teammates who might otherwise have perished to the top.

In his masterpiece, *Etoiles et Tempêtes* (*Starlight and Storm*), published in 1954, Rébuffat sang those six great ascents. Yet where nearly every other mountain writer in Europe (including Terray) would have narrated those tales in terms of all-out battles against enemies conjured up out of unforgiving cliff and icefield, Rébuffat stayed true to his vision.

A famous aside in the book, titled "The Brotherhood of the Rope," pushes that vision to a height of mystical ecstasy:

> Together we have known apprehension, uncertainty and fear; but of what importance is all that? For it was only up there that we discovered many things of which we had previously known nothing: a joy that was new to us, happiness that was doubled because it was shared, a wordless friendship which was no mere superficial impulse. . . .
>
> I wish all climbers an Elder Brother who can always be looked up to with love and respect, who will watch the way you rope yourself up, and who, as he initiates you into an exacting life, looks after you like a mother hen.
>
> The one who shares with you his fleeting sovereignty at 12,000 feet and who points out the surrounding peaks as a gardener shows his flowers.
>
> The one at whom we all gaze with envy, for the mountain hut is his lodging and the mountain his domain.
>
> The friendship of a man as rich as that cannot be bought.

ANNAPURNA HAD FIRED ME, by the age of sixteen, with the passion to become a mountaineer. Under its influence, exploring the ranges of my native Colorado, I graduated from easy "walk-ups" such as Mount Elbert (the state's highest peak) to more challenging objectives: a solo traverse of the treacherous Maroon Bells, near Aspen; a winter attack on the east ridge of Pacific Peak, in the Tenmile Range. Yet I continued to hesitate short of the real plunge—learning to climb with rope and piton and carabiner and the tight-fitting special footgear called *kletterschuhe*.

One day in 1959, in a local bookstore, I held in my hands *Starlight and Storm*. I knew Rébuffat from *Annapurna*, but had no sense of his individual voice or character. The nine climbers in that heroic saga remained in Herzog's telling little differentiated one from the other; they were all idealized "knights of the sky." Now, as I browsed through the small book, Rébuffat began to assume his own personality. Of the six great north faces of the Alps, I knew nothing, but the photos in *Starlight and Storm* made it clear that these savage, dark walls were far more daunting than any mountain in Colorado.

In the book, I could see, Rébuffat had somewhat chimerically adjoined his accounts of the six north faces to a pragmatic manual titled "The Beginning Climber"; perhaps the French publisher had thereby beefed up an otherwise dangerously slender volume. It may have been that how-to treatise that made me dig deep into my pockets and buy *Starlight and Storm*, for I was still too green to know that you couldn't learn to climb from a book.

Yet it was not the Chamonix guide's succinct advice about sunglasses and shoulder stands that captivated me, but the lyrical prose in which he recounted the harrowing bivouacs, the gutsy leads up frozen pitches, that had won him his great faces. The author himself had evidently wearied of the pedestrian job of explaining how to climb, for time and again in "The Beginning Climber" he burst into philosophy: "Of course, technique is a poor thing, even a wretched thing, when separated from the heart which has guided it: this is true in rock climbing, or playing a piano, or building a cathedral."

In these deftly romantic pages I found a view of climbing utterly different from what I had discerned in the pages of *Annapurna*. Yet at sixteen I was still too naive to comprehend that those two views were fundamentally incompatible. Nor did I entertain even a glimmer of a suspicion that Rébuffat's Annapurna might have made for a different story from Herzog's. No one in America, as I was to find in subsequent years, doubted the veracity of Herzog's perfect saga of the world's first 8,000-meter ascent.

Starlight and Storm became for me a sacred text. The book closed with an affirmation every bit as revelatory as Herzog's famous final words, "There are other Annapurnas in the lives of men." "Life, the luxury of being!" Rébuffat pealed, then laid down his pen.

Still without any inkling that I might ever climb a big wall myself, I thrilled through each rereading of the author's struggles on the Walker Spur and the Eigerwand. A few years later, at the age of twenty, by then a junior instructor at Colorado Outward Bound School, I was asked to give a dawn inspirational reading to the ninety-six students it was our job to toughen up in the Elk Range. With trembling voice but the passion of an acolyte, I read "The Brotherhood of the Rope" from my favorite mountain book.

It might seem odd that a Colorado boy should have taken as his climbing heroes men from far-off France. By 1959, on the crags only a few miles outside of Boulder, a six-foot-five bricklayer named Layton Kor was putting up the hardest and most daring routes ever climbed in Colorado. One of my high school classmates even climbed with Kor—or rather, was dragged bodily up pitches far beyond his ability by a demon so possessed he would pair up with anyone capable of tying in to the other end of the rope. Kor would go on to become a climber every bit as legendary as Rébuffat. Though I was in awe of his deeds, however, I never chose Kor as a hero.

Similarly, at age fourteen I had gone on a hike with Charley Houston, an Aspen physician who was a friend of my father's. Houston, I knew, had led the 1938 and 1953 American K2 expeditions, gallant failures on the world's second-highest mountain. And with longtime partner Bob Bates, Houston had written an account of the latter journey, called *K2: The Savage Mountain*, that would become a classic. Houston would later serve as a mentor to me—but never as a hero in the sense that Rébuffat became on first reading.

I was hardly alone in my infatuation with the men of Annapurna. As I grew into my mountaineering prime, I encountered one American climber after another who confessed that reading Herzog's book as a teenager had turned him irreversibly toward alpinism. After 1959, Rébuffat published a series of gorgeous picture books, such as *Neige et Roc* (*On Snow and Rock*), *Entre Terre et Ciel* (*Between the Earth and Sky*), and *Mont-Blanc, Jardin Féerique* (*Mont Blanc, Enchanted Garden*) that by themselves created a kind of cult. The photos of Rébuffat in action—always wearing the same patterned pullover, caught in profile against a vertical cliff, rope dangling from his waist into the void, hands resting gently on wrinkles of granite while toes clung to invisible holds—adumbrated an alpine acrobatics far more graceful than any climbing his readers had performed. The dreamy lyricism of the text elaborated further on the radical aesthetic of the Alps as an "enchanted garden" that Rébuffat had invented.

It was the poet of the mountains who had inspired me at sixteen, writing, in *Starlight and Storm*, "I am immensely happy, for I have felt the rope between us. We are linked for life." That the same man could have penned, in his private notebook, "Depersonalization . . . a certain Nazification," after the oath-swearing at the CAF, would have utterly surprised me.

All his life, even as his books made him mildly famous, Rébuffat kept his other side—the skeptical individualist, distrustful of all things grandiose and chauvinistic; the satirist, armed with a gift for the mordant phrase—under close wraps. His friends knew that side, but not the public, and so it came as a great surprise to learn, with the publication of Ballu's biography in 1996, just how disenchanted Rébuffat had been on Annapurna.

In April 1999, pursuing the "other Annapurnas" that Michel Guérin's confidences had alerted me to, I met Françoise Rébuffat, Gaston's widow, in Paris. Rébuffat had died in 1985, a rare male victim of breast cancer, after an agonizing deterioration stretched over ten years. Françoise had remarried, but she continued to guard her husband's legacy with a fierce loyalty.

In her chic apartment high above Montparnasse, I encountered an elegant and forceful woman of seventy-five. Françoise had met Gaston rather improbably one day in 1946 in Chamonix, in the *salon de thé* of the Hôtel des Alpes, a favorite hangout of both climbing guides and modish tourists that doubled as a dance parlor. The daughter of an architect from the Côte d'Azur, studying fashion at an elite school, she was on holiday with her friends. At twenty-two, Françoise was a great beauty.

"I'd like to meet a mountain guide sometime," she impulsively told her friends.

One of them pointed out the tall, angular Rébuffat, who was dancing with a Dior model. "That's one there," she said.

Françoise thought her friends were teasing her, the *méditerrannéenne* ignorant of the mountains. In her conception, a guide would be dressed in ragged trousers, wearing hobnailed boots, his visage leathery with exposure to sun and wind, sporting perhaps a fine mustache—not that young man in elegant tweeds with his face expressive of urbane character. "That one," she said with a laugh, "he must be a *guide d'opérette*"—a vapid know-it-all.

Thus Françoise and Gaston met, fell in love, and married. He took her climbing; she introduced him to her world of artists and aristocrats and fine restaurants.

As we talked on in her Paris apartment, and later, as I read a moving unpublished memoir Françoise had written about her husband after his death, I realized that despite the social inequality in their upbringings, theirs had been that rare union of two souls as devoted to one another thirty years after they met as when they had first plunged into the delirium of courtship, a pair who had never begun to fall out of love.

As he headed off to Annapurna at the end of March 1950, Gaston was twenty-eight years old, Françoise twenty-six. She had given birth to a daughter, Frédérique, two years before. Supporting the couple with his earnings as guide, Gaston had begun, if rather tentatively, to realize his ambitions as a writer. In 1946 he had published a book for aspiring climbers called *L'Apprenti Montagnard;* in 1949, a picture book about the Calanques.

Two days after the press conference at the CAF, culminating in the pledge of unquestioning obedience to their leader, the Annapurna team met at Orly airport to board the first of a series of planes that would eventually disgorge them in New Delhi. Françoise, there to see her husband off, remembered the moment vividly.

"I was standing behind a glass window. Just before they got on the plane, I saw Maurice [Herzog] hand Gaston a contract to sign. I saw Gaston read it, then I saw them arguing."

If the oath of obedience had come to Rébuffat as a shock, the contract seemed a far more stunning blow. With rising incredulity, he read the legalese that forbade him from utilizing his Annapurna adventure for "publication in any form, public speeches, radio or television broadcasts, books, articles, interviews, conferences, official statements, published photos or films." It was this coerced abnegation, designed by Devies and Herzog to keep the story of Annapurna the property of the expedition's patron and its leader, sprung on the team at the very last moment, that Herzog obliquely alluded to in the pages of *Annapurna* as if it demonstrated the voluntary altruism of his teammates: "From the start every one of them knew that nothing belonged to him and that he must expect nothing on his return. Their only motive was a great ideal."

"Gaston came very close to turning around and leaving, right there, in the airport," said Françoise. In the end, with the deepest reluctance, he signed.

So, even before the expedition members left France, the team was torn by conflict and resentment. Lachenal was similarly disenchanted. It was a hardship for the three Chamonix guides to give up a season's earnings to join the expedition. With two small sons of his own, Lachenal, and his wife, Adèle, felt the pinch. According to Françoise, the wives of all three guides were promised a pension of 400 francs a month for the duration of the expedition, but none of them received a sou.

On April 2, in New Delhi, the climbers attended a reception at the French ambassador's house. "High society dinner in a high society apartment," Lachenal wrote dryly in his diary. "Bored me to tears." In the *Carnets du Vertige* edited by Gérard Herzog and published in 1956 after Lachenal's death, the latter sentence was suppressed.

Rébuffat's melancholy funk persisted during the long hike

through the lowlands toward Annapurna. In a letter to Françoise, he complained: "I don't even have a friend. I've sacrificed a lot for friendship, and today, in this adventure, in The Adventure, I am alone."

Remembering the silent pantomime she had witnessed through the glass window at the airport, as her husband and Herzog had vehemently argued over the contract, Françoise told me, "Everything went badly after that moment."

THREE

Looking for Annapurna

As THEY SET OFF from the Indian border to trek north across Nepal toward the distant Himalaya, Herzog's team faced a quandary that effectively doubled the difficulty of their mission. Unlike such mountains as K2, first attempted in 1902, or Nanga Parbat, even earlier, in 1895, Annapurna had never been reconnoitered (let alone attempted) by Westerners. As mountaineers had found out the hard way on other Himalayan peaks, simply sorting out an 8,000-meter peak's defenses could exhaust the resources of the strongest expedition. Mount Everest, for instance, would be the goal of three full-fledged reconnaissances and seven all-out attempts before its summit fell to Hillary and Tenzing in 1953.

Between 1950 and 1964, all fourteen 8,000-meter peaks in the world were first climbed, beginning with Annapurna in 1950 and ending with Shishapangma in 1964. One measure of the quality of the French achievement is that, within that roster of first ascents of the world's highest mountains, only Annapurna would be climbed by the first expedition to reach its foot.

Knowing how vexsome merely approaching an unknown mountain could prove, Devies and the Himalayan Committee had defined the team's mandate as an attempt on either Annapurna or its neighbor, 26,811-foot Dhaulagiri (also previously unreconnoitered). Once they had acquainted themselves with the topography surrounding these two towering peaks, the team was to choose the easier of the objectives. For much of April and May 1950, Herzog's men bent their best efforts toward getting to Dhaulagiri. Annapurna came almost as an afterthought.

The approach to the mountains was fraught with setbacks. The usual porter strike materialized, to be solved by the Gurkha officer deputed by the Maharajah of Nepal to accompany the expedition, who beat a particularly obstreperous "coolie" and sent him fleeing as a lesson to the others. The Sherpas, who would prove so vital on the mountain, were more loyal. "It thrilled me," wrote Herzog, with the unconscious condescension of his day, "to see these little, yellow men, with their plump muscles. . . . The expedition was to give them plenty of opportunity to show what they were made of."

Terray was afflicted with a persistent stomachache, Rébuffat with lassitude, headache, and insomnia. As they gained altitude, eventually surpassing the height of Mont Blanc (the highest any of the men except Ichac had been before), Herzog seemed to acclimatize better than his teammates.

After fifteen days of trekking, the team reached the mountain village of Tukucha, equidistant between Dhaulagiri and Annapurna. Four days before, they had caught their first sight of Dhaulagiri, "an immense pyramid of ice, glittering in the sun like a crystal," its remote summit 23,000 feet above their lowland trudge. The sight was both joyous and discouraging. "Just look at the east arête, on the right," one team member blurted out. "Yes, it's impossible," rejoined another. (In Herzog's text, which is rich in dialogue, the identities of the speakers often go unspecified.)

The team used Tukucha as base, setting out, usually in pairs, to untangle the lay of the land and try to find a way to the foot of Dhaulagiri. It was now that they began to realize that their Indian

Survey maps were seriously in error. On the map, the valley of the Dambush Khola, bent like an arm around a sharp elbow, led directly from Tukucha to the northeast face of the great mountain. In reality, a high ridge blocked the river's headwaters, barring all access to Dhaulagiri from this side.

In *Annapurna*, though suffering from various ailments and driven to distraction by their failures, the men keep up a jaunty banter and an unflagging optimism. Here, the art of Herzog's writing serves the tale well. Clearly he has made up the copious dialogue that laces the pages; in his hospital bed months after the expedition, he cannot have remembered every exchange down to the exact word. Yet this dialogue has an air of authenticity; it sounds like climbers talking:

"Good Lord! Look at that! A valley starting here—"

"It's not marked on the map," said Ichac. "It's an unknown valley."

"It runs down toward the north and divides into two great branches."

"No sign of Dhaula! It couldn't be that pale imitation, that fake mountain, in front of us, could it?"

(This version of the passage, retranslated literally from the French to capture its colloquial ease, avoids the arch Anglicisms of the 1952 English translation.)

Does it matter that, in Herzog's concocted dialogue, no individual voice emerges? That all nine climbers sound alike? Not to most readers, for the chat serves as it should, to advance a story that gains momentum with every page.

Herzog does not entirely whitewash the personal conflicts that marred the weeks of reconnaissance. Rather, he presents a series of vignettes that all resolve in the same fashion: with the wisdom of his own leadership prevailing over the impetuous antics of the others. On an attempt to climb through an icefall toward Dhaulagiri, Herzog, Rébuffat, and Lachenal, each roped to a Sherpa, blunder into a nightmare, as a violent hailstorm hits and the seracs around them creak and shudder. Both Rébuffat and Lachenal counsel retreat. Then, with his characteristic wild haste, Lachenal starts tearing down the slope, dragging his Sherpa with him.

Herzog, alarmed, yells after him: "Watch out for the Sherpas! Don't let them fall off." Lachenal does not slow down.

Later, in safety, Lachenal laments only the missed opportunity to reach a benign plateau above the icefall: "We were so close!"

His leader admonishes: "You can't push on when it's like that." Then Herzog moralizes: "I realized that even if we had reached the plateau, it would have been madness to try to bring the main body up this way. The risk was far too great."

What takes the edge off these scoldings and I-told-you-sos is Herzog's magnanimity. At every turn, he acknowledges his teammates' skill on rock and ice. Of Lachenal and Terray, for instance, he pauses to observe: "This celebrated partnership, which had conquered all the finest and most dangerous of our alpine faces, was today living up to its reputation." Terray's stoic perseverance particularly impresses Herzog. "The next day," he writes of an early march, "Lionel Terray set a rapid pace from the start. During his illness he was so weak that he had only been able to walk with considerable effort, but now it was as much as we could do to follow him."

The chapters in *Annapurna* that cover the demoralizing search for an approach to either Dhaulagiri or Annapurna subscribe to an old, deeply satisfying narrative convention. Like Odysseus's shipmates, Herzog's partners dodge one lethal trap after another. They are headstrong individualists and brilliant climbers, but what holds the team together is its common pursuit of a goal as precious as life itself.

How different sounds the kindred musing of Rébuffat, in one of his letters to Françoise:

> [The others] have the air of being completely at ease in their egotism. Among us there is no team spirit, only a necessary politeness. What hypocrisy! . . . So, I live, I exert myself, I give, and I receive. But here, we are not on the same shore as one another. Here, we are reunited to bag an 8,000-er. The rest doesn't matter.

Rébuffat was homesick: he missed Françoise and his small daughter badly. With him he carried his wife's last letter, pausing to reread it now and then. It seemed to him that the other married men on the team—Lachenal, Terray, and Couzy—hardly suffered at all from the absence of their wives.

Back home on his native turf, Rébuffat could be a gregarious and charismatic companion. As a self-made intellectual, he loved to discuss philosophical and artistic matters. Here on the expedition, however, he withdrew into his melancholy privacy. Despite his deep friendship with Terray and Lachenal, he could not find on Annapurna that distillation of perfect comradeship that had floated him through the cold bivouacs on the Walker Spur and the Cima Grande.

In his own very different way, Lachenal marched, during the weeks of reconnaissance, along a similar gauntlet of irritations and disappointments. His diary, always plainspoken, clipped, and pragmatic, never blinks at the tensions and follies of the group's effort. Early during the approach, after he had settled in at the night's campsite, Lachenal impatiently waited for the rest of the entourage—porters, Sherpas, and fellow "sahibs." Finally the caravan arrived. "They had the courage to come all the way up to here on ponyback," he wrote sarcastically, "which seemed to me at first grotesque, then completely contra-indicated, since most of the other team members are totally lacking in conditioning."

On April 9, Lachenal dryly recorded Easter Sunday: "For us, a day like all the others, except a few more hassles than usual." The sentence was suppressed in the 1956 *Carnets du Vertige*.

Even the most laconic daily jottings ("Evening, the eternal chicken and potatoes") were excised from the *Carnets,* as edited by Gérard Herzog. Yet the sentence, "At noon, we opened a bottle of white wine, which devilishly reminded us of our native land, truly the most beautiful we have seen to date," was preserved.

On April 11, Lachenal witnessed an eerie rite:

I am going to attend the burial of a young girl who was carried on a stretcher. A hole is dug near the river, the girl put inside it, and after a little ceremony, covered with stones. The body will be

carried away by the floodwaters to fertilize the plains of Nepal.
[Suppressed]

Lachenal's record has the virtues of a true diary, in that it notes the homely, quotidian verities by which the party measured out its progress. From Herzog alone, for instance, the reader would little guess how constantly beset the team was with annoying ailments and illnesses.

> *18 April.* Everybody has been sick, except Schatz and Noyelle [the liaison officer]. Tonight Lionel [Terray] had really bad indigestion with diarrhea. I woke up feeling fine. I ate and then I took off.
> En route the urge to vomit and diarrhea made me stop several times. . . . Today was for me the most terrible since we started.

> *23 April.* Lionel was sick all night, with constant stomachache.

> *25 April.* . . . Always I have a bit of diarrhea. This morning I shat in my pants—not pleasant.

> *29 April.* . . . I have a boil that started on my sternum. I just hope it's the only one.

> *30 April.* . . . My boil only gets bigger, and I already have some ganglions under my arms.

(All these passages were suppressed, as if to admit to developing a boil on one's chest were unworthy of the crème de la crème of French mountaineering.)

Likewise Lachenal's candid observations of the native Nepalis the team passed daily. "The women seem to have very small breasts—even, if I'm not mistaken, not to have breasts at all." (The second half of the sentence was suppressed.)

If in Herzog's text, the nine climbers blur together, all hearty team players, all knights of the sky, the occasional passages in Lachenal's diary hinting at interpersonal conflict or quirks of character bring his comrades to individual life. "The night was pretty short, because in our tent Lionel held forth at length on his youth, his love life, and a bit about his career as a skier. We had to go to sleep at last at 1:00 A.M." "I took two sleeping pills to try to sleep, which gave me very funny dreams: I caught Thivierge [a fellow Chamonix guide] and Momo [Herzog] stealing cans of food!" (Both passages suppressed.)

One of the most interesting entries in Lachenal's diary hints at a serious argument between Rébuffat and himself. "With Gaston, discussions take on a macabre character," he wrote, softening the conflict with an edge of irony. "It's important not to have them too often, because they engender a certain melancholy, a nostalgia for our return, which puts a bad aspect on the adventure." Referring to their dispute, he writes, "We talked again about the business on the central spur of the Grandes Jorasses with the College. Gaston stuck to his position. He's wrong."

With typical bluntness, Lachenal thus brought up a painful episode in the men's shared past. In 1947, Lachenal and Rébuffat had led a group of five aspirant guides from the Collège des Praz, an elite guides' school near Chamonix, on a climb of the central spur on the great north face of the Grandes Jorasses—a route only marginally less serious than the Walker to its left, of which Rébuffat had made the second ascent two years before. On the descent, the team bivouacked just below the summit on the south side of the mountain. Just as the team settled in to sleep on their ledge, a huge block of rock came loose thirty feet above. Rébuffat and the aspirant Georges Michel were knocked from their perch. Michel plunged 1,500 feet to his death. In mid-fall, Rébuffat miraculously jammed himself into a chimney thirty feet below, saving his life at the cost of a broken foot, kneecap, and rib.

In *Starlight and Storm*, Rébuffat narrated that accident in an oddly dreamy passage. For the poet of the Alps, death was not easy to countenance: on the following day, the guides found their protégé's corpse lying face up on the glacier.

> The expression on his face was serene. The morning before, as we started up the spur, he had said to me, "Gaston, think of doing the north face of the Grandes Jorasses! I've dreamed of this all my life." And he added with a laugh: "After, I don't mind dying."

What Rébuffat neglects to mention is that at the last minute, he had talked Lachenal out of an easier route. The central spur had been climbed only four times before, never by Frenchmen. Apprised of the formidable objective Rébuffat proposed, the aspirants were at first taken aback; then, swayed by their faith in their tutors, they voiced wholehearted enthusiasm.

The passage in Lachenal's Annapurna diary seems to indicate that, three years later, he held Rébuffat at least indirectly responsible for the death of Georges Michel. Perhaps he felt his friend had let personal ambition get the better of his judgment. Whether other peers—including the school's director, the premier alpinist Jean Franco—were of like mind has escaped the record. (All mention of this debate on the night of April 28, 1950, was expunged from Lachenal's *Carnets* published six years later.)

The posthumous censoring of Lachenal's diary is so extreme that it cannot be explained simply as stemming from a concern that Lachenal's version might contradict Herzog's. Many of the most vivid vignettes having to do with native peoples have been excised. One day Lachenal attends a funeral of another young native girl, at the culmination of which a priest cuts open her corpse "from the vagina to the breasts"; extracts, Lachenal thinks, her liver; then sews the body closed again before burning it on a pyre. In a remote village, the sahibs are offered girls for four rupees apiece. When they turn down the proposition (mainly, Lachenal indicates, "because these were very dirty Tibetans"), the locals offer them young boys. Both scenes were left out of the *Carnets* as originally published.

One might argue that such raw vignettes would have been routinely excised by publishers in the 1950s. Yet it is not merely such shocking episodes as the sahibs being offered children for sex that were censored in the *Carnets*. Most of the common fleshly details that underline the human vulnerability of the teammates— their boils and headaches, their diarrhea and vomiting—were expunged as well. Knights of the sky do not suffer from diarrhea. And any hint of interpersonal conflict, such as Lachenal's quarrel with Rébuffat over the Grandes Jorasses, was similarly left out.

On the typescript of the diary that Michel Guérin rescued

from oblivion appear the marginal jottings of Lucien Devies and Maurice Herzog. Most of the excision marks bear Devies's hand. The final pruning and rearranging were done by Gérard Herzog, who was a professional editor.

When the unexpurgated *Carnets* appeared in 1996, journalists demanded of Maurice Herzog an explanation of the censoring that took place four decades before. "If none of those passages were published," he told *Montagnes* magazine, "it's because they didn't interest the editors."

One passage "the editors" did not suppress gives the lie to Rébuffat's intuition that he was the only married team member to miss his wife. On May 16, nearly seven weeks gone from France, Lachenal paused beside a pretty stream in a calcite gorge. "I filled my hand with water, looked at it carefully, then threw it back into the torrent, telling it to evaporate and transport itself in a cloud all the way to Praz where this bit of water might fall on the head of my wife."

By May 14, however, such private, happy moments were few and far between for the beleaguered team. They had spent most of those seven weeks trying to get to Dhaula (as the team had nicknamed the great mountain) and find a feasible route up it, only to be thwarted at every hand. "Morale is really low," Lachenal noted as early as May 5. Terray had came back disgusted from a reconnaissance up the Dambush Khola: "Lionel's first words were of Dhaula: 'You can just stick it up your ass.' " (Needless to say, this outburst appears not in *Annapurna* but in Lachenal's unexpurgated diary.) Terray went so far as to venture the opinion that Dhaulagiri would never be climbed. (The mountain finally succumbed in 1960 to a Swiss team led by Max Eiselin.)

Impressed by his power on the trail and his ability to carry very heavy loads, the porters had nicknamed Terray "the strong man." Throughout those seven weeks, even while ill, he had pushed the search as vigorously as any of his teammates. Now even the strong man seemed ready to throw in the towel.

The monsoon could arrive within as little as two weeks, and the expedition had accomplished nothing grander than sorting out the errors on the Indian Survey maps. The team faced the prospect of returning to France empty-handed, without even having set foot on either of the 8,000-meter peaks that Devies had sent them off to conquer.

WHEN TERRAY HAD MET LACHENAL five years before Annapurna, one of the great partnerships in mountaineering history was born. Its inception, however, was far from auspicious. During the last months of the war, in the spring of 1945, Terray was changing trains in Annecy. A "poorly dressed young man," as Terray later recalled, came up to him, pushing a bicycle with one hand and holding a can of milk in the other, and said, "Aren't you Lionel Terray?"

When Lachenal offered his name, Terray realized that the two had been briefly introduced on the streets of Chamonix three years before. Then Lachenal had been wearing his Jeunesse et Montagne uniform, which made him "a rather more dashing figure" than the apparent vagabond in the train station ("The youth's rather pitiful condition made me wonder if he was out of work").

Lachenal's reputation as a climber had reached Terray's ears. The two adjourned to a bistro for a beer. Yet at the outset of their chat, a fundamental difference in values nearly quashed any chance of friendship. Though no Gaullist, Terray was a patriot. With Germany in retreat, he had joined the underground Compagnie Stéphane, a crack outfit devoted to guerrilla warfare in the mountains. Terray would later recall, "The eight months I spent in [the company] were among the most wonderful in my whole life." In the middle of winter, Terray and his comrades climbed technical routes in the Alps to gain aeries from which they might direct grenades and bullets against high Nazi outposts. Several of his friends were killed, and he had a number of close calls.

Now, in the bistro, as Terray later put it, "I extolled the thrilling life we were leading on the Alpine Front." Instead of agreeing, Lachenal "vehemently proclaimed his horror of war and of the army." Lachenal was a pacifist, who, rather than face the compulsory labor service his country demanded, had fled to Switzerland.

Terray left that first meeting with Lachenal with mixed feelings: "I liked his uncomplicated passion for the mountains, but his way of talking and his anti-militarism rather irritated me."

Terray himself, however, harbored a deep ambivalence about the war. The mountain campaigns he pursued so skillfully seemed in an important sense to corrupt his beloved climbing. Even as he prepared to fire upon a company of Germans who, unaware of the French patrol that had climbed above them, sunbathed and skied around their outpost, his feelings were torn. "After a few minutes of this cruel game," he later wrote, "we grew weary of shooting at men who were unable to defend themselves and withdrew, satisfied at having carried out our mission."

After a pivotal alpine battle at Pointe de Clairy, Terray "went back down to the valley through the peaceful forests full of disgust." The battle had given him an epiphany.

> Spring was beginning to burgeon. Creamy snowdrops speckled the ground, and the air was full of odors evoking peace and love. As I descended through this poetic landscape I realized that the hell I had just left, in which so many men had meaninglessly lost their lives, could never again have anything in common with the naively sporting game I had played through the winter months. The whole abomination of war was suddenly and overwhelmingly apparent to me.

In the summer of 1945, with Europe at peace for the first time in six years, Terray went climbing with Lachenal. On the very first route they shared, Terray was awestruck at Lachenal's technique:

> I began to admire his extraordinary ease of movement. Whether on ice or on snowed-up, loose rocks, he already gave proof of that disconcerting facility, that feline elegance which was to make him the greatest mountaineer of his generation.

The first major accomplishment for the pair came the next day, with the second ascent of the east face of the Moine. To their surprise, Terray and Lachenal reached the summit by midday. They basked in sun on top, staring across at the 4,000-foot north face of the Grandes Jorasses. That very day, they knew, Rébuffat was attempting the second ascent of the Walker Spur with Edouard Frendo.

They discussed Gaston's chances on the imposing route, rating them at well less than fifty-fifty. They spoke in hushed tones of the dazzling deeds of Ricardo Cassin, who had pioneered the Walker in 1938. At the time, both Terray and Lachenal were twenty-four years old.

If Rébuffat succeeded, Terray tentatively mused, he might be interested in having a crack at the Walker himself. "But the great problem is to find someone to go with . . . would you be interested?"

Lachenal was dizzied by the idea. "Are you kidding? The Walker's my dream. But do you think I'm up to it? I haven't done much yet."

"You may not have done much, but I've been watching you these last two days. You're a natural, it's enough to make anybody jealous. Done. If they get up, we'll have a shot."

In that moment, the partnership was forged.

LIONEL TERRAY WAS BORN IN 1921, the same year as Rébuffat and Lachenal, in Grenoble. His parents were *grands bourgeois* with instinctively aristocratic tastes. Terray's father had started a chemical engineering business in Brazil, grown modestly rich, and at the age of forty chucked his job in industry for a career in medicine. Terray's mother had studied painting and made some ambitious horseback trips into the Brazilian wilderness.

The family house, a ramshackle three-story château in the oldest part of Grenoble, backed up against the limestone spur at whose foot the town spreads. It made a halcyon playground for young Lionel. "I grew there almost without constraint," he wrote in 1961, "running through the woods, clambering the rocks, trapping rabbits, foxes, and rats, shooting blackbirds, thrushes, sparrows and sparrowhawks." Using guns and knives his parents had brought back from Brazil, Lionel played cowboys and Indians with his schoolmates in the woods. With one friend, Terray skinned the rats he had trapped, dried and tanned the hides, then sewed them into "picturesque costumes which, we hoped, resembled those of Attila's Huns."

Terray's parents had been avid skiers, his father the first Frenchman to master the telemark turn. But when Lionel showed an interest in climbing, they voiced a withering disapproval. "It's a stupid sport," said his mother, "which consists of dragging yourself up rocks with your hands, feet and teeth!" His father inveighed, "A man must be completely crazy to wear himself out climbing a mountain, at the risk of breaking his neck, when there isn't even a hundred franc note to be picked up on the summit."

A cousin of Terray's had been crippled in a climbing accident. His parents held up this tragedy as a lesson for their son. Seeing German students hung with gear in the streets of Grenoble, Terray *père* would sneer, "Take a good look at those idiots. A lot of good they'll have done themselves when they're walking on crutches like your cousin René!"

Such vehement opposition only reinforced the young Lionel's interest in climbing. When he was twelve, his mother took him for the school holidays to Chamonix. The boy was stunned by his first close encounter with really big mountains, as opposed to the lime-stone *préalpes* near Grenoble. One of his friends, the housekeeper's daughter, Georgette, three or four years Lionel's elder, belonged to a hiking club. The ambitious young *montagnard* talked Georgette into a secret attempt on the Dent Gérard, a fairly serious climb in the Vercors. "Perhaps I have never come as close to death as I did on that day," recalled Terray at the age of forty, after two decades of ex-treme climbing all over the world. On the crux of this desperate as-cent, Lionel used his rope to haul Georgette bodily up a pitch he had just almost fallen off himself, succeeding "despite the sobs and protests of my half-suffocated companion."

At boarding school, Terray became a champion skier, though in his own estimation, "I was a very bad student. . . . [T]he trouble came from a complete incapacity to concentrate: I was at the school physically, but my mind could not succeed in settling there." Ad-dicted to a vigorous outdoor life, Lionel grew up strong, rugged, al-most burly. Though a family legend reported that as a baby he had such a full head of hair that his parents had to call in a barber at the age of four days, by the time he was twenty-one he was going bald. By late adolescence, Lionel had a round, powerful countenance and a piercing gaze; he was quite handsome, with a certain Italianate sensuality about his mouth and eyes.

Having survived his ordeal on the Dent Gérard, Lionel more sensibly hired a guide on his next trip to Chamonix. There followed some stiff classic climbs, including the traverse of the Grépon. By now, his parents had separated, and his mother had moved to Chamonix, where she owned a small chalet. Lionel was installed in a boarding school in town, but he devoted all his efforts to skiing and climbing. His schoolwork had been so poor that he had to repeat a year, and he knew the chances were all but nil of his ever gaining his *baccalauréat*. The turning point came when he was invited to the French national ski championships in the Pyrenees in the middle of the school term. The "juvenile prison" in which he was incarcerated refused to give Lionel leave, so he went to the championships anyway, knowing the school would expel him.

At this point in Terray's life, his father in effect disowned him. Writing in maturity, Lionel could afford to treat this breach with irony: [M]y father, by now completely dispirited at having engendered such a monster, seemed not to take much further interest in my fate." At the time, however, his father's disdain sorely cost the young man, and Terray would devote an inordinate effort after he became a guide and famous climber to proving to his distant father that he had after all amounted to something.

After the war broke out, Terray joined Jeunesse et Montagne, in whose ranks, in 1942, he met Rébuffat. To Terray's astonishment, this tall, craggy Marseillais had become at the same age a mountaineer even more ambitious than himself. They talked of wild projects, then climbed together, their efforts culminating in the perilous but brilliant first ascent of the Col du Caïman.

It would have been logical had Terray and Rébuffat formed the perfect partnership that Terray later formed with Lachenal. Yet temperamentally, the men were not a good match, and that disparity emerged on snow and rock. "The climbs we did together," Terray reflected in 1961, ". . . were quite good for those days but not

really exceptional . . . [E]ven taking into account poor conditions
and equipment our times were quite slow."

Rébuffat "was an extremely good rock climber," Terray later
wrote.

> By contrast, however, he was deficient in some of the qualities
> which distinguish the mountaineer from the climber, such as a
> sense of direction and ease of movement on mixed ground and
> snow and ice. I was completely his opposite. I was rather nervous
> and lacking in confidence and, apart from occasional flashes, a very
> mediocre rock climber. But I had an unusual sense of direction and
> was completely at my ease on all types of high mountain terrain.

Quixotically, instead of forming the ideal *cordée,* or rope team,
during the middle years of the war, Rébuffat and Terray bought a
farm together in Les Houches, a hamlet just down the Arve valley
from Chamonix. Their bizarre experiment in pastoralism was an
attempt, as Terray put it, "to find a way of living in the mountains,
so that I could continue climbing and skiing." But Rébuffat had
had, since childhood, a mortal fear of cows. In addition, both men
were far too restless to settle down to the grinding discipline of
farm life. The agricultural lark ended in 1944.

A concomitant factor was that in the meantime, Terray had
fallen in love with a teacher from Saint-Gervais-les-Bains. Marianne was "very blonde, with porcelain-blue eyes . . . young and
pretty . . . [with] a taste for things elegant and intellectual." The
last sort of life she wanted was to become a farmer's wife. In love
herself, Marianne agreed to marry Lionel in 1942, but from their
wedding on, the ménage at Les Houches was doomed.

Terray scraped a living out of teaching winters in the ski
school at Les Houches, and during the last year of the war he performed his daring jaunts of mountain warfare as a member of the
Compagnie Stéphane. Just like Rébuffat, however, Terray had set as
his highest ambition becoming a Chamonix guide. His birthplace of
Grenoble was not as glaring a stigma as Rébuffat's hailing from
Marseille, but there was no question Terray was a "foreigner." Yet

his skill and tenacity won out. Shortly after the war, and shortly after he met Lachenal, Terray was accepted into the elite fraternity of the Compagnie des Guides de Chamonix.

LACHENAL GREW UP IN ANNECY, the winsome lakefront French village south of Geneva. If Terray's parents had become *grands bourgeois* through industrial success, Lachenal's remained *petits bourgeois* through and through. Sober, frugal, and conservative, they ran an old-fashioned grocery store on a busy Annecy street. From childhood on, Louis felt the pinch of near-poverty.

Temperamentally, he was the opposite of his parents. Intensely curious, he was both an avid reader and a restless adventurer. The driven impatience that became the hallmark of his climbing stamped his spirit from his earliest years. At a tender age, he realized he was addicted to risk. The passion first took the form of a systematic campaign, with Louis's best friend, to sneak without paying into every movie theater in Annecy. Each theater required a different technique. The thrill was the chance of getting caught. Once the boys had succeeded in sneaking in, Louis would laugh with uncontainable joy. Yet in truth, he hated movies. As soon as the first scenes came on the screen, he would tell his friend, "Come on, let's go, it's over."

In adulthood, Lachenal wrote memorably about the appeal of risk:

> Definition: a taste for risk is inborn and later made rational. For certain men, it is a necessity. It is the desire to perfect oneself, to raise oneself, to attain an ideal. It implies a taste for responsibility. Mastery of oneself and conquest of fear.

Louis grew up as a choirboy and, starting at thirteen, as a scout; yet he was at the same time not far from what in America would be called a juvenile delinquent. While still young, he acquired a taste for the sharp cider of Savoie, known as *biscantin* in the local patois. "Biscante" became Lachenal's lifelong nickname, the moniker by which his teammates addressed him on Annapurna.

From his first hikes with fellow scouts onward, Louis was obsessed with mountains. When he cornered an elder who had real climbing experience, he would bombard him with earnest questions: Was Whymper a guide? Was Lochmatter? Were there no French guides? What was the name of the mountain in this photograph? How high?

On a small crag overlooking Annecy, Lachenal and a few chums taught themselves to climb. For a rope, they borrowed the halyard with which their scout troop hoisted its flag; for shoes, they wore "sneakers," soled with woven cord rather than rubber. From an early age, Louis was a born craftsman. One day his pals found him shod in what looked an expensive pair of after-ski boots. Where had he gotten them?

"I made them myself," he answered proudly.

"With what?"

"With my hands."

"But the leather?"

"I found an old scrap that I reworked."

"And the soles?"

"Some old satchels."

From his first leads on rock onward, Louis was so much more agile and skilled than any of his friends that they were dazzled by his technique. At the age of sixteen, he bicycled to Chamonix, where the giants of the Mont Blanc massif smote him, just as they had Terray at an even earlier age. Two years later, with a childhood friend, still innocent of any formal training, Lachenal rashly undertook an ascent of the Grépon. The pair survived a descent in a furious storm and a bivouac in the snow. His friend never climbed again.

Louis grew up thin and lanky, with powerful shoulders. His hairline began to recede in his twenties, though he never become as bald as Terray. He wore his intensity in his narrow face. Gradually over the years, a look almost of anguish printed itself on his countenance: the high forehead and the sensuous lips were dominated by the fixed arch of his eyebrows, a perpetual frown on his brow.

One of Louis's adolescent playmates was Adèle Rivier, a tomboy who climbed and camped with the best of them, notwithstanding the overprotective instincts of her parents. Once Louis and Adèle fell in love, the parents grew more and more vigilant. Her father was an important engineer in Annecy, descended from an aristocratic Swiss family. Though he treated Louis with a certain stern kindness, it was clear that he did not expect his daughter to marry the son of a grocer.

The obstacles to their romance, like the challenge of sneaking into a movie theater, only made Lachenal's passion keener. Meeting furtively, the pair courted, then secretly affianced. Suspecting something, M. Rivier called Lachenal to account and acerbically cross-examined the *séducteur*.

In 1939, as he turned eighteen, a series of events threw Lachenal's life into upheaval. He and Adèle passed their *baccalauréat* together, but suddenly her father died. His passing only stiffened Mme. Rivier's opposition to her daughter's match: now she forbade Adèle all contact with Louis.

The war broke out in early autumn. No one went climbing. Casting about for a métier, Louis worked desultorily in his parents' shop, went for long walks in the mountains alone, and fell into a kind of bitterness that alarmed his friends. In view of the course of the rest of his life, that prolonged depression at age eighteen would come to seem a kind of lost year.

It was only the next summer, when he returned to Chamonix for a series of climbs with a veteran alpinist from Annecy, that Lachenal set his compass. One evening, from the terrace of a high mountain refuge, the two men stared at the surrounding peaks turning dull with dusk. Lachenal poured out his questions about guiding, then asked his friend why he had never become a guide.

"I never gave it a thought," said the man.

"Because you have a true passion for the mountains," mused Lachenal. Moments later, he pronounced his conclusion: "To be a true guide, you have to love the mountains more than anything in life."

UNDER THE INFLUENCE OF *Starlight and Storm*, in the spring of my final year of high school, I signed up for a beginning rock-climbing course taught by the Rocky Mountain Rescue Group. After only five Saturdays on easy routes on the Flatirons above Boulder, I considered myself a "real" climber. I scraped together enough cash to buy a 120-foot rope (it cost twelve dollars), a few soft-iron pitons, and a half dozen carabiners. Fired all the more by Rébuffat's lyrical evocations of the great north faces of the Alps, I grew ambitious. In June 1961, with a pal who had climbed for two years (versus my four months), I ascended the east face of Longs Peak, a 2,000-foot precipice of steep snow interrupted by short vertical pitches of clean granite. Because of a recent tragedy on the face, when two experienced mountaineers had frozen to death after getting caught in a storm, the whole east face was officially closed at the time my friend and I sneaked in to its base. After finding our names in the summit register, a ranger tracked us down to Boulder, where a benevolent elder in the Rescue Group talked him out of arresting us.

The east face of Longs seemed a grand exploit, pushing my sketchy technique to its very limit. On one smooth rock traverse, with my arms giving out from fatigue, I just managed to clip a carabiner into a fixed piton before losing my purchase altogether. Late in the afternoon, only a few hundred feet below the top, as he led on perilous mixed snow and rock, my friend screamed, "Get ready! I'm about to come off!" Fortunately, he kept his cool and swarmed past the tricky part.

Despite this bold deed, I did not find the track that would lead me toward serious mountaineering until I arrived at Harvard in the fall of 1961. At the time, the college's mountaineering club (the HMC) comprised the most ambitious collection of undergraduate alpinists in the country. At my first meeting, I was dazzled to learn that certain juniors and seniors had come back from summer expeditions to the Coast and Saint Elias Ranges of Canada, where they had reached the summits of such storied mountains as Waddington and Logan. Until that moment, the idea that I might ever emulate Rébuffat or Terray and go to the great ranges had remained an improbable fantasy.

The summer after my sophomore year, I was invited on my first expedition. That July, six HMC cronies and I made the first direct ascent of the Wickersham Wall on Mount McKinley, a 14,000-foot-high precipice of ice and rock that forms the tallest single mountain face in the Americas. Our adventure was capped by a week-long vigil at 17,000 feet as we waited out a blizzard so severe that our bush pilot—who had flown through the storm to see our tracks disappearing into avalanche debris—reported us missing and feared dead.

On the Wickersham Wall, I cemented a partnership with a classmate named Don Jensen. Stocky, strong, moody, and painfully sincere, Don had hardened his high school apprenticeship with three-week solo outings in the Sierra Nevada of his native California. During our junior year, we met every day in the dining hall and talked obsessively about mountains. Already we were scheming a return to Alaska. On McKinley, we had been tutored by the more experienced men a year or two older than us. Now Don and I wanted to organize our own expedition, and find a mountain route even more challenging than the Wickersham Wall.

Sometime in 1963, Don and I came across a book with the awkward title *Conquistadors of the Useless*. First published in France two years before (as *Les Conquérants de l'Inutile*), the 351-page tome had just been translated and published in Great Britain. (How we found a copy, I have forgotten: perhaps an older bibliophile in the HMC had sent away for the book.)

To say that Don and I devoured *Conquistadors* is an understatement. Every page brimmed with revealed truth—for we were reading the autobiography of Lionel Terray. At once, the book replaced both *Annapurna* and *Starlight and Storm* as my favorite work of mountain literature. In blunt, vivid prose, Terray went straight to the heart of the mystical calling in which Don and I had started to become acolytes. Not for him the rapturous poesy of Rébuffat, the idealized drama of Herzog. We relished every detail. Even a sentence like, "As I went on, it became more and more difficult to let go with one hand even for a moment, and the axe was getting in my way," rang with a clarion purity. Here was the very stuff of extreme climbing, laid out in all its logistical and technical minutiae. The book met the ultimate criterion of adventure writing, for as Don and I read Terray's pages, our palms grew damp with sweat.

Of the six principal climbers on Annapurna, only two—Jean Couzy and Lionel Terray—ever went on another expedition. Yet after 1950, Terray became arguably the greatest expedition mountaineer in history, as he spearheaded small expeditions to some of the remotest and most daunting mountains in the world. Fitzroy in Patagonia, Jannu and Makalu in the Himalaya, Chacraraju and Taulliraju in the Peruvian Andes—always with the indomitable Terray solving the crux pitches that led to victory. This was the kind of mountaineer Don and I aspired to become: an expeditionary expert, seeking out not so much the highest unclimbed mountains as the hardest and most beautiful.

More than anything else in *Conquistadors of the Useless,* however, what stirred Don and me to the core was the account of the partnership Terray and Lachenal forged after 1945. By that year, Lachenal had found his direction in life. He had worn down the haughty opposition of Mme. Rivier and married his beloved Adèle. After a brilliant stint in Jeunesse et Montagne, where he came in first in virtually all the competitions waged among the finest young skiers and alpinists in France, he had won a job as a ski and climbing instructor in the Contamines, near Chamonix. And despite his flight to Switzerland to avoid his labor service obligation, after the war Lachenal was voted into membership in the Compagnie des Guides de Chamonix.

With Terray, Lachenal started knocking off one prize after another among the hardest routes yet essayed in the Alps, starting with the Walker Spur on the Grandes Jorasses. Driven by Lachenal's impatience, the pair set extraordinary time records on these formidable ridges and walls. The first ascent of the northeast face of the Piz Badile, in Italy, had been accomplished by Ricardo Cassin with four partners in 1937. The climb had taken this strong party three days, and they reached the summit in an all-out storm. On the descent, two of Cassin's teammates died of exhaustion.

In 1949, Terray and Lachenal stormed up this wall—one of the six great north faces of the Alps, as categorized by Rébuffat—in the astounding time of seven and a half hours. Their ascent had been three times as fast as the fastest previous success, four times as fast as the hitherto matchless Cassin.

In "The Brotherhood of the Rope," that lyrical set piece in *Starlight and Storm*, Rébuffat had sung the virtues of the *cordée*—the pairing of soul mates bound together by a nylon rope. Yet it seemed that Rébuffat himself, while treasuring the companionship of any number of loyal teammates, had never found his ideal partner, the man with whose destiny he wished to intertwine his own. Now Don and I discovered, in the example of Lachenal and Terray, what the *cordée* meant at its most crystalline.

In one canny passage in *Conquistadors* (I think I learned it by heart), Terray analyzed that partnership:

> We climbed very much better together than either of us did apart. Our differing characters and physical aptitudes complemented each other, each of us making up for the other's weaknesses.
>
> Lachenal was by far the fastest and most brilliant climber I have ever known on delicate or loose terrain. His dexterity was phenomenal, his vitality like that of a wild beast, and his bravery amounted almost to unawareness of danger. On his day he was capable of something very like genius, but strenuous pitches gave him trouble, and above all he was unpredictable. Perhaps because of his very impulsiveness and incredible optimism he lacked patience, perseverance and forethought. He also suffered from a bad sense of direction.
>
> For myself, I was the less gifted partner on any kind of ground; but I had more stamina and was stronger, more obstinate and more reflective. I suppose I was the moderating element in the team, but it also seems to me that I gave it the stability and solidity necessary for the really major undertakings.

The apotheosis of the *cordée* came in 1947, when Lachenal and Terray made the second ascent of the Eiger Nordwand, the deadliest wall in the Alps. Terray had devoted a long and wonderful chapter in *Conquistadors* to this stunning climb. Don and I each read the chapter again and again.

Inevitably, we began to identify with Terray and Lachenal. The analogy was not perfect, but close enough to allow our fantasy to blossom. Like Terray, Don was stocky and strong, with immense stamina. He was far more deliberate than I, and could wait out any storm with a placid repose that it was hopeless for me to try to emulate. Like Lachenal, I was thin and relatively lithe. My forte in the mountains was the same as Lachenal's, loose and mixed rock and snow. And, as Don once told me, I was the most impatient person he had ever met.

We climbed together every chance we could get—on spring and autumn weekends at the Shawangunk Cliffs in New York state, in winter on the frozen ice gullies of New Hampshire's Mount Washington, over Christmas on ten-day trips into the high Colorado Rockies, where we made a number of first winter ascents. And in the summer of 1964, we locked fates on a two-man expedition to the unexplored east ridge of Mount Deborah in Alaska. That expedition—a grinding forty-two-day failure in the course of which several times we came close to getting killed—remains the most intense ordeal of my life. Near the end of that demoralizing journey, Don, with his Terray-like perseverance, still longed to head east through the Hayes Range in search of other mountains, while I wanted only to flee south to the Denali Highway and hot showers and cheeseburgers in greasy cafes.

At some point, our identification with Terray and Lachenal took on a power that transcended mere hero worship. Like the kids I had grown up with, playing pickup baseball in the vacant lots of Boulder, pretending to be Mickey Mantle or Willie Mays, Don and I started to share the conceit that we *were* Terray and Lachenal. We went so far as to address each other as "Lionel" and "Louis."

Passages from *Conquistadors of the Useless*, as well as other chronicles we could come across that detailed our heroes' conquests, became canonic mottos on our lips. On the crux move of a route on Cannon cliff, for example, Don might shout out, "Guido, the sardine tin!" In M. A. Azéma's *The Conquest of Fitzroy*, which told the story of the 1952 first ascent of the hardest expeditionary mountain yet climbed anywhere in the world, Terray and Guido Magnone had solved nearly all the technical difficulties, only to be stumped by a short blank wall just below the summit. Out of pitons, they thrashed around, unable to solve the wall, until Terray cried, "Guido, the sardine tin!" Earlier that day, the pair had used a knife-blade "ace of spades" piton to pry open their sardine can. Terray dug the piton out of his rucksack, pounded it into a thin crack, aided the wall, and sprinted to the summit.

In *Conquistadors*, Terray had devoted a long chapter to Annapurna. By and large, it complemented Herzog's famous story, though Terray performed the invaluable service of following up on the lives and careers of the team members in the eleven years after the expedition. It seemed to Don and me that the *cordée* we idolized ought to have found its paired glory on the first 8,000-meter peak to be climbed. (The ideal plot would have had Terray and Lachenal going to the summit together.) Yet in neither Herzog's *Annapurna* nor in Terray's *Conquistadors* was there much evidence of that legendary partnership playing a pivotal role. The pairs and trios of climbers setting off to look for Dhaulagiri and Annapurna permutated relentlessly, as if Herzog were trying to keep strong bonds from forming among his team. The knights of the sky were in this sense interchangeable.

Only a vignette here and there in the Annapurna chapter of *Conquistadors* hinted at the sense of twinned invincibility Lachenal and Terray had hammered out on the Walker Spur, the Piz Badile, the Eiger. On the long march in to Tukucha, the two guides were designated as the scouting party. Wrote Terray.

> Lachenal was also very interested by all that went on around us, but patience was never one of his characteristics, and he found my halts too frequent. When he got tired of waiting he would lope off on his own, and I would find him asleep under a banyan a few hours later.

Seven weeks into the expedition, Terray reminded us, the team was plunged into despair. The most vigorous possible reconnaissance of Dhaulagiri had deemed the mountain virtually unclimbable. Time was running out.

On May 14, the whole team assembled once more in Tukucha. In the mess tent, Herzog presided over what he called "a solemn council of war." He gave a speech, summarizing the expedition's discoveries. A freewheeling discussion ensued. No one had any heart to pursue further approaches to Dhaula; Terray, the strongest member, was the most vehemently opposed. One by one, the teammates turned their thoughts to Annapurna, which still lay hidden in a haze of topographical ignorance.

By the end of that discussion, the die was cast. Ever the loyalist, Terray summarized the fateful moment:

> Maurice Herzog hesitated before the choice. Should he abandon a prize, however doubtful, in favor of a mystery so insubstantial? Could he expose men who had taken their oath to obey him to mortal danger? In full awareness of his terrible responsibility Maurice chose the more reasonable but uncertain course: we would attempt Annapurna.

FOUR

Breakthrough

THE INDIAN SURVEY MAPS were every bit as confused about Anna-purna as they were about Dhaulagiri. As the team, running out of time, turned its attention to this second 8,000-meter objective, it had little notion of where to begin. In 1961, Lionel Terray would recall:

Annapurna . . . remained a complete enigma. We had seen the mountain from afar off, lording it over groves of seven-thousanders, but the closer we got to it the hazier our ideas of its topography became, for all our painstaking reconnaissances.

The parties scouting Dhaulagiri had run head-on into one impasse after another. Now, however, Herzog and his companions stumbled upon some good luck.

In late April, as they had ascended the valley of the Kali Gandaki toward the mountain village of Tukucha, they had noticed a savage, narrow ravine entering on the right. The natives called this chasm the Miristi Khola. The valley looked too small to offer a highway into the hidden sanctuary of Annapurna, but the climbers were given pause by the huge volume of water plunging out of the gorge. It looked to the eye as though the Miristi Khola headed against a relatively minor massif called the Nilgiris; but that torrent suggested a massive glacier at its source. The unreliable map, moreover, indicated that the Miristi Khola led straight north of Annapurna to a pass labeled the Tilicho Col. Yet when the Sherpa sirdar Ang-Tharkey questioned the locals, no one had any knowledge of either the Tilicho Col or of any path leading up the gorge.

The lower stretches of the chasm, in any event, looked impossible to traverse. Yet on April 27, Herzog sent Schatz, Couzy, and the team doctor, Jacques Oudot, along with Ang-Tharkey and several other Sherpas off on a foray to see if they could climb to the top of the long south ridge of the Nilgiris and peer over into the Miristi Khola from partway up its course. The steep slope leading up to the ridge was covered with jungle, but the reconnoiterers found a faint path through the trees and thickets, with cairns here and there and even disused terraces. Despite local ignorance of the Miristi Khola, evidently shepherds and farmers over the years had climbed high toward the Nilgiri ridge.

At last the party topped out in a narrow notch in the ridge. The view that greeted them was provocative and confounding. Fully 3,000 feet below, the Miristi Khola plunged through cataracts. In the distance rose Annapurna, magnificent and daunting, but of the map's purported Tilicho Col, they could see no vestige. It looked as though the Miristi drained at least the west face of Annapurna, and possibly the north face, but all the men could see in the form of a climbing route was a precipitous arête of rock and ice. The Northwest Spur, as the team began calling this arête, looked as though it would present a formidable challenge were it in the Alps, let alone at altitudes above 18,000 feet in the Himalaya. What was more, the men could not tell whether the top of the spur linked up with the summit snowfields of Annapurna, or simply dead-ended in yet another high ridge the map had failed to record.

Couzy and Schatz pushed on from the notch, traversing four miles along the steep southwest shoulder of the Nilgiris. A narrow, broken ledge offered the only possible nontechnical passage, and the exposure—that 3,000-foot drop to the raging river—was giddy in the extreme. Schatz and Couzy managed to work their way down to the river, cross it, and push on to the base of the gigantic Northwest Spur. But as to whether the ravine gave access to the broad icefields on the north face of Annapurna—which other team members had seen from the Dhaulagiri reconnaissance, and which seemed the most likely route for an attack on Annapurna—they could not say.

Now, at the conclusion of the May 14 "council of war," Herzog deputed Lachenal and Terray (guided by Schatz) to lead a committed probe with porters carrying loads along this improbable route. Terray was overjoyed by this call to action, after fruitless weeks trying to sort out the range's topography. As he set out from Tukucha, he remembered later, "I struck up a Chasseur [light infantry] song and led off, twirling my ice-axe over my head like a drum-major's baton." That evening, the old comrades Lachenal and Terray lay in their tent, counting up, in their amiably competitive way, the number of climbs each had made in the Alps at the level of difficulty of the Grépon or harder. Terray enumerated 157, Lachenal 151.

On May 16, the caravan reached the crossing of the Miristi Khola. Already frightened by the vertiginous slope they had traversed on the narrow ledge, the porters refused to ford the river—or even, Lachenal noted with disgust in his diary, "to make a one-meter jump" where the stream pinched between boulders. (An observation suppressed in the 1956 edition of *Carnets*.) Instead, the three Frenchmen hoisted the loads themselves and waded the torrent. Even unladen, the porters had a bad time at the crossing, which, Terray noted, "gave rise to some picturesque scenes, with a cowboy Lachenal lassooing coolies as they were swept away." Eventually the Frenchmen built a bridge of branches.

By May 18, the six principal climbers had at last reached the foot of Annapurna. Here, however, they made a serious mistake, which ended up costing them five wasted days and came close to extinguishing their chances of reaching the mountain's summit. Carried away by the prospect of confronting steep rock and ice after weeks of wandering about the lowlands, Terray pleaded for an attack on the Northwest Spur. Herzog agreed, immediately assigning the task to the "celebrated partnership" of Lachenal and Terray.

At this juncture, the four sources of the story that have come down to us—Herzog's *Annapurna*, Terray's *Conquistadors*, Lachenal's unexpurgated *Carnets*, and the letters and interviews that went into the making of Yves Ballu's biography of Rébuffat—curiously diverge. All agree that Terray, with his limitless energy, was the driving force behind the attack on the spur. During the last few days, in fact, his mood had soared to something like euphoria. Now he was exhilarated to perform the first real climbing on the expedition with his old partner. Looking back in 1961, Terray remembered the joy of reconstituting the matchless *cordée* on Annapurna:

> At 4:30 the following morning Lachenal and I once more formed the partnership which had so often brought us success. . . . We were back on our old semi-divine form, each reacting to the other so as to double his normal skill and strength almost in defiance of the laws of nature. In this supercharged state we literally played with the obstacles, running up them like cats.

The climbing, however, was harder than either man had anticipated, and snow flurries and clouds made the going all the more tricky. One pitch that Lachenal led, on steep rock coated with a skin of ice called *verglas,* was rated, both men agreed, Grade V—a very stiff pitch for that era in the Alps, and almost certainly the hardest passage that had ever been climbed at an altitude of more than 18,000 feet. At the end of the day's probe up the spur, the indomitable Terray wanted to bivouac and continue on the morrow, but Lachenal talked him into descending.

Lachenal's own diary entry for May 18, written that evening or the next morning, rather than after an interval of eleven years, bears none of the ebullience of Terray's account. No hint of any nostalgic glow at the reuniting of the old *cordée* emerges in Lachenal's laconic phrases. Instead, he is fretful and dubious. A chilling sleet makes the rock-climbing more hazardous, and a traverse across rotten slabs seems "extremely exposed." On the descent, Lachenal notes, the pair make three dangerous rappels, two of them anchored by bad pitons. The sleet turns to steady snow. The two men regain their camp on the moraine "completely soaked."

Given the difficulty of the climbing, Lachenal wanted no more of the Northwest Spur. But the stubborn Terray had only grown more optimistic in the face of the severe pitches he and Lachenal had so skillfully led. Against Herzog's objection that the team could never get the Sherpas up the spur, he argued that (in his own words) "with the aid of eight or ten fixed ropes it would be perfectly possible to get Sherpas up to the point we had reached, and probably also to Point 19,685 ft., since the snow ridge did not look particularly difficult."

Herzog was evidently convinced, for after a rest day, he spent the next three days climbing with Terray to push the route up the Northwest Spur. Both men grossly underestimated its difficulty. "In the event," wrote Terray ruefully in 1961, "it took Maurice and me three days of top-class climbing to reach even the first pinnacle of a fantastic ridge of purest snow lace, utterly invisible from below." Four days of brilliant gymnastics had pushed the Frenchmen only into a cul-de-sac nearly 7,000 feet short of the summit. "We were beaten again. Days of mortal combat had led us to no more than an unheard-of little summit."

In 1961, with his decade of big-range mountaineering behind him, Terray could see his pigheaded enthusiasm for the Northwest

Spur as the folly it was. In *Conquistadors,* he was unsparing: "What ignorance of Himalayan conditions! What an accumulation of errors of judgment!"

Yet for all that, Terray retained a certain pride in his effort on the spur: "Nothing will ever surpass those desperate days when I gave myself up to the struggle with all the strength and courage at my command." To this day, the full Northwest Spur remains unclimbed.

HERZOG'S OWN ACCOUNT of the five days of wasted effort exemplifies his penchant for the retrospective I-told-you-so. In *Annapurna,* he presents himself as skeptical from the start about the Northwest Spur. In the face of his demurrals, "Lachenal and Terray stormed away at me. They thought we ought to decide to attack at once, and kept on insisting that this was the right route." The leader chalks up the pair's "wild enthusiasm" to "a very excitable state after their day's climbing."

"I've no intention of hazarding the whole strength of the expedition on a route we know so little about," Herzog quotes himself as saying. Yet as if to humor Terray, he agrees to the three days' push on the spur. In his detailed account of the fierce climbing the duo performed, Herzog seems to lapse into the same blithe enthusiasm as the headstrong guide. Yet at the high point, staring at their defeat, he concludes: "No long discussion was necessary. Even if no other obstacle cropped up to hinder our progress . . . it would have been madness to launch an expedition on this route."

The true skeptic regarding the Northwest Spur was undoubtedly Rébuffat. Despite his lanky, acrobatic grace on vertical rock, the guide from Marseille saw the spur as a seductive distraction from the start. To him, the self-evident best hope of attaining the relatively low-angled north face of Annapurna was to climb the glacier that sprawled west from unseen basins to the very foot of the spur. Even as Terray and Herzog flailed away at the difficult pitches on the spur, Rébuffat set off with a now-disillusioned Lachenal to scout a route among the crevasses and seracs. The choice of line of attack was Rébuffat's, and it turned out to be a sub-

limely canny piece of route-finding, leading without major difficulties up to a snowy plateau from which the north face began to
unfold.

For the rest of his life, Rébuffat harbored a bitterness toward
Herzog for not sufficiently acknowledging the critical jump-start
in the expedition's fortunes that his reconnaissance up the glacier
had provided. Writes Ballu, his biographer:

> Rébuffat felt a great satisfaction at his discovery of this "favorable
> and rational" itinerary. Thanks to his instincts, he had, he thought,
> perfectly exercised his métier as guide, by finding this route that, on
> the face of it, would become *the* route.

Indeed, in *Annapurna,* Herzog seems to appropriate the intuition of the glacier route from Rébuffat, crediting himself with or-
dering the reconnaissance:

> As I looked once more at the glacier, and the enormous icefall down
> below, I felt in my bones that if there were a way up Annapurna,
> that was where it lay. So another plan began to take shape in my
> mind. Rébuffat and Lachenal . . . [would] attempt to force a way—
> which to all appearances would be found along the right bank—up
> the glacier to the plateau.

Having topped out on the plateau at 11:15 A.M. on May 22,
Lachenal and Rébuffat immediately scribbled a note for the Sherpa
Adjiba to carry down to Herzog. Though it is not clear which man
wrote the note, Lachenal gives its whole text in his diary, and the
impatient exhortations of its closing lines sound like that most
driven and impetuous of climbers:

> Come up, and bring supplies as quickly as possible, for we are
> expecting good weather and a solid route almost certainly climbable
> in a few days. Come en masse with all the Sherpas and the
> maximum food and gear. We think we need to act very fast.

So too does Lachenal's voice speak in the single ironic sentence the note contains: "The sluggards are ready to dash." The context of the remark is obscure. Had Herzog earlier denigrated some of his team-mates as "sluggards"? No epithet could have more sharply insulted Lachenal, who seemed to run on sheer nervous energy, and it would have been like the man to throw the derogation back in Herzog's face.

Immediately after quoting the text of the note, Lachenal wrote in his diary, "We are very happy. Today is the first day in the Hi-malaya that I felt this much pleasure."

During the previous week, in fact, Lachenal had often been in a terrible mood, wracked with annoyance and irritation, lashing out at what he perceived as the idiocies of his teammates. On May 19, he noted of a campsite ordered by Herzog: "A huge waste of time, which disgusts me." Of a parallel reconnaissance of the glacier along its left-hand side, ordered by Herzog and undertaken by Schatz, he remarked, "an exploration that seemed completely ridiculous to me." (Both passages were suppressed in the 1956 edi-tion of *Carnets*.)

Over another campsite that Lachenal favored but Herzog dis-dained, a "bitter altercation" raged. On May 20, still bent on attack-ing the Northwest Spur, Terray and Lachenal had hiked up through a snowstorm to find Rébuffat and Herzog lolling in their tent at the foot of the spur at 10:00 A.M. Lachenal exploded in fury: "What the hell are you doing here?" he demanded.

"Can't you see the snow?" one of the "sluggards" rejoined.

"We've seen it as much as you! More than you, since we've been climbing since dawn to get here."

Lachenal persisted in his tirade, calling his teammates "a bunch of schoolgirls" and "weaklings."

Rébuffat protested, "It would be crazy to go up in this. I have no desire to 'come off' here."

"We'll show you who's going to 'come off'!" Without another word, Lachenal flung himself at the dangerous first pitch, climbing with a reckless abandon born of his anger.

Curiously, this scene appears not in Lachenal's diary, but in *Annapurna*. Though Herzog marvels at Lachenal's skill, he is dis-mayed by his fury. "I wasn't at all happy," Herzog writes: "it seemed to me that it was wrong to take such risks in the present conditions." In the end, the tableau, which on the surface of it takes the chance of painting the author and his fellow sluggard Rébuffat as not as tough or daring as the stalwart *cordée* of Lachenal and Terray, serves to build up a portrait of Lachenal that subtly accretes through the book—of a genius-madman of ascent, unmatched at sheer ability but nearly devoid of judgment, his impetuous rages driving him beyond reasonable human limits.

MARCEL SCHATZ AND JEAN COUZY were a *cordée* as well, though a far less experienced one than Terray and Lachenal. Only a couple of years younger than the three stellar Chamonix guides, these two were "amateurs" like Herzog. Couzy, who hailed from the Southwest of France, was a promising aeronautical engineer; Schatz, a Parisian, was a physicist who earned his living as manager of one branch of his father's tailoring business.

Schatz would quit mountaineering altogether less than a year after Annapurna. After turning thirty, he returned to his research, which he performed so capably that he eventually had a hand in the development of the French atom bomb.

Couzy, on the other hand, went on to become one of the greatest mountaineers of his generation. On Makalu, the world's fifth-highest peak, in 1955, he was the "tiger," the climber whose will drove the whole party to success on the only other 8,000-meter peak first climbed by Frenchmen.

In 1950 on Annapurna, however, these two alpinists played a largely supporting role, accomplishing important reconnaissances (including the key penetration of the Miristi Khola), but leading virtually none of the pitches on the mountain itself. (They would, to be sure, participate in a heroic act of rescue on the descent.) Perhaps the pair were simply in awe of the three great guides; perhaps they were further intimidated by the strong personalities of their four elders. (Along with the others, moreover, they had sworn unflinching obedience to Herzog.) Couzy in particular never seemed fully to acclimatize. In all the accounts of the expedition, he lurks in the background, a silent collaborator who gets along with his team-mates by never thrusting his own character to the fore.

Whether or not in recognition of Couzy's poor form on the mountain, as the team at last came to grips with Annapurna, Her-zog took the young engineer aside and said, "Couzy, you are going to have a thankless job." He then ordered the twenty-seven-year-old to take charge of the grunt work of organizing the porters and Sherpas to carry their loads to a permanent Base Camp at the foot of the north face. The chore would take days, and Couzy would have to hump loads himself, while his five teammates soared across untrodden terrain above.

In *Annapurna*, Couzy responds to this disheartening directive with staunch loyalty: "It certainly doesn't sound much fun, but if the job's really got to be done . . ."

Herzog praises the self-sacrifice of this youngest knight of the sky:

> He did [his job] to perfection and without a single word of
> complaint, although he knew that, when the final attack was
> launched, he would not be sufficiently acclimatized and so would
> lose the chance of being on it. It is this admirable spirit of self-denial
> which determines the strength of a team.

Couzy's private thoughts on this matter have escaped the record. But in 1999, Couzy's widow, Lise, told this writer, "It was Marcel [Schatz] and Jean who found the passage [up the Miristi Khola] in a very tight valley. Herzog later said, 'We decided. . . .' But it was Marcel and Jean who found it."

Choosing her words cautiously, Lise Couzy added, "When you bring together men like this on an expedition, there are always problems and disagreements. Jean was correct with Herzog, but there was not an affinity between them. They did not have the same passions. Herzog was not an enemy, but he was not a great friend, either."

What with the loss of five days on the Northwest Spur, it was not until May 23 that the team established Camp I, at an altitude of

16,750 feet—a discouraging 10,000 feet below the distant summit. Herzog had received a radio bulletin about the weather farther south, in India. In *Annapurna,* he gives voice to the hectic urgency the whole team now felt: "The arrival of the monsoon was announced for about June 5. *We had just twelve days left.* We'd have to move fast, very fast indeed."

Now Lachenal, hitherto so cranky and out-of-sorts, was seized with a fervent optimism. In his diary on May 22, with no rational reason to make such a sanguine judgment, he wrote, "Finally today we sense that victory is very close—as long as the weather stays good. . . . Life is beautiful."

"An astonishing sight greeted me next morning," wrote Herzog. "Lachenal and Rébuffat were sitting outside on a dry rock, with their eyes riveted on Annapurna. A sudden shout brought me out of my tent: 'I've found the route!' cried Lachenal." As Herzog watched and listened, Lachenal linked features on the icy face above, which glittered in the sun, while Rébuffat—ever the skeptic on this expedition—raised doubts and problems that Lachenal brushed aside. The debate ended on an upbeat note. "A hundred to nothing! Those are the odds on our success!" pealed the genius-madman of Herzog's portrait. Of the route Lachenal had sketched in the air, even the dubious Rébuffat conceded, "It's the least difficult proposition and the most reasonable."

So began what Terray would call the "fantastic up-and-down ballet" of establishing a series of camps on Annapurna and hauling gear and food to them. During the week that followed, the strongest team member was Terray. A close second, however, was Herzog himself. There is no reason to doubt the leader's own self-appraisal in this matter in *Annapurna.* When it came to taking the lead and plowing through deep snow up avalanche-prone slopes, getting the tents pitched at a new campsite, and maintaining the high morale needed to counter the team's setbacks, even the accounts of his teammates confirm that Herzog was a paragon. A sample entry in Lachenal's diary, from May 28: "Couzy and I descended once more to Camp II. There we found Momo [Herzog] in great form." Terray recorded a discussion with Herzog on the day before, in which the leader bemoaned his teammates' low spirits: "His own form at around twenty-three thousand feet, by contrast, was very hopeful, and he still felt confident of victory as long as the daily snowfalls did not exceed six to eight inches."

At 31 the eldest of the six principal climbers on Annapurna, Maurice Herzog had grown up in Lyon. His father was an engineer and a casual alpinist who had served in the French Foreign Legion in World War I. Wounded in battle, he had been repatriated to Toulouse, where he met Herzog's mother. The couple eventually had eight children, of whom Maurice was the first. In a telling phrase embedded in the memoir he published in 1998, Herzog reflected, "As the eldest, I felt myself invested with the mission of guardian of order."

That memoir, titled *L'Autre Annapurna* (*The Other Annapurna*), appearing in Herzog's eightieth year, represents only the second personal narrative to flow from the pen of France's most famous mountaineer. During the intervening years, Herzog had coauthored a picture book with Marcel Ichac about the expedition, called *Regards vers l'Annapurna* (*Looking at Annapurna*) and issued a historical tract titled *Les Grandes Aventures de l'Himalaya* (*The Great Adventures of the Himalaya*). There are some passages of considerable power in the memoir, particularly those recounting with fresh detail the agony of Herzog's retreat from the mountain and his convalescence in the hospital.

In sum, however, *L'Autre Annapurna* is a feeble performance, riddled with parables of character-building and self-congratulation, marred by an unfortunate predilection for name-dropping. Nonetheless, *L'Autre Annapurna* stands as the primary source for Herzog's youth and early adulthood. In his full celebrity, the leader of the 1950 expedition would blossom as a man of consummate charm and personality. Women found him irresistible: his looks were often likened to Clark Gable's. It is interesting, then, to learn that at eighteen, Herzog thought himself not only "taciturn and introverted," but a veritable misogynist (his own word). Everything feminine, everything to do with romantic love, seemed to him soft and weak. His heroes were Wagner's Lohengrin and Siegfried; his masters, Nietzsche and Schopenhauer.

Just like his teammates Lachenal, Rébuffat, and Terray, Herzog discovered Chamonix early in life, thanks to a family chalet at the foot of the Glacier des Bossons, which spills northeast from the summit of Mont Blanc. On solitary excursions, he explored the wonders and terrors of the great glacier, graduating to more and more ambitious ascents of the granite peaks and aiguilles that tower above it.

Chamonix was Herzog's "little native land," but school took him increasingly to Paris, where he earned his *baccalauréat* in mathematics and philosophy and an advanced degree in business from the Ecole des Hautes Etudes Commerciales. In 1945, just as Terray and Lachenal were becoming Chamonix guides, Herzog was hired as a director at Kléber-Colombes, the mammoth tire company.

Herzog thus remained firmly an "amateur" in mountaineering. In his memoir, he recounts an exchange with Terray, whom he had befriended in Chamonix. Terray asks Herzog why he doesn't want to become a guide.

"I suppose I could," he responds, "but I wouldn't enjoy squeezing money out of the mountains. Living off what I love."

"Nature is nobler than offices and labs and factories," retorts Terray.

"Exactly! A passion should remain free."

"For Christ's sake," bursts out the guide, "the point isn't to make money, but just to get by!"

"There's another reason," Herzog adds. "I would think that being a mountaineering professional means endlessly repeating the same routes. Isn't that tiresome? And finally, a true burnout?"

"Yes, but you can constantly change clients."

As so often in *Annapurna*, here, with Terray's meek rejoinder, Herzog in effect gives himself the last word.

In any event, in the 1940s Herzog became a good but not a great alpinist. With his usual bluntness, Terray addresses the question in *Conquistadors* as he acknowledges the fact that the choice of Herzog to lead the Annapurna expedition "caused a great deal of argument both then and later. . . . The objections were mostly on the grounds that he had done none of the greatest ascents of his day, and could therefore not be considered one of its leading climbers." Still loyal in 1961, Terray counters the objections by insisting that Herzog had "made himself into a good rock climber; and above all he was a complete mountaineer with all the right qualities for the Himalayas." Moreover, Terray insists, "If Herzog's selection was justified on technical grounds, it was even more so on intellectual and human ones."

In *L'Autre Annapurna*, Herzog dances all around the question of just what level of ability he attained as a climber. The gulf between Herzog's expertise and that of the three Chamonix guides, however, emerges somewhat inadvertently in the book. Herzog devotes thirteen pages to an exciting account of what must have been his greatest climb in the Alps: the 1944 first ascent of the Peuterey Ridge on Mont Blanc via the north face of the Col de Peuterey, with his brother, Gérard, and Rébuffat and Terray. The epic ascent culminates in a summit dash in the midst of a violent lightning storm, as the four men avoid a potentially fatal bivouac.

Reading between the lines, one realizes that the *cordée* of Rébuffat and Terray led virtually the whole climb, with the brothers Herzog trailing behind on a second rope. In *L'Autre Annapurna*, Herzog calls the climb "the greatest ascent in the Alps" (to date). Though a highly creditable new route, the Peuterey Ridge was not in the same class as the Walker Spur on the Grandes Jorasses or even Terray and Rébuffat's first on the Col du Caïman. In *Conquistadors*, Terray relegates the Peuterey ascent to a single sentence. Rébuffat seems never to have bothered to write about it.

Another key to Herzog's makeup lies scattered through the pages of *L'Autre Annapurna*. At the age of seventy-nine, long after Rébuffat's radical aesthetic of the mountains as an "enchanted garden" had gained the day, Herzog still automatically conceives of ascent in martial terms. He speaks of his youthful climbs as "victories" and "conquests." One passage is explicit: "Adventure is a war. It determines the character of the combatant, who pledges at every instant his very existence."

War, indeed, has been central to Herzog's conception of himself, and long passages in *L'Autre Annapurna* detail his deeds in the Résistance and later as a captain of a high mountain troop. Unlike Terray, with his epiphany after the battle of Pointe de Clairy, Herzog felt no ambivalence about the war against the Germans. He had only contempt for the collaborators of the Vichy regime.

Herzog's account of the actions in battle of his alpine comrades-at-arms is unabashedly heroic. Terray puts a slightly different spin on his friend's role in the war:

> As a newcomer he was not treated with any great respect by the leaders of the A.S. [the *Armée Secrète,* or underground army]. He was so annoyed by this that, although he had no affiliations with the Communist Party, he turned, on the rebound, to the F.T.P. [the left-wing *Francs Tireurs et Partisans,* or French Partisans and Riflemen]. They were short of men, and Herzog was received with open arms and made a captain.

According to Terray, though beseeched by Herzog to join the F.T.P., Rébuffat wanted no part of a communist outfit. Terray himself also declined, since he then "was not very impressed by all the muddles and internecine quarrels of the new army." For the time being, Terray tolled on as a farmer in Les Houches.

In recent years, amidst the blizzard of revisionism around Annapurna 1950, several French journalists have tried independently to verify the particulars of Herzog's war record. Some have concluded that there is little evidence that the captain performed many of the campaigns he claimed in *L'Autre Annapurna.* By their very nature, however, the underground army and other fugitive battalions of the Maquis left little to document their activities. Perhaps on this question—as on the vexed issue of whether certain famous ascents were in fact hoaxes—one must start from the principle of taking a man at his word. There is no denying the fact that Herzog received two citations of the Croix de Guerre after the war. Nor is there any reason to doubt that his opposition to the Nazis was as fierce and steadfast as that of his general and mentor, Charles de Gaulle.

Oddly enough, while purporting to be an intimate memoir, *L'Autre Annapurna* tells us relatively little about Herzog's personal life. There is not a word in the book about either of his marriages, nor about his four children. From *Who's Who in France* and assorted clippings, we learn that in 1964 Herzog married a countess with the imposing name of Marie-Pierre de Cossé-Brissac, with whom he had a son (now deceased) and a daughter; and that in 1976 he married an Austrian woman named Elisabeth Gamper, who bore him two more sons. In a recent interview in the magazine *Sport et Vie*, asked about his family life, Herzog avowed, "I've always taken my role as a father seriously. In fact, I try to be an ordinary human being. I don't want my children to be proud of having a well-known father." Herzog went on to describe the "hell" that—according to Anne Morrow Lindbergh, whom Herzog knew well—her own children had endured as the offspring of the famous aviator.

So guarded has Herzog been about his private life that, paradoxically, we know less about this most famous mountaineer in French history than we do about his colleagues Rébuffat, Terray, and Lachenal. The habit of self-concealment seems to have set in early.

HERZOG'S MEMOIR does offer certain details of the Annapurna expedition that, while agreeing in their general outlines with the narrative in *Annapurna*, cast new light on the famous ascent. In the very first pages of *L'Autre Annapurna*, Herzog insists that his selection by the Himalayan Committee as leader of the expedition was unanimous, and that he in turn chose the rest of the team. Herzog alludes to two leading candidates who were vetoed by the committee, and one who was accepted only on probation.

One of the most famous Chamonix guides, Herzog states, was excluded because he demanded to be paid for his participation on the expedition. The cognoscenti, puzzling gleefully over this aspersion in 1998, agreed that Herzog must have been referring to Armand Charlet, a generation older than Terray, Lachenal, and

Rébuffat and otherwise an obvious choice for Annapurna. About the identity of the second anonymous rejectee, impugned by Herzog for his "excessive character," the experts were divided. The canard was too vague to point unambiguously at one member of the celebrated company, though the name André Contamine was raised more than once.

Herzog then let slip his juiciest insider gossip:

> The fate of another of the best-known [Chamonix guides] was resolved by conditionally accepting him. In case of any major difficulty during the expedition, I had the absolute power, without appeal, to send him back to France, that is, to banish him. I never had to exercise this clause (which some might judge rather leonine) because—despite what was apparently divulged much later—everyone conducted himself as a true comrade on the mountain.

Vague though these bureaucratic sentences sound, expert observers almost unanimously agreed that they referred to Lachenal. "Despite what was apparently divulged much later" seems an oblique disclaimer of Guérin's edition of the *Carnets*.

If so, one wonders whether Lachenal knew that he was under probation on Annapurna, and that Herzog was ready to send him home at the first sign of rebellion. In any event, the tensions and the barely checked contempt that sprinkle the candid passages in Lachenal's diary give vivid testimony to the strain under which Herzog's knights of the sky prepared to launch themselves toward Annapurna's summit.

DURING THAT LAST WEEK of May, Terray became a demonic workhorse. Most of the arduous trail-breaking that gave the team access to the upper slopes of the north face was performed by him or Herzog. Terray later recalled those days of grueling effort.

> I was trudging on like a sleep-walker, just as on those occasions when I had shot my bolt by doing too many climbs in succession as

a guide. But for all that I was in no mood to give in, and could still find the energy to curse the others when they slumped down exhausted.

In *Annapurna*, Herzog saluted Terray's indomitable spirit: "He was an invaluable man. I know of no one in France who comes nearer to being the ideal member of an expedition."

Having established Camp II, with Herzog, at 19,350 feet, Terray volunteered for a thankless task. There was not enough room in the tents at this "poor little camp" for the Sherpas, who had carried loads behind the trail-breaking of the two Frenchmen, and it seemed unsafe to send them down on their own past teetering seracs and avalanche slopes. So Terray accompanied them back to Camp I, from which an easy trail in the snow allowed the Sherpas to descend all the way to Base Camp. Meanwhile, Terray bivouacked alone, without a tent, at Camp I, preparing to climb again to II in the morning.

Heavy snow and strong winds turned the bivouac into an ordeal. Terray shivered through a virtually sleepless night, "reviewing the whole of my past life."

> I felt no regrets. On the contrary, I blessed the providence which had vouchsafed me to experience this marvelous adventure. . . . My whole lifetime of platitudinous mediocrity seemed as nothing beside these hours of perfect happiness and total absorption in action.

Meanwhile, Lachenal and Rébuffat were having a rough go of it. The "long man," as the Sherpas had nicknamed the lanky Rébuffat, felt his feet go numb every day. Obsessed with a fear of frostbite, he stopped often on the trail to take off his boots and massage his feet. On top of this problem, he suffered from nearly constant intestinal disorders.

Lachenal's diary during the last week of May records a succession of minor woes. "I am with Gaston and we didn't sleep very well." "The night was beautiful, but my sunburned lips gave me a lot of pain." "The last hundred meters up to Camp [II] were a veritable torture for me." "It is now more than two months since I left my kids."

On May 23, above Camp II, the four principal climbers trudged in single file, carrying heavy loads, with Terray and Herzog alternating in the lead. "The other two seemed utterly worn out," wrote Herzog.

Suddenly Lachenal burst out bitterly, "We're not Sherpas!"

Rébuffat seconded him: "We didn't come to the Himalaya to be beasts of burden."

The indefatigable Terray turned scornfully on his teammates: "A climber ought to be able to carry his gear. We're as good as the Sherpas, aren't we?"

Bent panting over his ice axe, Lachenal inveighed, "If we wear ourselves out with this ridiculous porterage, how the hell can we manage in a few days' time?"

Terray lost his temper. "And you call yourselves Chamonix guides! You're just damn amateurs, that's what you are!"

This scene, a rare instance of open conflict acknowledged in *Annapurna*, is corroborated by Terray and even by a terse entry in Lachenal's diary: "Lively altercation with Lionel over this method of proceeding." In Herzog's telling, the episode redounds favorably on the "supermen," as Lachenal mockingly calls Herzog and Terray: "You're supermen, real supermen, and we're just poor weaklings."

Yet the truth of the matter was that by now Herzog and Terray were in far better form than the rest of their teammates. The next day, angling for the first time above 20,000 feet, Terray broke trail through the worst snow yet, thigh-deep powder. He was unable to gain even three feet a minute: one whole hour to climb a paltry 150 feet. In his wake, the Sherpas Pansy and Aila carried heavy loads.

That night the trio camped at 21,650 feet, three in a two-man tent, with only two sleeping bags. Recalled Terray,

> We spent a night of terror listening to the avalanches that
> thundered down the couloir less than fifty feet from our tent,

which shook with the wind of their passing. The Sherpas never closed an eye all night, but just sat there smoking cigarette after cigarette.

The next day, exhausted, Terray forced the route another 600 feet, climbing a 60 degree ice wall. "Deep inside me, I was beginning to doubt. If it went on like this every day we should all be worn out long before reaching the summit, even if an avalanche didn't settle the matter before then."

The north face of Annapurna is not very difficult technically. There is virtually no rock on it that needs to be climbed, and only a few really steep pitches of ice. Yet the face is an extremely dangerous one—a huge open bowl of ice and snow torn with daily avalanches in April and May. During the half century since the French expedition, Annapurna has proven itself arguably the most dangerous of all the fourteen 8,000-meter peaks. For every two climbers who have reached its summit, another has died on the mountain.

The constant strain of worrying about avalanches began to take its toll on the Frenchmen. With Terray momentarily worn out, now Herzog came to the fore, performing a prodigious feat of trail-breaking that pushed the team's progress to 23,500 feet. There, on May 28, he pitched Camp IV beneath a huge, arching ice cliff the team had named the Sickle. On this exposed slope, a small serac served as a protecting wall uphill from the tents.

As well as Herzog was climbing, his morale soared even higher. "I felt . . . complete confidence in our victory," he wrote later. "Annapurna was practically in the bag." Nor can this optimism be attributed to retrospect: Terray, assailed by his own doubts, marveled at his partner's sanguine faith in the team's success.

Recuperating at Camp II on the night of May 28, Terray and Herzog discussed the situation in exhaustive detail.

Maurice was very put out by the poor physical and moral state in which he found the others. Although he had spent no more than a few minutes in their company he considered them sick, discouraged, and altogether incapable of effective action.

Out of that evening's analysis, a plan was born. It was clear to Herzog that if anyone would be capable of making the summit, it would be himself and Terray. The next day, he proposed, the better-rested Terray would carry a load with two Sherpas up to Camp III, then descend again to II. On the following day, with four Sherpas rebreaking trail, Terray and Herzog would climb all the way to Camp IV. On the third day, the pair would carry the essentials for a light camp up through a notch in the Sickle, find a site for Camp V somewhere on the bare, windswept snowfield above, and go for the top the following morning. The monsoon was now firmly predicted to arrive by June 5. If all went according to Herzog's plan, he and Terray would stand atop Annapurna on June 1.

Yet there was a flaw in the plan. Even as Terray and Herzog plotted in Camp II, the other four climbers were trying to carry loads to Camp IV. Their support was vital, for without a well-stocked garrison at IV, a summit dash was far too risky.

On the 29th of May, as Terray climbed toward III, he met Couzy and Lachenal coming down. To his great dismay, Terray learned that the other four climbers had been too exhausted to haul their loads to IV. A little later, he crossed paths with a dejected Rébuffat and Schatz.

"As a result of their lack of form," Terray wrote succinctly in 1961, "my companions had been unable to fulfill their mission . . . and this threw the whole operation out of phase." That night in Camp III, Terray struggled with a moral dilemma few Himalayan climbers have confronted. Camp IV had not been supplied. The summit push with Herzog would therefore have to be delayed. And someone—clearly not the played-out quartet of descending teammates—would have to get gear and food to IV. The fittest Sherpas could pull off the job, but it would be irresponsible to send them, with their rudimentary alpine skills, up high without a Frenchman to accompany them.

Terray's dilemma was whether to climb back down to II, as Herzog had ordered, or to undertake the load-hauling to IV by himself, picking up the slack his teammates had dropped. In the end, he resolved to make the ultimate self-sacrifice. As Terray analyzed his thoughts in Conquistadors,

Was I to obey orders and go back down, or should I stay where I was with the Sherpas and carry out the uncompleted task? By doing this I would lose my chance of teaming up with Herzog, who at present was in the best condition and best placed for the summit dash, so that a bitter paradox would make a disinterested action the frustration of all my hopes. It would be so easy to obey orders and bow to a fate another had ordained. Nobody would ever hold it against me: after all, I was only a simple foot soldier who had taken an oath of obedience. And yet, and yet . . . it seemed to me that by going down at this juncture I would be letting down the side. The very idea gave me a pang such as one might feel at the suggestion of committing a crime.

In *Annapurna*, Herzog handsomely saluted Terray's act of self-abnegation. Equally dismayed at his teammates' failure to carry to IV, he began to concoct a backup plan.

Despite Herzog's poor opinion of the physical and psychological state of the four "sluggards," the fact is that Lachenal had, in his own idiosyncratic way, begun to round into great form. (Such a delayed acclimatization often occurs in the Himalaya, so that a climber who spends weeks suffering from lassitude and headaches low on the mountain suddenly sprints to the head of the pack.)

Lachenal's diary records this transformation. Sunburned lips, exhaustion, insomnia notwithstanding, he is seized by May 25 with an optimism nearly as heady as Herzog's. "Victory now seems assured," he writes on that day. And finally, on May 31, "This morning, one more time, I set out not to descend again until after I have made the summit."

At Camp III, Terray had rallied Rébuffat to his altruistic cause. On May 30, the two men and their Sherpas took seven exhausting hours to climb with loads to Camp IV. They spent the night in an all-out blizzard: "By dawn the tents were half buried in the snow. There was so little space left inside that one could hardly move. We had to dig them out with our mess tins and re-erect them as best we could."

That morning Terray and Rébuffat climbed all the way down to Camp II to recuperate. "Victory seemed farther off than ever," thought a discouraged Terray. On the way down, they crossed paths with Herzog, Lachenal, Ang-Tharkey, and Sarki, who were heading up.

Herzog had replaced Terray with Lachenal in his plan for a summit dash. Camp IV was now stocked. Only two days had been lost from his original scheme, and the monsoon still held off. If there was hope still to claim the summit, it lay in Lachenal's remarkable comeback. "Lachenal was a new man," Herzog wrote in *Annapurna*.

That night the two Frenchmen slept at a new Camp IV (dubbed IVA), which they had pitched just above the ice cliff of the Sickle. In the morning, Ang-Tharkey and Sarki, who had carried yet another load high, joined them for the push into terra incognita.

Meanwhile, down at Camp II, Terray's spirits underwent a revolution. He had come to the belief that Lachenal and Herzog still lacked adequate support to go safely to the summit. It was intolerable for him to loiter low while his friends pushed above 24,000 feet. Terray talked Rébuffat into one more foray, and despite the agony of his recurringly numb feet, the "long man" agreed. After a day's rest, on June 2, carrying light packs, Terray and Rébuffat moved faster than ever before (one and a half hours from III to IV, versus the seven hours it had taken them on May 30) and succeeded in installing themselves in the tent at IV, just below the Sickle. The next day, they would follow their friends' track leftward across the featureless slope, looking for Camp V. Carrying their own tent and sleeping bags, they hoped to move into position for a second attempt on the summit on June 4. Having convinced himself that Herzog and Lachenal "were simply deceiving themselves" in hoping to gain the top on June 3, Terray savored the prospect of making the first ascent of Annapurna with his old Chamonix comrade—not the partner of his charmed *cordée*, but the man with whom he had accomplished his first great climb in the Alps way back in 1942. Even should Lachenal and Herzog precede them, a second summit dash a day later would still be a glorious deed.

As Rébuffat and Terray moved smoothly up to Camp IV on June 2, Herzog and Lachenal, trailed by the doughty Ang-Tharkey and Sarki, broke new ground above the Sickle. Herzog was in an ecstasy. "Not for a single moment," he later wrote, "did either Lachenal or myself entertain the slightest doubt about our victory."

In the early afternoon, the men came to a rib of rock on the far east edge of the bare summit snowfield. The rib offered no natural campsite, but by dint of relentless chopping with their ice axes the men carved out a platform, pitched a tent, and anchored it with pitons driven into the rock.

Herzog offered the Sherpas a chance to go to the summit with them, but the men declined. Their feet starting to freeze, Ang-Tharkey and Sarki headed instead down to the relative safety of Camp IVA.

That evening, wrote Herzog.

> I had great difficulty in concentrating and I couldn't get up an interest in anything. Conversation languished. With great effort, and only because we urged each other on, we managed to make some tea on the stove. . . . It was impossible to swallow any food down at all.

In the night, the wind rose, driving gusts of new snow across the barren slope. Lachenal's diary recorded the sleepless vigil:

> The night was very bad. Violent storm. The rear of the tent collapsed on top of us under the weight of the snow. I passed the night holding on to the tent poles to keep them from falling. We were completely covered with new snow.

For Herzog, the ordeal in the dark at 24,600 feet was worse than "our very worst Alpine bivouacs." In the first light of dawn, as the wind died down and a metallic cold ruled their world, the two men felt "worn out and utterly weary." It would have been tempting to take a rest day, but there was neither time nor food to waste.

After two months of failure and frustration, the French team had finally put itself in position to reach the top of Annapurna, less than 2,000 feet above, across easy-looking ground.

At 6:00 A.M. on June 3, Lachenal and Herzog closed their tent and started climbing toward the sky.

FIVE

Deliverance

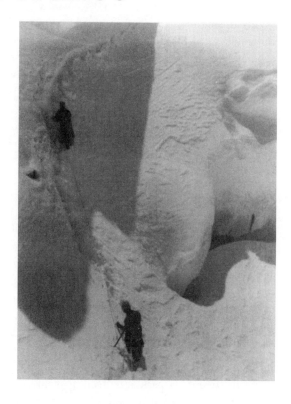

THE CENTRAL MYSTERY of the 1950 Annapurna expedition is what happened on June 3.

For the time being, let us pass the question by, and follow not Lachenal and Herzog as they press through the cold, thin air toward the summit, but Rébuffat and Terray as they climb out of Camp IV, planning a second summit foray the next day. Upon arriving at the serac-sheltered camp the night before, the two Chamonix guides had encountered Schatz and Couzy, who had at last completed their assigned task of hauling loads in support of the summit duo.

Throughout the expedition, it had been Terray who was the stickler for early starts. In that respect, he was ahead of his time, often rousing his teammates at 3:00 or 4:00 A.M., thereby boldly applying the Alpine gambit of the predawn start to the Himalaya, a range where his predecessors had by and large been too discouraged by cold and altitude to brave a launch in the dark.

Happily assuming the lead on June 3, Terray plowed through chest-deep snow as he angled toward a notch in the Sickle. Higher up the soft snow gave way to ice, in which Terray chopped steps for the teammates who followed him. The plan was for all four Frenchmen and two Sherpas, Pansy and Aila, to carry to Camp V, then reassess the situation in light of what they might find out there about Lachenal and Herzog.

Topping out above the Sickle, the climbers soon came to the solitary tent at Camp IVA, where they found Ang-Tharkey and Sarki, who recounted in detail the establishing of Camp V the day before. "They had frostbitten feet and seemed in poor shape," noted Terray. "Our own two Sherpas were also complaining about their feet and lost no time scrambling into the tent to get warm."

On the bare slope above the Sickle, the four Frenchmen took turns breaking trail, the footsteps from the day before having drifted in during the storm in the night. Pansy and Aila followed gamely in the track. All six men felt their feet go numb, and their progress was slowed by the necessity of stopping to take off boots and rub their toes back into feeling inside the protection of a *pied d'éléphant*—a half sleeping bag normally used for bivouacs. Though the men had come to Nepal with the finest footgear money could buy, the best leather boots in the world in 1950 were inadequate for the cold and lack of oxygen above 8,000 meters. (It would not be until the invention of plastic double boots in the 1980s that footgear equal to the task of preventing frostbite at such altitudes would become available.) Bottled oxygen had been used on Everest as early as 1922, but the French team had chosen to do without it. This purist decision in turn contributed to the problem of cold feet, for a climber breathing supplemental oxygen above 24,000 feet normally has far better circulation than one without.

With Terray doing the lion's share of the trail-breaking, the six men reached Camp V around midday. There they found a single tent half buried in snow. There was no note from Herzog or Lachenal. Laboring mightily, the men hacked out a second platform and erected their tent. Terray chopped away with his axe in an efficient fury: "At times I would force so much that a black veil began to form in front of my eyes and I fell to my knees, panting like an overdriven beast."

The day had deteriorated into a gathering storm. Even before the second tent was pitched, Terray sent Pansy and Aila down to Camp IV, counting on their being able to follow the trail before wind and snow could fill the steps again. At last Rébuffat and Terray crawled into one tent, Couzy and Schatz into the other.

It seemed obvious that Lachenal and Herzog must be making their summit bid, despite the storm. "Time went by without our seeing anything," recalled Terray. "Outside the furies of the storm were in full cry, and we began to get seriously worried." As the afternoon waned, it became apparent that it would soon be too late for anyone to go down to Camp IV. With the return of Lachenal and Herzog, there would be six men crammed into two two-man tents—an intolerable prospect in a storm. Couzy and Schatz, both altitude-sick, offered to head down to IVA. As soon as they had parted, Terray moved to the empty tent and started melting snow to brew up malt drinks for his teammates. "As time went by we became more and more anxious," he later wrote. "I kept on sticking my head out of the tent to see if I could see anything, but there was nothing but the pitiless blizzard."

At last, toward the end of the afternoon, Terray heard the crunching of footsteps in the snow. He thrust himself outside the tent and saw Herzog, alone, his beard and clothing coated with rime. "We've made it," the expedition leader said. "We're back from Annapurna."

What happened next appears in both *Annapurna* and *Conquistadors of the Useless*, in passages that strikingly agree. Wrote Herzog,

Terray, who was speechless with delight, wrung my hands. Then the smile vanished from his face: "Maurice—your hands!" There was an uneasy silence. I had forgotten that I had lost my gloves: my fingers were violet and white and hard as wood. The other two stared at them in dismay—they realized the full seriousness of the injury.

In Terray's telling:

I seized him by the hand, only to find to my horror that I was shaking an icicle. What had been a hand was like metal. I cried out: "Momo, your hand is frostbitten!" He looked at it indifferently, and replied: "That's nothing, it'll come back."

"What about Biscante?" Terray anxiously asked, using Lachenal's nickname.

"He won't be long," Herzog answered. "He was just in front of me!"

Rébuffat got Herzog into his tent, while Terray started heating water on the stove. Lachenal's failure to appear deeply troubled Terray. Once more, he thrust his head outside the tent to look for any sign of his friend in the deepening murk of the storm.

Then the raging wind carried a faint but unmistakable "Help." I got out of the tent and saw Lachenal three hundred feet below us. Hastily I dragged on my boots and clothes, but when I came out of the tent again there was nothing to be seen on the bare slope. The shock was so terrible that I lost my self-control and began to cry, shouting in desperation. It seemed that I had lost the companion of the most enchanted hours of my life. Overcome with grief I lay in the snow unconscious of the hurricane that howled around me.

Abruptly, the clouds cleared for a moment. Terray saw Lachenal once more, seemingly even farther below the tent than he had been at first sighting. Without even putting on his crampons, Terray seized his axe and launched into a high-speed glissade, sliding on his boot soles. The crust was so hard that the ski champion from Grenoble had trouble stopping.

It was evident that Lachenal had taken a long fall. He was missing his ice axe, one crampon, his hat, and his gloves. In a state of near hysteria, Lachenal had only one thought. "My feet are frozen stiff up to the ankles," he told Terray. "Get me down to Camp II quickly, so Oudot can give me an injection. Quick, let's get going."

To try to descend now, with darkness gathering, in full storm, would have meant certain death. Yet Terray could not reason with his friend.

> When he heard me starting to argue, he suddenly grabbed my ice axe and started running across the slope. His single crampon impeded him, however, and he crumpled onto the snow weeping and screaming: "We must get down. I've got to have some injections or I'll be ruined for life. They'll cut off my feet."

At last Terray wore down his partner's resistance. Chopping steps with desperate energy, he cut a staircase back up toward the tent. Lachenal followed, literally crawling on hands and knees.

Inside the tent, Terray tried to unlace Lachenal's boots, but they were frozen and intractable. Eventually he had to cut them open with his knife. "My heart sank at the sight of his feet inside, white and utterly insensible." Eleven years later, Terray recalled his thoughts at that moment:

> Annapurna, the first eight-thousander, was climbed, but was it worth such a price? I had been ready to give my life for the victory, yet now it suddenly seemed too dearly bought.

Thus the account in *Conquistadors*. Once more, Herzog's version dovetails closely with Terray's. "My feet are frostbitten," he quotes Lachenal raving to his friend. "Take me down . . . take me down, so that Oudot can see to me." Lachenal, Herzog confirms, "was obsessed by the fear of amputation."

Lachenal's own account of his fall (written, apparently, within two or three days) is vivid in its details:

> A little before arriving at Camp V, I took a fall of 150 meters, due to what cause, I don't know. Throughout the fall, I had time to say to

myself, "This is it, this time I've wiped myself out." After turning over and over again in the air, getting stripped of one of my crampons, my ice axe, my gloves, and my hat, for no reason I stopped, stupefied. Completely transfixed with cold, my hands frozen. I still had my pack. I thrust my hands inside it and started yelling for help, incapable as I was of climbing by myself back up to the tents.

No one came! It was a long time. The occupants of the tents had to put their boots back on. Between two patches of fog I saw Lionel descending toward me. I wanted to descend at least to the next camp [Camp IV]. He convinced me that I wasn't in good enough shape for that. I had a great fear that in the morning we wouldn't be able to find the route. Finally, I climbed back up with a great deal of trouble.

With darkness upon them, the four survivors huddled in their tents. Terray brewed hot drinks long into the night, as he and Rébuffat tirelessly performed what was then considered the necessary torture prescribed for saving frozen digits. Each took the stiff end of a rope and lashed away for hours, Terray whipping Lachenal's toes, Rébuffat Herzog's toes and fingers. All they accomplished, as medical science would later learn, was to exacerbate the damage.

In April 1999, I interviewed Maurice Herzog in Paris. He had turned eighty just two and a half months before. By now, he and Francis de Noyelle, the expedition's liaison officer, were the only surviving French members of the 1950 expedition.

We met in Herzog's posh office on the Rue de Louvre. Traffic delayed his arrival, and as I waited for some forty minutes, having been ushered by Herzog's assistant into his inner sanctum, I noted the furnishings. The huge brown desk behind which Herzog habitually sat had a brass nameplate perched on it. On the floor, before the black-and-white marble fireplace, spread a luxuriant potted orchid. An original painting by the alpine artist and cartoonist Samivel hung on one wall, a framed and signed photo of de Gaulle on another. One bookshelf was wholly given over to editions of *An-napurna* in various languages.

Herzog arrived, nattily dressed in suit, vest, and tie. As he offered his apologies for being late, he shook my hand vigorously, and I had an instant of squeamishness as I clasped the shortened stumps of his fingers. Herzog installed himself behind his desk. Through much of our hour together, he laid his hands on the desktop facing me, or brought them together in a low arch, as if praying.

Remarkably handsome in his ninth decade, Herzog spoke lucidly in French and without hesitation. A jackhammer tearing up the sidewalk outside drowned out some of his responses, which I had to ask him to repeat. He seemed patient, open, sincere, as though his only wish were to answer my questions. An old-fashioned courtesy radiated from this dignified man.

It had been three years since the publication of Ballu's biography of Rébuffat and Guérin's edition of Lachenal's diary, three years of controversy and reexamination. Had the furor troubled his sleep?

Not at all, he maintained. "I have a clear conscience," he said, "and the experience of the truth. No one has doubted what I wrote."

The remark puzzled me. In the wake of the recent publications every mountaineering journalist who had taken up the issue had expressed doubts about the whole truth of *Annapurna*.

Gradually we edged back toward the events of June 3, 1950. On the summit, as Herzog had made plain in *Annapurna*, Lachenal had been consumed with a frenzy to descend at once, while he himself lingered, awash in his beatific trance, attaching the various flags to his ice axe for summit photos, staring at the horizon.

Now Herzog said something that dumbfounded me. "The hour on the summit didn't exacerbate the frostbite. We were well protected. Losing the gloves didn't cause it. The journalists always say that, but they're wrong. I just put my hands in my pockets as I descended.

"No, it was digging in the crevasse for our boots [two days later, on the morning of June 5] that caused the frostbite. Raking with my fingers in the snow. I knew I would freeze my hands. But we had to find the boots—otherwise we would have died."

What was going on here? I wondered. After forty-nine years of remembering that fateful day, had Herzog changed his story? In *Annapurna*, he had seemed unequivocally to blame the loss of his gloves (and his failure to remember to use the spare socks he had stashed in his pack) for the frostbite that would cost him his fingers. The sentence recording Terray's and Rébuffat's shock at seeing his frozen hands—"The other two stared at them in dismay—they realized the full seriousness of the injury"—said it all.

In *Annapurna*, there had been no mention of sticking his hands in his pockets. Later, I read the opening chapter of *L'Autre Annapurna*, Herzog's memoir that had appeared only the year before. In those pages, he retold the events of June 3, 4, and 5, and the story had indeed changed. No mention of dropping his gloves and watching them roll away. (In *Annapurna*, "The movement of those gloves was engraved in my sight as something irredeemable, against which I was powerless. The consequences might be most serious.")

Instead, *L'Autre Annapurna* contained a long passage about searching through the snow at the bottom of the crevasse, where the four men bivouacked through the night of June 4–5, as Herzog looked for the boots that alone would ensure his and Lachenal's survival, frantically raking the snow with his fingers:

> My hands mattered little, if the boots could be recovered. . . . Each boot that I might recover promised me the life of my comrade or myself. The price, alas, would be my frozen fingers.

Reading on in Herzog's 1998 memoir, I came across another passage that was at odds with *Annapurna*. After Terray had glissaded to the rescue of the fallen Lachenal, late on the afternoon of June 3, the pair struggled back up to the tents at Camp V. Now Herzog recounted what Terray had said to him and Rébuffat on returning.

In broken phrases, Lionel told us that Louis, collapsed in the snow at the edge of a crevasse, had refused to get up. He preferred to die nobly in the mountains in a rage rather than perish in the midst of this army in full rout. Despite his protests, regardless of his delirium, Lionel seized him with force and determination. Throwing caution to the winds, he dragged him up to camp, without hesitating to resort to invectives and even violence.

This version of Lachenal's behavior after the fall cannot be reconciled with the accounts in both *Annapurna* and Terray's *Conquistadors* (which has Lachenal wildly demanding an immediate descent to Camp II to save his toes). It is even further afield from Lachenal's own account, which attributes his frenzy to descend to a quite rational fear that the storm would wipe out the men's tracks and leave them lost on the mountain. (Indeed, this is precisely what happened on June 4.)

In his office, Herzog mused on the difference between his two books. "At one point we had the idea of each of us writing a chapter of the expedition book, each on his specialty," Herzog told me. "Oudot on medicine, Ichac on cinematography. . . . If we had done that, the book would not have been so interesting. It would have sold maybe one thousand copies.

"Why did it sell fifteen million copies? *Annapurna* is a sort of novel. It's a novel, but a true novel.

"It was easy to dictate it in the hospital. It came straight from my heart. I have a good memory. There were times when I was crying for myself as I dictated it, like at the bottom of the crevasse. As for the dialogue, sometimes I paraphrased, but I knew my comrades well. I could imagine them speaking. Even when I wasn't there, I slipped in some dialogue."

I was uncertain how to understand this avowal. Did Herzog mean that, as a novel, *Annapurna* was not to be held to the standards of truth of a factual memoir? Or simply that the book read like a novel, which explained its immense popularity?

About *L'Autre Annapurna*, Herzog insisted, "These are the feelings of fifty years later. The first book, *Annapurna*, was for the whole world. *L'Autre Annapurna* was written for me, to express myself. One is objective, the other subjective. The new book is what I feel now about all my adventures."

For weeks after my interview, I chewed on the bones of Herzog's strange and provocative remarks. In those two critical discrepancies—concerning the cause of his frostbitten hands, and Lachenal's behavior after the fall—I could discern three possible explanations.

The first was that Herzog had simply started to become forgetful, misremembering events on which he had already gone clearly on record. The second was that the new version, in *L'Autre Annapurna*, was a deliberate attempt to manipulate a whole new generation of readers, many of whom had perhaps not read *Annapurna*.

I laid to rest the first hypothesis: in his office, Herzog seemed too lucid to be forgetfully revising his own past. And the second seemed unlikely, too. Surely the discrepancies begged critics to accuse him of dishonesty. The new, more self-serving version might cast a better light on Herzog, but it was an open invitation to readers such as myself to call his rewriting bluff.

The third possibility, I thought, was that this is indeed how memory works, in all its fallible reinvention of the past. After nearly fifty years, Herzog's emotions about those dramatic days high on Annapurna had perhaps restructured his memories into what *should* have been. He should have lost his fingers not because of the stupid mistake of dropping his gloves, but by saving the companion whose diary would later impugn him, as he raked with bare hands through the snow, sacrificing his fingers to find the boots. As for Lachenal's asking to be left to die after his fall—it was the logical culmination of the portrait of the genius-madman Herzog had slowly built up in *Annapurna*. The suicidally reckless climber, who would rather die in a demonic rage than limp pitifully back to ordinary human safety.

These reconstructions need not be cynical, or even fully conscious, on Herzog's part. They could be the fruit of memory's seizing again and again on disturbing, pivotal events, reshaping them with each rehearsal, trying to find meaning where there was only happenstance. They might exemplify the process so ruefully predicted in Robert Frost's great (and much misunderstood) poem about memory's sentimentality, "The Road Not Taken." In that poem, the speaker clearly recognizes that the two paths are equally worn: his choice of one over the other is a flip-of-the-coin decision. Yet in the last stanza,

> *I shall be telling this with a sigh*
> *Somewhere ages and ages hence:*
> *Two roads diverged in a wood, and I—*
> *I took the one less traveled by,*
> *And that has made all the difference.*

THROUGH THE NIGHT of June 3–4, the four men at Camp V got almost no sleep. For the first time, the storm showed no signs of abating toward dawn. For all the men knew, the monsoon had arrived. Wrote Herzog in *Annapurna,*

> As the night wore on the snow lay heavier on the tent, and once again I had the frightful feeling of being slowly and silently asphyxiated. I tried, with all the strength of which I was capable, to push off with both forearms the mass that was crushing me. These fearful exertions left me gasping for breath and I fell back into the same exhausted state. It was much worse than the previous night.

According to Terray, the wind was so violent that it threatened to tear the tents loose from their anchors.

At last, in the wee hours, Herzog and Rébuffat drifted into an exhausted sleep—only to be wakened by Terray, that demon of the early start. As Terray tried to help Lachenal get dressed, he ran into a seemingly insoluble problem. Lachenal's feet were too swollen to force back into his cut-open boots. There was no way the man could descend the mountain in stocking feet and survive. But what could be done?

Suddenly the only possible answer dawned on Terray, bringing with it a gust of terror. His own boots were two sizes larger than

Lachenal's. If he gave them to his partner, then forced his own feet into Lachenal's inadequate boots . . . The exchange could easily cost Terray his own feet. He hesitated, then performed an act of supreme self-denial. As he later wrote,

> To give way would be dishonor, a crime against the name of friendship. There was nothing else for it, and with the feelings of a soldier going over the top I hauled off my second pair of stockings and stuffed my feet into these new instruments of torture.

Terray and Rébuffat had arrived at Camp V the day before full of hopes of going to the summit themselves. Now there was no possibility of that. Instead, their utmost efforts would be devoted to saving their friends' lives.

For Terray and Rébuffat, there was no other possible course. This was what a mountain guide did. In later life, however, Rébuffat's bitterness about Annapurna was deepened by the sense that Herzog had never fully acknowledged either the two men's sacrifice of their own chance for the summit, or their heroism in saving the frostbitten pair's lives. For all Herzog's considerable magnanimity in crediting the others' achievements on the way up the mountain, *Annapurna* is curiously thin on such benedictions on the descent. In place of any expression of true indebtedness, within moments of his return to Camp V Herzog tries to bathe his partners in his own joy: "This victory was not just one man's achievement, a matter for personal pride . . . it was a victory for us all, a victory for mankind itself." (That sentence from *Annapurna* seems unconsciously telling, as if, with "one man's achievement," Herzog had already started to write Lachenal out of the story.)

At this point, Terray seemed once again to take charge. As the men packed up on the morning of June 4, with the storm in full fury around them, he alone had the wits to urge a course that, had it been followed, might have saved the men much of the agony that lay in wait for them. Terray stuffed food and his sleeping bag into his pack, urging Rébuffat and Herzog to do likewise (neither man heeded the advice). Terray then started to collapse a tent and pack it up as well. All his training as a guide told him that to carry a tent and bag with him would give the team a huge extra safety margin in case the men lost their downward track. But Lachenal's impatience forestalled this canny instinct. Already roped up, Lachenal yelled, "Hurry up! What the hell do you think you're doing with a tent? We'll be at Camp IV in an hour." Terray allowed his partner's optimism to persuade him.

In the chaos of the previous night, Terray had laid down his ice axe somewhere near the tents. Now he could not find it under several inches of new snow. With time at a premium, he and Rébuffat seized the two remaining axes, and each took charge of a frostbitten teammate, to whom he was roped. Herzog and Lachenal had had virtually no sleep for forty-eight hours, and both men were almost exhausted. With his frozen fingers, Herzog had been unable to dress himself, so Rébuffat had put on his clothes and boots for him.

As the four men started down, Lachenal's apprehension that the track would have disappeared proved true: not a trace of their steps showed in the newly drifted snow. Lachenal led the blind stumble through the storm, his impatience screwed to a new pitch, trying to find the way from his memory of the occasional landmark—a serac here, a crevasse there.

By midday the wind had calmed almost to nothing, yet still the thick flakes of snow fell and piled up alarmingly fast. Terray and Rébuffat now alternated in the lead, breaking trail with painful slowness through first thigh-deep, then waist-deep powder. The mountain around the men turned into a blurry, featureless universe of white. "We kept colliding with hummocks which we had taken for hollows," wrote Herzog. A heavy despair settled over the quartet, as they recognized they were lost. Now and then, Terray urged a halt so he could take off his boots and massage his feet. "Though ready for death," he later wrote, "I had no wish to survive mutilated."

Herzog responded to the party's increasingly dire predicament by lapsing into a kind of robotic apathy, following Rébuffat, as Terray put it, "without a murmur." Retracing their steps to try to find a landmark, crisscrossing the slopes almost randomly, the men sought a way out of their maze. They sensed they had reached a point somewhere near the great ice cliff of the Sickle, but could see no hint of it. Camp IVA must lie somewhere hereabouts—a single tent in a miasma of white.

Even in these extreme circumstances, it would suit Herzog to perpetuate the notion that informs *Annapurna* from start to finish—that his was the counsel of reason and deliberation, trying to rein in the rash impulses of his teammates. "Terray, when his turn came, charged madly ahead." "Lachenal gave him considerable trouble. Perhaps he was not quite in his right mind. He said it was no use going on; we must dig a hole in the snow and wait for fine weather." "Each in turn did the maddest things: Terray traversed the steep and avalanchy slopes with one crampon badly adjusted. He and Rébuffat performed incredible feats of balance without the least slip."

In hopes that they were in the vicinity of Camp IVA, and that Schatz and Couzy or some of the Sherpas might be ensconced there, the men cried for help in unison. Only the swish of softly falling snow answered their plaints.

The hours had passed almost unnoticed: night was approaching. The last-ditch suggestion of Lachenal—according to Herzog the whim of a madman—loomed in fact as the men's best hope: to dig a hole in which to bivouac, hoping to survive until the weather changed. Recognizing this fact, Terray started to carve out a hollow with feckless swings of his axe.

As he did so, Lachenal suddenly let out a cry. Terray jerked around, but saw nothing of his friend. Without realizing it, Lachenal had been standing on a thin snow bridge over a hidden crevasse. The bridge had broken, plunging him into the depths of the crevasse, unchecked by any belay. Yet the potential disaster turned out to be a deliverance. Lachenal had fallen a mere twelve to fifteen feet into the hole, checking up unhurt in a perfect nook for an emergency bivouac.

In *Annapurna*, Herzog renders the exchange between the two old friends at the moment of the crevasse plunge:

> "Lachenal!" called Terray.
> A voice, muffled by many thicknesses of ice and snow, came up to us. It was impossible to make out what it was saying.

"Lachenal!"

Terray jerked the rope violently; this time we could hear.

"I'm here!"

"Anything broken?"

"No! It'll do for the night! Come along."

Forty-eight years later, in *L'Autre Annapurna*, this dialogue has been revised to make it sound more colloquial. Lachenal curses his friends on the surface as a "bunch of *babotsh*" (local slang for the inhabitants of the valley below Chamonix). Which version better represents the "true novel" Herzog aimed at in *Annapurna*? Both, no doubt, are products of Herzog's memory. For that matter, Terray's *Conquistadors* is equally a partial fiction—as, some would argue, are inevitably all memoir and biography. Even Lachenal's diary is a construct at odds with the whole truth.

In that diary, Lachenal delivers his own I-told-you-so:

> The whole day, we stirred up the snow without knowing where we were, climbing, descending, retracing our steps, only to come finally, at 6:30 P.M., to a decision we should have made long before: to find a crevasse in which to spend the night. We found one, into which I fell by accident.

Self-congratulatory that diary account may be, but in its clearheadedness, it undercuts the portrait of both of Herzog's books, and even, at times, of Terray's—of Biscante as an impetuous climber operating on reckless instinct, having to be restrained, after his fall, like a madman on a leash. If we can trust Lachenal's account—written, after all, for himself, and not for publication—then it was he who most cogently summed up the four men's plight on June 4 and sensed the way out of it.

In any event, one by one, Terray, Herzog, and Rébuffat dropped down what Herzog called "a regular toboggan-slide" into the crevasse to join Lachenal. Terray says it was a plunge of merely twelve to fifteen feet; Herzog measures it at thirty feet in *Annapurna*, forty feet in his later memoir. (Terray's estimate is the more likely, for a thirty-foot drop could easily have caused broken ankles.)

So began one of the legendary bivouacs in Himalayan annals. The grotto was just big enough to accommodate the four men, who broke off icicles and rearranged the snow underneath them to make their huddled vigil marginally more comfortable. All night, whenever any man moved, or jolted suddenly as a cramp seized his leg, he disturbed the other three.

Terray pulled out his sleeping bag and slithered inside it, "carried away on a tide of voluptuous bliss." It was only now that he learned that Rébuffat and Herzog had neglected to pack up their own sleeping bags. Sitting on their packs, the others shivered stoically in silence. As Terray recalled, "I soon began to feel my disgusting egoism, however, and after some contortions Herzog, Lachenal, and I all managed to squeeze our lower portions into the providential bag."

All four men had taken off their boots: to leave them on was to invite certain frostbite. Rébuffat rubbed his own feet, complaining out loud of the pain. Terray rubbed Herzog's and Lachenal's feet for hours each.

In *Annapurna*, Herzog reveals that even in this wretched bivouac, the euphoric trance that had seized him on the summit detached him from his surroundings.

> I was astonished to feel no pain. Everything material about me seemed to have dropped away. I seemed to be quite clear in my thoughts and yet I floated in a kind of peaceful happiness.

In his next breath, however, Herzog admits that he had given himself up for dead. "All was over, I thought. Wasn't this cavern the most beautiful grave I could hope for?"

Shortly before dawn, the men heard "a queer noise from a long way off . . . a sort of prolonged hiss." Suddenly they were inundated with powder snow. A small avalanche had swept the slope above them, spilling loads of fine spindrift into the hole by which they had entered the crevasse. By the time the avalanche stopped, the men were buried in powder. They struggled to free themselves, but now their belongings—including their precious boots—lay lost beneath the new debris.

At this critical juncture in the men's survival ordeal, the various accounts diverge once more. In *Annapurna,* someone breaks the silence: "Daylight!" To which Rébuffat wearily answers, "Too early to start."

Terray admits to having fallen asleep, despite the misery of the crevasse, only to be awakened by the avalanche, which he places at first light. Lachenal alone records the hour of the avalanche—4:30 A.M., when it would still have been pitch dark.

With the "ghastly light" of dawn, the men struggle to find their belongings beneath the piles of new snow about them. According to Terray, Rébuffat found his boots first, put them on, and scrambled to the surface. In Herzog's account, Lachenal was the first to find a pair of boots; when he tried to put them on, he realized they were Rébuffat's. Terray found his boots shortly after.

All sources agree that Rébuffat was the first to emerge from the crevasse. In *Annapurna,* Terray calls up, "What's the weather like?"

"Can't see a thing," answers Rébuffat. "It's blowing hard."

Terray follows Rébuffat to the surface. Impatient as ever, Lachenal gives up the search for his own boots and—in Herzog's words—"called frantically, hauled himself up on the rope. . . . Terray from outside pulled as hard as he could."

In Herzog's telling, "When [Lachenal] emerged from the opening he saw the sky was clear and blue, and he began to run like a madman, shrieking, 'It's fine! It's fine!' " Thus the team realizes that, having taken off their goggles to navigate through the previous day's storm, Rébuffat and Terray have become snow-blind. They confuse the milky blur before their eyes with a continuing tempest. Only the sighted Lachenal can see the blue sky that promises the men salvation.

Terray reinforces the image of Lachenal as madman: "No sooner was he up than he started bellowing again: 'It's fine! It's fine! We're saved! We're saved!'—and ran off toward the end of the trough in which our cave was situated."

Lachenal's diary, however, tells a quite different story. Having failed to find his own boots, he climbs to the surface, not hauled like a sack of potatoes by Terray, but under his own power, by "planting the tips of my frozen feet in the snow." In *Annapurna*, only Terray and Rébuffat are snow-blind; according to Lachenal, Herzog is also. On emerging from the crevasse, Lachenal confirms the fact that a storm still rages, with a strong wind. There is no mad running in the snow, no screams of deliverance. Instead, "Finally I see a corner of blue sky, then little by little all the sky clears. The weather is good. We're saved if we have enough strength."

Far below him, Lachenal sees Camp II. Hoping to attract someone's attention down below, he waves his arms and shouts. Despite being snow-blind himself, Terray treats his partner's actions as the folly of a deluded man. "Lachenal, now completely hysterical, was shouting and semaphoring in the direction of Camp II, which he claimed he could see at the bottom of the slope."

What is the truth here? One can forgive Lachenal for his joyous shouts at the moment when the tide in the men's luck seems to have turned. One can imagine him running across the snow as he urges his friends to get on with their descent. In all the photos and diagrams of Annapurna, it looks eminently possible to see Camp II from the top of the Sickle, some 3,300 feet above. Perhaps that was too large a gap for voices to carry across, but who could blame a man for shouting? And once the weather had cleared, of course Oudot and Ichac and Noyelle, down at Camp II, would have been searching the mountain with binoculars for any sign of their missing teammates.

Meanwhile, all accounts agree, Herzog continued to search at the bottom of the crevasse for the last two pairs of boots. In *Annapurna*, he is fairly matter-of-fact about the effort, thinking logically, "The boots *had* to be found, or Lachenal and I were done for." It is only in *L'Autre Annapurna*, with its glaze of long-sifted memory, that that mission takes on the guise of martyrdom. In that book, instead of resigning himself to a euphoric death in the crevasse, Herzog focuses on his impending role: "From that instant on, I sensed that I would have to sacrifice a part of myself."

After finding the boots and sending them up on a rope, Herzog is hauled in turn to the surface by Terray, only to collapse in the snow exhausted. Both of his own versions of the story indicate that at this point, he urged the others to go on without him. In *Anna-*

purna, he says to Terray, "It's all over for me. Go on . . . you have a chance . . . you must take it."

Terray rejoins: "We'll help you. If we get away, so will you."

In *L'Autre Annapurna,* however, this exchange has been hugely expanded, into a drama of interpersonal loyalty that, if it really took place, further elevates Terray's nobility. On the edge of the crevasse, Herzog beckons Terray close, then whispers into his ear: "Leave me, Lionel. I beg you. I'm finished. It's impossible to stand up. My feet and hands are frozen. . . . Leave me here, beside the crevasse. Leave, leave! Hurry . . . save yourself."

"No, Maurice, I refuse."

"It's you who's crazy!"

"I RE-FU-SE," Terray hammers. "Either we escape together, or we stay here together. Here. With you."

"That's . . . blackmail?"

"No, that's the *cordée.* You never abandon a wounded man in the mountains. You know that. It's like in the war. And besides, Maurice, you are my brother in battle."

Something rings false about this scene. It reads like a fantasia on the theme of the solidarity so curtly voiced by Terray in Herzog's original telling. Once more, the considerable discrepancy between the two versions creates a problem of credibility for Herzog. Which really happened? If the entire, poignant dialogue invoking the fidelity unto death of former comrades-at-arms really took place, why did Herzog leave it out of *Annapurna,* that otherwise so dramatically crafted narrative?

In any event, Herzog's earlier, terser version seems corroborated by Terray's own account of the exchange in *Conquistadors:*

> As he lay there gasping it was his turn to feel a moment of despair, and he said: "It's all over, Lionel. I'm finished. Leave me and let me die." I encouraged him as best I could, and in a minute or two he felt better.

The plea to be left behind, whether briefly expressed or played out in the full exchange of the later memoir, raises yet another question. In changing his story about what Lachenal voiced after his terrible fall on June 3—from a demand to descend to Camp II for injections, in *Annapurna*, to a demand to be left to die, in *L'Autre Annapurna*—Herzog perhaps unconsciously projects his own moribund despair of June 5 onto Lachenal's plight two days earlier.

But in both versions, Herzog makes it clear that he is not snow-blind. "The weather was perfect," he writes in *Annapurna*. "The mountains were resplendent. Never had I seen them look so beautiful." Yet a few paragraphs later, he admits, "[Lachenal] was the only one of the four of us who could see Camp II below." If Herzog had escaped snow-blindness, why couldn't he see Camp II as well?

For the second morning, the men struggle to put on their boots. This time Herzog's have to be cut open before he can force his feet into them. Now, as the men prepare to stagger on down the mountain, they disagree as to which direction to start out. Herzog urges a leftward course, Lachenal a rightward.

Curiously, only Herzog's two versions mention anyone calling for help. In *Annapurna*, at first the other three think Lachenal's shouts toward Camp II are the final proof of his derangement. "Lachenal's frozen feet affected his nervous system. . . . Obviously he didn't know what he was doing. . . . They were shrieks of despair, reminding me tragically of some climbers lost in the Mont Blanc massif whom I had endeavored to save." Yet in the next moment, the others join in, hurling their feeble chorus of cries into the thin air.

Then the men hear an answering cry. "Barely two hundred yards away," Herzog writes in *Annapurna*, "Marcel Schatz, waist-deep in snow, was coming slowly toward us like a boat on the surface of the slope." Terray puts their rescuer even closer: "Suddenly Schatz emerged from behind a serac fifty yards away."

The four men, it turns out, had bivouacked in their crevasse only 200 yards from Camp IVA, where Schatz and Couzy lay in their sleeping bags. In *Annapurna*, Schatz and Herzog embrace, as Schatz murmurs, "It is wonderful—what you have done." The 1998 memoir elaborates on this most emotional of reunions, turning it into a mystical religious moment:

He clasped me in his arms, gave me a kiss of peace, breathed new life into me. Yes, in that moment this man transmitted to me something of sacred value. I would have liked to pray: "My God, I want so much to be a man, but I remain your infant." . . . With an infinite gentleness, my friend supported me and helped me take my first steps.

Lost in the persistent characterizing of Lachenal in extremis as a madman is the fact that, once again, on the morning of June 5, he had a better notion of what to do than the others did. Calling for help, far from a shriek of despair, was a pragmatic choice, and it brought, with Schatz's answering cry, the escape the men so dearly needed.

IN THE TELLING AND RETELLING of the Annapurna story, Schatz's discovery of the four stranded men has always been treated as the capstone of a miraculous series of close calls resolved by heroic deeds. Yet one need not be an iconoclast to ponder the circumstances leading up to that moment.

By the afternoon of June 4, in full blizzard, Schatz and Couzy would have known that the four men above them were in trouble. They would have guessed that, had they not already come to grief, the quartet would be descending in a desperate search for Camp IVA, and that the storm had wiped out the track. To go out and look for the men might have been impossible: it might well have caused Schatz and Couzy to lose their own way. But most climbers would at least have stood outside the tent and shouted, in hopes their friends would hear them and so be guided to the elusive camp. (On Everest in 1924, above Camp VI, Noel Odell whistled and yodeled for the better part of an hour in the vain hope of signaling his lost friends Mallory and Irvine.)

There is no evidence that Schatz or Couzy did anything on June 4 other than lie in their tent and wait. As Françoise Rébuffat bitterly complained in 1999, "What were they doing, Couzy and Schatz, sleeping in their tent like a couple of schoolboys, instead of going out to look?"

Indeed, as the four exhausted men followed Schatz back to Camp IVA, they found Couzy still in his sleeping bag. By now Terray was preoccupied with his own terror of frostbite. He asked his friends to leave him at IVA so he could massage his frozen feet; they might return the next morning, he urged, to fetch him in case his snow-blindness had not improved. Herzog quotes Terray as saying, "I want to be whole, or dead!"

In the tent, Terray attacked his own feet, rubbing and beating them for hours. "After a time," he later wrote, "the circulation came back and their rather greeny whiteness gave way to a fine healthy pink, but the pain was so great that I could not restrain myself from groaning out loud."

As the other five men climbed down the Sickle, they set loose a slab of snow that gathered into an avalanche, thundering down and engulfing Camp IV below, where the four Sherpas who had gone high on Annapurna awaited. Although the avalanche carried off one of the tents, by good luck none of the Sherpas was injured. Greeting Lachenal, who took off his boots to rub his feet, Pansy tried to comfort him, telling him the frostbite was nothing serious.

Both Herzog and Lachenal felt that the only hope to save their frozen digits was to go all the way down to Camp II the same day. Herzog roped up with Sarki and Alia, while Lachenal and even the snow-blind Rébuffat insisted on descending unroped. Meanwhile Schatz, Ang-Tharkey, and Pansy climbed back up to IVA to persuade Terray to descend. While Terray deliberated, Schatz performed a courageous task, sliding back into the crevasse of the bivouac to search for Herzog's camera, with its exposed summit photos. After much pawing through the loose snow, he found the Foca camera undamaged.

In the heat of the sun, after so much new snow had fallen, avalanches were breaking loose everywhere, creating a near-constant din. Below Camp III, Herzog and his two ropemates set off an avalanche and hurtled with it toward a 1,500-foot precipice. The three men bounced from serac to serac, before the rope fortuitously snagged over a crest of ice, suspending Herzog on one side—upside down, with the cord threatening to strangle him—and Sarki and

Aila on the other. Eventually the Sherpas were able to pull Herzog back to safety.

Strung out all up and down the mountain, the team descended like the army in full rout Lachenal would later conjure up. Lachenal, who had not been wearing goggles, stopped to take a short nap; when he awoke, he found that he too was snow-blind. He tried to proceed down the steep slope by feeling for holds, then thought better of it, waiting instead until Couzy caught up and guided him the rest of the way down.

As he slid down a rope that had been fixed in place over an ice cliff, holding on with bare hands, Herzog watched as pieces of skin were flayed from his fingers. At the bottom, he wrapped his bleeding hands in a handkerchief—in order, he would say in 1998, to avoid upsetting his teammates.

As the men severally approached Camp II, Sherpas came up to greet them and help them down the last, seemingly interminable slope. It turned out that Ichac and Oudot had indeed heard shouts that morning from up high. With binoculars, they had spotted two men on a patch of ice near Camp IV, whom they took for Schatz and Couzy. Deeply alarmed, Oudot had started to organize a rescue party, but the climbers had descended faster than their would-be saviors could climb.

In *Annapurna*, Herzog offers his first words to Ichac, Oudot, and Noyelle at Camp II: "We're back from Annapurna. We got to the top yesterday [actually the day before yesterday], Lachenal and I." Then, after a pause: "My feet and hands are frostbitten."

By 1998, Herzog's memory has restructured this speech, with a significant shift in pronoun. In *L'Autre Annapurna*, he says, "I bring you the victory."

"Bravo!" cheer his teammates.

"But my feet and hands are frozen!"

Herzog witnessed Terray's halting approach to Camp II. "He was blind, and clung to Ang-Tharkey as he walked. He had a huge beard and his face was distorted by pain into a dreadful grin." Then Lachenal: "From a distance it looked as though he was pedaling along in the air, for he threw his legs out in front in a most disordered way. His head lolled backwards and was covered with a bandage."

That evening, Lachenal closed his diary entry with a simple formula: "Our lives are saved. Thank you, my God." With only an easy walk down to Camp I ahead of them, the team was effectively off the mountain. Their ordeal, however, had just begun.

SIX

The
Woods
of
Lété

AT CAMP II, Oudot examined the invalids. Herzog's extremities were numb up to his ankles and wrists. Lachenal's toes and patches on the soles of his feet had turned black. Rébuffat had only frostnip on a pair of toes, and Terray had somehow avoided frostbite altogether.

Three years later, the British expedition to Everest would climb more than 2,000 feet higher than the French on Annapurna, yet contract no serious frostbite. It is worth pausing to wonder why Herzog and Lachenal suffered such appalling damage on a single day's push above 26,000 feet. The boots of the British insulated considerably better than those of the French, which had been designed for the Alps. Even so, back in the 1920s and 1930s teams had come home from high altitude in the Himalaya without serious frostbite.

On Everest in 1922, the British discovered that they could not afford to wear crampons up high, because the straps that fixed them to the boots inevitably cut off circulation. As long as footgear was made of pliable leather (as were the French boots), that sinister tradeoff would manifest itself. By choosing to wear their crampons all the way to the top, as indeed the terrain demanded, Lachenal and Herzog cut their margin of safety from frostbite.

In 1922, 1924, and 1953, the Everest climbers used bottled oxygen. The French on Annapurna eschewed it—one more factor possibly cutting thin that margin of safety. A hypoxic climber is thought to be more likely to develop frostbite than one breathing a steady flow of supplemental gas.

It seems unlikely that Lachenal and Herzog drank much, if anything, on the morning of June 3. Herzog says the pair could not face the chore of lighting the stove and making tea. Dehydration further increases climbers' risk of frostbite.

Reading *Annapurna*, one gains little sense of what drugs and medicines the men were taking, but Lachenal's unexpurgated diary makes clear that almost nightly the French were swallowing sleeping pills. In 1950, doctors had not yet warned against this practice, which can depress normal breathing and heighten the effects of oxygen deprivation. On Annapurna, most of the Frenchmen and many of the Sherpas smoked cigarettes daily. As a vasoconstrictor, nicotine makes frostbite more likely, though the science of the day had not yet deduced this possibility. (On Everest in 1922, George Finch, who performed as well as the unstoppable George Mallory, believed that cigarette smoking actually aided the process of acclimatization.)

Finally, among the expedition's generous supply of pills was a stimulant called Maxiton. In the 1950s, and even into the 1970s, climbers routinely took "uppers" such as Dexedrine to push their weary bodies through unavoidable ordeals. Maxiton, later users would learn, is a particularly dangerous drug, which even in small doses can produce, according to one source, "a kind of drunkenness, with a disturbance of one's sense of equilibrium." The drug "is a powerful stimulant that creates a sort of euphoria."

Though the stimulant would not have directly contributed to

the men's frostbite, it might have induced the euphoria Herzog testified to on the summit, causing him to linger far too long, and later carelessly to drop his gloves. (To this writer in 1999, however, Herzog denied ever taking Maxiton. Yet one can read *Annapurna* without realizing that, as they were carried out from the mountain after June 6, Lachenal and Herzog were dosed with morphine to kill the pain of their frostbite almost nightly. Only Lachenal's diary documents the constant morphine use.)

Alarmed at the extent of the frostbite, Oudot decided to give Lachenal and Herzog abdominal injections of novocaine. "I used them during the war," the physician told Herzog almost jauntily, "and it's the only treatment that's any use with frostbite." The injections were excruciating. "I should never, until then, have believed so much pain to be possible," wrote Herzog. It is poignant to know that this torture, which the two men endured with great courage, did nothing whatsoever to forestall their frostbite.

Steeling himself for his second round of shots, Herzog pleaded with Terray to hold him in his arms. Still wearing a bandana over his eyes as he recovered from snow-blindness, the "strong man" clasped Herzog. "I howled and cried and sobbed in Terray's arms while he held me tight with all his strength."

In *L'Autre Annapurna*, after an interval of forty-eight years, that simple act of brotherhood has taken on a mystical aura.

> Lionel held me in his arms like an infant. He transfused his humanity into me. During this long torment, I felt a sense of communion with my comrade-in-arms. . . . Between two howls of pain, I made the firm resolution to be buried later side-by-side with him in the alpinists' cemetery in Chamonix.

By now not only Lachenal and Herzog, but also the snow-blind and frost-nipped Rébuffat could not walk. Couzy was completely played out. With his limitless stamina, Terray moved under his own power, though still recovering from his snow-blindness. On June 6, Rébuffat was hauled on a Dufour litter (a sled used in emergency evacuations) down the easy track to Camp I. Herzog and Lachenal followed by litter the next day. "I was wrapped up like

a package," wrote Lachenal in his diary, "and saw absolutely nothing because I still had a bandana over my eyes."

Below the snow line, the Dufour sled was useless. On June 9,
Lachenal was carried from Camp I down to Base Camp by a single
Sherpa, in a device called a *cacolet:* a chairlike litter made of canvas
and webbing, to which the victim was strapped and bundled, facing
backward. The carry made an agonizing trip for the Sherpa, lugging
a burden heavier than he himself weighed. And it was agonizing for
Lachenal, too, who wrote, "It was a very, very hard march, because
my legs hung loose and the blood descended to the tips of my feet."
The next day, Herzog was similarly transported to Base Camp. By
now, Rébuffat could walk, though he was still in considerable pain.

The long-anticipated monsoon had arrived. Torrential rains
lasted all day, intensifying the team's misery and further threatening the frostbitten duo's health. Leery of septicemia, Oudot gave
the men penicillin. Herzog sensed that the monsoon could spring a
trap, for, swollen with floodwaters, the Miristi Khola might become
uncrossable. Schatz, who had gone ahead to scout a ford, sent a note
back reporting that the river's volume had doubled in a single day.

At last, Schatz and some Sherpas were able to construct a
flimsy bridge over the Miristi Khola, by using lianas to lash together four or five tree trunks. Adjiba gamely carried the two invalids across piggyback, one at a time. Both men were unnerved by
the passage.

Though bound together by such acts of teamwork, the expedition began at this point to unravel. There is no hint of this in *Annapurna*, with its fiction that from start to finish the party was glued
together by common purpose and loyalty to its leader. But on June
10, Lachenal complained to his diary:

> I have to ask for everything several times and wait forever before
> receiving it. Even the food—I must literally yell to get someone to
> bring me any. Everybody, sahibs and Sherpas alike, out of a natural
> attraction to the leader, fusses around Momo, who in my opinion
> knows how to make the most of it. All this might seem bad will on
> my part, certainly I probably shouldn't write it, but if not, will it be
> remembered afterward?

As the doleful retreat progressed, Rébuffat too sensed the dissolution of the team's solidarity. On July 2, he wrote Françoise, "The members, except for Oudot, are possessed of quite some egotism! They think only of eating and of doing nothing else."

Lachenal's diary methodically records the daily tribulations. On June 12, "Momo was awakened by the need to piss, so I had to help him get it done." The day before, "The descent for me was extremely painful, although a bit numbed by morphine." On the 12th, Lachenal took the dressings off his feet to look at the damage. "They have a lot of swelling. I have to hold them vertical, exposed to the air, until the swelling almost disappears."

On June 14, Lachenal and Herzog got involved in a "violent polemic," after disagreeing whether to camp at a notch in the ridge or, as Lachenal and Rébuffat desired, descend farther. Herzog's wish prevailed. Lachenal's congenital impatience could not drive the stricken party's retreat any faster than a halting plod. In one moment, he could take pity on the Sherpa carrying him on his back; in the next, he was fed up with everyone around him.

On the dangerous traverse to the pass on the south ridge of the Nilgiris, a laden porter slipped and fell to his death. *Annapurna* fails to note this tragedy, which only Lachenal's diary documents.

With time heavy on his hands, Lachenal wrote lengthier entries in his diary than he had earlier, when he had still been caught up in the daily tasks of the expedition. Fully a third of the diary is given over to the retreat, and those passages abound in vivid detail. In 1956, however, Lucien Devies and Gérard Herzog condensed thirty-four days' worth of entries into a scant two and a half undated pages in the published *Carnets du Vertige*. Those cobbled-together extracts disproportionately emphasize Lachenal's occasional happy remarks, as when he notices a beautiful countryside or rejoices at receiving letters from his wife brought by couriers from distant outposts. Virtually all evidence of conflict, disgust, despair—or for that matter, morphine—has been expunged.

Herzog himself was slipping into his own despair. Realizing that amputations were inevitable, he wept in Terray's arms. "Life's not over," Terray tried to reassure him. "You'll see France again, and Chamonix."

"Yes, Chamonix perhaps," answered the invalid, "but I'll never be able to climb again."

The ordeal of being carried wore Herzog's forbearance thin as well as Lachenal's. "The violent jerking caused me unbearable pain. To go on was madness, and, moreover, I just didn't feel capable of standing another couple of hours of this torture."

Herzog's patience snapped on June 15, when he thought his ice axe had been lost. In *Annapurna*, he says merely, "I set great store by it; as Lachenal had lost his, it was the only one to have been to the top of Annapurna. . . . I had intended to present the axe to the French Alpine Club on my return." (The tool was found two days later, in the last porter's load.)

In *L'Autre Annapurna*, nonetheless, with its sifting of decades of retrospect, the loss takes on heavy symbolic meaning. The ice axe is "my dear companion in combat"; crafted to Herzog's specifications by the master artisan Claudius Simond, it is "a work of art." Herzog goes on to claim, "For the alpinist, his axe is his legionnaire's sword. It is the extension of himself. . . . Should I add that an axe is also a cross?"

In this extravaganza, as in other key passages of Herzog's 1998 memoir, the author reveals how the myth of himself that memory has spun over almost five decades has transformed the events of Annapurna. Herzog was always adamant (*contra* Rébuffat) that the lessons learned and the virtues inculcated in the war made victory on Annapurna possible. Martial imagery mingles with Christian. As a child, Herzog had been smitten by a visit to the Cistercian monastery of Lérins, near Cannes, where he saw a vision of holy peace.

With all the references to communion, resurrection, the cross, the kiss of peace, and so forth in *L'Autre Annapurna*, Herzog adumbrates an implicit metaphor: himself as Christ, martyred by his triumph, sacrificing his hands and feet so that his fellow men might live. Later, that metaphor would become explicit.

By June 18, the ragtag caravan had left the mountains for good, entering the deep forest of Lété, where gnarled trees interwove with giant rhododendrons. Still unable to walk a step, Herzog and Lachenal were now carried on stretchers by four men each. It was the season of the rice harvest in the lowlands, and porters kept deserting. The team's progress was so sorely jeopardized that finally the sahibs, led by Noyelle, simply went into the fields and recruited bearers by force.

On the 18th, in the forest, Oudot called a halt so that he could trim dead flesh from the wounded men's limbs. Herzog felt little as Oudot's scissors snipped away at his feet, "but my hands were so sensitive that the slightest touch made me cry out in pain, and I broke down." "It was horrible to watch," noted Lachenal. Then it was his turn. After the surgical snipping, Oudot proceeded with the hated abdominal injections. "These made me suffer horribly," wrote Lachenal. "He had to jab me with the needle a dozen times. Tonight, the morphine was necessary."

Herzog had lapsed into a high fever, the thermometer at one point reaching 105 degrees Fahrenheit. By now, he writes in *Annapurna*, he had lost forty pounds. (In *L'Autre Annapurna*, the weight loss becomes sixty-five pounds.) Delirious, Herzog anticipated the end: "Gathering together the last shreds of energy, in one last long prayer, I implored death to come and deliver me. I had lost the will to live."

In *Annapurna*, that nadir of surrender in the Lété woods passes with the feverish night. In the 1998 memoir, however, it expands to lay the foundation for the central notion of Herzog's whole life—that with Annapurna, he came back from the dead to be born again. Lying on his mattress among the larch trees of Lété, he imagines himself already buried. "On the knoll where my tomb lay, a cross of wood had been erected—quite unprecedented among these Buddhist places, where our Christian crosses mean nothing." Herzog watches a long funerary procession—sahibs, Sherpas, porters—"paying me a last homage as they pass by my tomb."

Semiconscious once more, he feels life slipping away.

An ecstatic serenity enveloped me. . . . It had to do not with an end or with nothingness, but with another existence. . . .

Then came the miracle. I crossed again the boundary between the visible and the invisible. Once more, I saw the faces washed of all color, approaching me as if across an air bubble.

No sound reached my ears, but already I felt hands placed on me, stroking my face.

Despite all the years that have since passed, this great interior adventure remains the major event of my life. A second birth, more true in my eyes than the first—is that not a sacred mystery?

In *L'Autre Annapurna*, Herzog makes it clear that the vision of Lété was no mere feverish delirium. It constituted a genuine passage from one world to another. When I interviewed Herzog in Paris in 1999, he elaborated on this theme: "Annapurna changed my life. The man I became was very different from the man I had been. I had been given a second life. The American edition of *L'Autre Annapurna* will be titled *Born Twice*." From behind his desk, Herzog held the stumps of his fingers out toward me. "You can see what is lost, but inside, I feel what I have gained."

Some years after the expedition, Rébuffat, in an acerbic comment to the mayor of Marseille, who was presenting him with the Legion of Honor, remarked that he had had often to resist Herzog's "exhibition of his hands." His erstwhile teammate may thus have been the first to hint at the implied analogy that I felt Herzog was making, in that uncomfortable moment in his office, as he held out for me to see the mutilated evidence of his martyrdom, like Christ's stigmata.

The allegory played out in the Lété passage in *L'Autre Annapurna*—with the funeral procession passing by the tomb, the hands laying hold of his body and caressing his face, the wakening unto a new life, redeemed by his suffering—is clearly that of Herzog as Christ. Yet the fact that Herzog, in so remembering the ordeal of Annapurna, has invested it with such religious import is not necessarily a sign of grandiosity so much as proof of the man's genuinely mystical character. To the mystic, all experience partakes of the gods.

· · ·

MEANWHILE, the down-to-earth Lachenal cursed the delay in Lété. All his frustration and suffering are packed into an extraordinary sentence he wrote in his diary on June 20.

> My feet give me a lot of trouble and I have truly had enough of this, of the noise of the Kali [Gandaki, the river the caravan followed], always the same, of listening constantly to people around me talking in a shrill language that I don't understand, of suffering, of being dirty, of being hot, of being injected by idiots, of not sleeping, of not being able to move around, of being surrounded by no one who is kind to me, of passing whole days alone on my stretcher with at best one Sherpa as companion, with no sahibs, knowing full well that nothing will get done, not even ordinary tasks, without my having to ask many times and then to wait a long, long time.

In his misery, only one thought gave Lachenal any pleasure: to contemplate "my family, my kids, whom I have a mad desire to see again, my wife who alone will take care of me."

From Base Camp, Herzog had sent a Sherpa ahead as a runner to get the news of the expedition's success back to France. On June 16, while Herzog lay waiting for death in the woods of Lété, *Figaro* broke the news. Because the team had signed exclusive contracts with that newspaper and with the magazine *Paris-Match*, Herzog and Ichac had been vigilant, as they had periodically sent off dispatches, that news from the expedition not be intercepted and leaked. Even at the time, Rébuffat was scornful of these first efforts by Herzog to put his own spin on the story. In one undated letter to Françoise, he wrote, "Don't believe for a moment what the telegrams sent to *Figaro* say. It makes us laugh sometimes to hear the wording Ichac and Herzog give them!"

Slowly the caravan moved on. On the 21st Lachenal bore what he called "the most painful episode for me of the whole evacuation," when Adjiba carried him across a bridge over the Kali Gandaki. At the start of the crossing, Lachenal's left foot (the worse frostbitten) struck a big stone; then, as Adjiba stumbled on, both feet banged repeatedly against the chains that suspended the bridge. "He left me weeping beside the trail on the other side," wrote Lachenal; "he dumped me literally on the ground as he went off to look for the Bara Sahib [Herzog]."

So the entries in Lachenal's diary stream on, noting small indignities and rare moments of pleasure, giving the day-by-day details of the long march home that Herzog's account is too well crafted to include. "A pretty bad night. Didn't have any morphine. Besides, I was nibbled by fleas." "In the middle of the night, a huge need to take a shit which I satisfied in an old box." "It rained in torrents almost the whole night and it's still raining this morning." "I believe I have never been so dirty in my life. It's been two months since I washed—not even my hands."

"All the young females in this region are beautiful, with eyes like coals." "In the evening, the countryside was very beautiful, a mixture of the green of vegetation and the ochre of the cliffs." "When I'm not suffering too much, life seems almost good."

Lachenal's sole distraction on the slow march out was a mystery novel Ichac lent him, which had the ominous title, *The Man Without a Head*. That, cigarettes, and morphine got him through his days.

Lachenal's able-bodied teammates seemed to him to have little compassion for his sufferings. Even Terray was distant on the march out from Annapurna. Only Rébuffat seemed truly solicitous. "He was very nice to me last night and this morning," wrote Lachenal one evening, and some days later, "He offered me several very kind words, not idiotic ones. Several heartfelt words in the right tone, not the ritual phrases of consolation."

On July 1, with the return of a courier, Lachenal was overjoyed to receive several letters from Adèle. Yet reading them filled him with a deep melancholy at the thought that his house in Chamonix, in July, "would be all beautiful (flowers, grass), waiting for me, and that I would return terribly deformed."

On July 2, Oudot performed his first amputations. The penicillin had reduced the men's septicemia, but many digits were clearly unsalvageable. On a meadow beside the river, Oudot first went to work on Herzog. Lachenal says that four of Herzog's toes, including both big toes, were the first to go; Herzog's own account has a little finger cut off first. "This gave me rather a twinge," writes Herzog in *Annapurna*, with a kind of gallows humor. "A little finger may not be much use, but all the same I was attached to it!" According to Herzog, the operation was performed without anaesthetic (why, if Oudot had novocaine?).

Then it was Lachenal's turn. As Oudot snipped away with his scissors, "I cried like a baby and howled. Ichac and Lionel held my foot." Later that night, however, "calmed by morphine, I spent an excellent evening with Pansy with a pack of Gauloises and a bottle of cognac."

By now, the halting caravan of Annapurna survivors had spent a full month on the march out. Wrote Herzog, "The expedition had turned into a limp and anemic body straggling without much spirit on a course the reason for which escaped us. We were buoyed up by a single wish: to get to India as quickly as possible." As always, Lachenal was beside himself with impatience. "What a lot of time we're wasting!" Herzog quotes him as complaining toward the end of the long march.

"We'll have to be patient, Biscante; things aren't always easy."

Finally, on July 6, three trucks that Noyelle had gone ahead to arrange arrived at the men's camp. After the wounded had been loaded aboard, the trucks drove them to the railway terminus at Nautanwa. From there, the train would speed the men to Delhi.

Yet on the first leg of that journey, in 113 degree heat inside the railway car, Oudot performed a last set of amputations. After Lachenal had removed his own dressings, the doctor waited for the brief halts of the train at successive stations, then quickly cut away with his scissors. "At the station before Gorakhpur," wrote Lachenal laconically, "two toes fell from my right foot. At the stop at Gorakhpur, three more from the right foot."

In his sweaty haste, Oudot dropped his smaller pair of scissors down the window slot. Cutting with the larger pair, he sliced into living flesh. Lachenal screamed and jerked his foot away, whereupon Oudot scolded him, telling him to be more cooperative. Incredulous, Lachenal wrote in his diary that night, "I will remember this forever."

The jocular tone of gallows humor bathes this nightmarish scene in the railway car in *Annapurna*.

Things had to be cleaned up now; the nauseating smell drove even the natives away. Sarki and Foutharkey set to work, they opened the the door wide and with a sort of old broom made of twigs, they pushed everything onto the floor. In the midst of a whole heap of rubbish rolled an amazing number of toes of all sizes which were then swept onto the platform before the startled eyes of the natives.

In his diary, Lachenal wrote at the end of this wretched day, "I suffered something truly horrible, but after all, so much the better. Is not memory proportional to suffering?"

In a 1999 documentary about Annapurna filmed by Bernard George, Herzog looks back with a certain disdain on Lachenal's agonies. "He was obsessed with this story of his feet," says Herzog, in measured tones. "There was a kind of obsession that was painful. It breathes in all his writings: 'My feet, my feet, my feet.' . . .

"In climbing, one must adapt. I lost both my feet and my hands, but it didn't ruin my life."

What was the cause of Oudot's haste in the railway car? Surprisingly, Herzog had chosen to divide the party. He, Oudot, Ichac, and Noyelle would change trains at Gorakhpur and ride to Kathmandu. Lachenal, Terray, Rébuffat, Schatz, and Couzy would proceed to Delhi. The rationale for this separation, according to Herzog, was that "I intended to make every effort possible to keep the promise I had given at the start to visit the Maharajah of Nepal."

It was no accident that Herzog took the expedition doctor with him. By now, on July 6, all the climbers wanted nothing but to get back to France as soon as possible. Not only psychologically, but in terms of the worsening condition of Herzog's and Lachenal's feet and hands, the sooner the men could fly to France the better.

In the end, however, it would be eleven more days before the Annapurna team boarded its airplane. Those eleven days of waiting drove Lachenal deeper into fury and despair.

IN THE CIRCUMSTANCES, it is puzzling that Herzog would have delayed his whole team's return to France for any ceremony, no matter how prestigious. In *Annapurna*, he devotes three and a half of the last five pages of the book to his audience with the Maharajah, which unfolds as a pageant of jewel-encrusted uniforms, of Gurkha soldiers presenting arms, and dignitaries giving formal speeches. At the climax of the ceremony, the Maharajah conferred on Herzog the country's highest military honor, the Gurkha Right Hand for valor, saying, "You are a brave man, and we welcome you here as a brave man."

Yet the book also makes clear that attending the ceremony taxed Herzog to the limit. As he sat watching the long performance, pus and blood oozed through his bandages. Ichac whispered, "How's it going?"

"Pretty awful," Herzog whispered back. "I don't think I can hold out much longer."

Later, in Delhi, Oudot discovered that Herzog's feet had become infested with maggots. When he tried to use tweezers to remove them, they withdrew into holes in the man's dead flesh.

Even if Herzog felt it vital to attend the audience of the Maharajah, why could the five climbers in Delhi not have flown at once back to France?

When I interviewed her in 1999, Françoise Rébuffat gave me one answer, based on her late husband's understanding of the situation. "Herzog said at one point that his company, Kléber-Colombes, had asked him to work, to go see the Maharajah. They knew Nepal would need rubber.

"Herzog took away all the men's passports, so they couldn't go home early. No one was to get back to France before Herzog. He even insisted on being the first off the plane when it landed at Orly. This embittered Gaston."

In fact, it was Lucien Devies who, acting in consultation with Herzog, secured tickets for a return flight on July 16. Meanwhile, in Delhi, the five climbers loitered, with nothing to do. Lachenal's diary records this ordeal by monotony, which became for him even worse than the agonies of the retreat by stretcher.

"All my comrades are dawdlers who think only about themselves, never about me," he writes on July 8. That evening the men attended a dinner party for all the French citizens in Delhi—all fifteen of them. "My feet felt really bad, and in addition I was sick to my stomach with colic, and at every instant I was afraid I would have to ask someone to carry me to the bathroom."

July 9: "I changed my dressings, which were oozing [with pus] and which smelled really bad. There is a lot of rotten flesh. . . . I change positions a thousand times a day, a thousand times a night. My ass, on which I sit day and night, gives me a lot of trouble."

July 10: "The afternoon was very slow, it seemed it would never end. Several times I asked myself what day it was. Yes, at 6:00 P.M., as at 3:00 P.M., as at 1:00 P.M., it was still always the 10th and to get to the 11th, it was necessary to wait half the night. And after—after that it will be the 11th, just like the 10th, with the same suffering, the same pains."

July 11: "Bored to death. The onset of the night was very slow. Morphine."

Appalled by the gangrene that was developing in his feet, Lachenal twice begged his companions to fetch doctors to attend to him. These native physicians were in over their heads, as they confronted the ravages of frostbite.

> The doctor undid my dressing with a great deal of delicacy. He proceeded with much propriety. He sterilized his tools over an alcohol flame. He seemed a bit frightened, he didn't know what he ought to do, so he asked me. . . . In the end, he was content with covering my feet with gauze soaked in Mercurochrome and wrapping them back up again.

By July 12, on learning that the flight home was to be delayed another day, Lachenal had reached the ragged end of his patience. "Does Momo think of no one but himself?" he raged in his diary.

Finally, after the return of the Kathmandu party, Lachenal consented to one more treatment by Oudot, who amputated his last toes. "I suffered horribly. He gave me an intravenous shot of morphine, which did me little good. . . . At each attack of the scissors, the scalpel, the lancet, my big toe jumped. For me this was a huge disappointment, for I had truly believed I could keep part [of my toes]."

"Will I still be able to ski properly?" Lachenal wondered in his diary on July 15. "Tomorrow is the departure toward my wife." At last the 16th arrived. The men boarded the airplane, then whiled away the hours of the endless flight. Just before landing at Orly the next day, Lachenal and Herzog put fresh dressings on their wounds.

Their reception on arrival was more tumultuous than anyone had predicted. Before a wildly cheering throng, Herzog was hoisted first off the airplane, his feet and hands covered with enormous bandages. Rébuffat followed, then Couzy, then Terray, carrying Lachenal in his arms like a child. Reporters swarmed around the worn-out climbers, demanding at once the whole story of Annapurna. Herzog's mother, father, and siblings embraced him. Adéle took Lachenal's head in her hands and kissed him, tears streaming down her face.

For the French, still sunk in the humiliation of World War II, the conquest of the first 8,000-meter peak ever climbed became at once a matter of incalculable national pride. Indeed, it could be argued that no triumph of sport in the nation's history ever meant so much to its people. Nor was the glory to be short-lived. Fifty years later, Annapurna still occupies a sovereign place in the French soul.

For Herzog, the ordeal of recovery had just begun. *Annapurna* ends with the arrival at Orly, with Herzog's ringing *envoi:* "There are other Annapurnas in the lives of men." The most moving passages in *L'Autre Annapurna* concern the author's convalescence. In the end, he would spend a full year in the American hospital at Neuilly, undergoing twelve major operations and a number of skin grafts. His spirit would plummet to a bedrock despair, before the "new life" could truly commence.

Early on in his hospital stay, Herzog underwent a moment of deep horror. Surrounded by doctors, the patient lay still as nurses unwrapped the dressings on his feet. The head physician offered soothing words: "Maurice, be brave while I change this last bit of gauze."

Suddenly Herzog heard a chorus of cries. Doctors and nurses

alike jerked back involuntarily. "They're jumping!" someone screamed. "They're jumping!"

The maggots that had infested Herzog's feet in Nepal had gorged on his dead flesh. Now, each one as thick as a pencil, at the moment of release from their prison of gauze, they leapt into the air in every direction.

Herzog could not control the tears of an utter desolation.

SEVEN

The
Meditation
of
Rébuffat

WITH THE TEAM MEMBERS bound
by their contract to publish no account of the expedition for five
years after its conclusion, it would
seem that Devies and Herzog had
planned from the start for Herzog
to write the official book. In *L'Autre
Annapurna,* however, Herzog insists that this was not the case—
that as he lay recuperating in the
hospital, he had no notion of writing about the expedition.

In that memoir, he attributes
the spark of the idea to a head nurse
named Irène Kravchenko, whose
blue eyes, blond hair, and "ravish-
ing" smiles boosted the invalid's

morale. Kravchenko's beauty, writes Herzog, camouflaged "an inflexible will." One day she let her patient know that she considered him psychologically as well as physically damaged. What he needed, she counseled, was a purpose in life.

"A purpose?" Herzog protested. "My god, what? Reading? Is that your idea?"

"Why not write?" proposed Kravchenko.

"You're joking. What about my hands?"

"You could dictate a book. Your book. Your life, your death. A new life. . . . You must do it. You *can* do it!"

Is this story disingenuous? Is it a complete fiction? How could Herzog not have planned to write the book a voracious public was already clamoring for? In its portrait of the maimed victor of Annapurna as a reluctant celebrity, the Kravchenko vignette mirrors a stance Herzog would come to perfect in his lecture appearances.

As soon as its editors could put together a story, on August 19 *Paris-Match* ran its exclusive account of the expedition. The cover featured the now-famous summit photo of Herzog holding aloft the Tricolor attached to the shaft of his ice axe; inside were splashed sixteen pages of color and black-and-white photos. (These photos were credited to Ichac, although Rébuffat took the ones high on the mountain, Lachenal the summit photo.) The issue broke all the magazine's previous sales records.

On January 25, 1951, 2,500 spectators crowded into the Salle Pleyel in Paris to watch the premiere of the film Ichac had brought back from Annapurna. The audience included the president of France, Vincent Auriol, and five ministers. Herzog, holding the stumps of his hands pressed together before him, limped across the stage, with his eight teammates following in single file, to the wild applause of the congregation.

In *L'Autre Annapurna* the reluctant celebrity gives us a glimpse of the climbers nervously lingering backstage before their procession. Everyone feels intimidated by the grand occasion. His friends counsel Herzog to lead the procession on stage, but he demurs, urging they appear as a group. Terray clinches the debate: "You were the first on the summit. Here, you should be first as well. Go ahead."

After the premiere on January 25, it would require thirty more showings of the film in Paris, and some 300 lectures and individual appearances by the climbers in other French cities, to satisfy the public's passion for details of the great adventure.

On February 17, *Paris-Match* ran another cover story on Annapurna, focusing on the film premiere at the Salle Pleyel. This time the cover photo showed a still emaciated Herzog, clean-shaven and dapper in jacket and tie, holding his truncated hands out toward the audience as he spoke into a microphone. The cover blurb announced, "Paris salutes the triumph of the conquerors of Annapurna"; then, "Herzog—his life, his struggles, his defeats, his victories." The text hailed Herzog as "our number one national hero." As for the film premiere and the subsequent *séances* at the Salle Pleyel, the reporter gushed about the "enormous crowd" that "every night shouts itself hoarse, crying out its pride in the conquerors of the Himalaya."

The article devolved into a profile of Herzog. Incredibly, in six pages of adulatory prose, not once did the reporter mention Lachenal. Instead, "On June 3, 1950, at 2:00 P.M., Maurice Herzog marked the triumph of his tactical campaign by planting his ice axe at 8,078 meters on the summit of Annapurna." The photos dwelt on Herzog at his parents' house in Saint-Cloud, Herzog as a young climber, Herzog front and center in a group photo with all "the greatest explorers of France." The reporter had visited Herzog at home, surrounded by his souvenirs, including "The 'Foca' that took, at 8,078 meters, the famous photo immortalizing the French victory, which was a cover photo of *Paris-Match*." A caption referred to "the Foca that accompanied him to the summit." It was as if the camera had been Herzog's only teammate on the summit, and the photo had taken itself.

Thus began the insidious process by which Lachenal would come to be all but written out of the story. Whether this focusing on the leader to the exclusion of his teammates was due to the workings of Lucien Devies's publicity machine (in his preface to *Annapurna*, Devies wrote, "The victory of the whole party was also, and above all, the victory of its leader"), or whether the credulous public needed to single out a "number one national hero," a myth had begun irreversibly to form about the distant mountain. "*Paris-Match* . . . today presents you the man who has won the greatest glory because he underwent the greatest suffering."

Six months after returning from Annapurna, Herzog could walk in special shoes only with short, shuffling, uncertain steps. He had learned to grasp a pencil with several stumps on his right hand and produce a shaky scrawl. In the Neuilly hospital, Herzog prepared to "write" his book.

According to the version of that process described in *L'Autre Annapurna*, each morning Herzog's personal secretary, Nicole, sat by his bedside taking dictation. In the afternoon, back in her office, she typed up the text. The pair then went over it, making corrections.

> Like the strings of a violin, Nicole cried or laughed with me, as was the case. . . . Profoundly moved, even scarred, by my sometimes violent emotions, she announced, after the last sentence had been written, that since our mission was accomplished she was going to enter the Dominican order of the Campagnes under the name Sister Marie-Isaïe.

Published on November 24, 1951, *Annapurna* became an instant sensation. For almost a year, it stayed in first place on the nonfiction best-seller list in France. Forty-eight years later, Herzog maintains in *L'Autre Annapurna*, the book has been "translated into almost all languages" and has sold fifteen million copies. (Conservative observers place the number at closer to eleven million. In either case, *Annapurna* stands as far and away the best-selling mountaineering book ever written.) If all the copies of the book sold over the past forty-seven years were stacked in a pile, Herzog brags, they "would surpass the height of a dozen Annapurnas."

The book, however, did not make Herzog rich, for from the start all the royalties were earmarked for the Himalayan Committee. It is no exaggeration to say that several decades' worth of French expeditions to the great ranges (including several undertaken by Terray) were bankrolled by the profits from *Annapurna*.

When I interviewed him in 1999, Herzog said he was especially gratified whenever he got a letter from someone (like myself) who had been inspired to climb by reading *Annapurna.* "I receive many letters from young Americans," he said. "All these letters, from boys, from girls, touch me equally. I answer them all.

"I showed the book [in manuscript] to all the members of the expedition," Herzog insisted. "They all approved it. I tried to give each his due. They were all impressed by it—even Lachenal."

In *L'Autre Annapurna,* Herzog relates a curious exchange from the first year of his convalescence, when the Archbishop of Marseille visited his bedside. According to Herzog, the cleric forced upon him the comparison to the martyrdom of Christ that would come to inform his own sense of the meaning of Annapurna. This dignified man categorized his own visit to Herzog as a "pilgrimage."

"My son," spoke the archbishop, "in the light of your own tribulation [*calvaire*], have you been able to imagine, if only in flashes, what the passion of Christ must have been?"

Herzog admitted that the analogy of the nails driven through Christ's hands and feet to his own suffering had sometimes occurred to him.

"So the mountain was your cross?"

Herzog demurred. "My story, alas, concerns only myself. It contains no mystery. Neither on the summit, nor during the interminable tragedy of the descent, had I any revelation or vision. Thus—and I am aware of disappointing you, Monsignor—I don't consider myself the carrier of any message."

"The most edifying message is your example. You must bear witness to it."

As so often in this memoir, Herzog puts the words that praise him in another's mouth. Did such a conversation really take place between the archbishop and the mountaineer? To convince the reader of the authenticity of his memory, Herzog reproduces a forty-seven-year-old dialogue verbatim, as though he had a tape recording of it.

All the fetes and soirees that Herzog attended, in the wake of Annapurna, brought him into contact with the famous and the great. They, in turn, were eager to learn more about the ordeal of France's newest hero. The "tacitum and introverted" adolescent that Herzog once thought himself had by now been well submerged in a charming, gregarious adult.

When I interviewed her in 1999, Françoise Rébuffat acerbically mimicked the public performer that Herzog became: "He can cry whenever he wants. He puts on a trembling voice. 'I have in my pocket a letter from a little boy in deepest France. No, I can't show it to you. Yes, I shall. No. Yes.' Finally he reads it: ' "M. Herzog, you are the greatest hero in the world." ' "

When Charles de Gaulle came into power in 1958, he appointed Herzog Minister of Youth and Sport, a post he held for the next eight years. With that appointment, he ended his work as a director of Kléber-Colombes. During the next decades, Herzog would serve on advisory boards for all sorts of businesses, but he never again had to hold down a true desk job in a company. From 1968 to 1977, he was mayor of Chamonix; then, from 1981 to 1984, president of the company in charge of the Mont Blanc tunnel.

Over the years, Herzog served as a consultant and representative to a number of bodies, ranging from Olympic committees to parliamentary missions for nuclear affairs. His résumé bristles with titular honors: President of Ofexport (an organization exporting sports equipment), President of Triton France (an oil and gas consortium), President of Forces Motrices de Chancy-Pougny (a Swiss dam project).

Some observers give Herzog high marks for his public career. Benoît Heimermann, a writer for L'Equipe magazine, says, "In the 1960 Olympics, the French performed awfully. De Gaulle said, 'We have to do something about this.' As Minister of Youth and Sport, Herzog was responsible for opening lots of stadiums, swimming pools, and so on. He did lots of good things.

"As an industrialist, Herzog was very influential. He was a good Minister of Youth and Sport. But it's hard not to be disappointed in this guy. He built his whole life on Annapurna. He did one thing, and after that he became a politician."

Writing about that public career in L'Autre Annapurna, Herzog lapses into shameless name-dropping and ill-disguised pats on his own back. On meeting John F. Kennedy, then the junior senator from Massachusetts, Herzog shares his idea of creating an "army" of young people pledged to work in underdeveloped countries—evidently the germ of the Peace Corps. "An admirable suggestion, Maurice," says Kennedy, according to Herzog. "We need an ideal for our youth."

One day, in conversation with André Malraux, Herzog comes up with a spontaneous *pensée:* "What is culture, if not knowledge become conscience [*connaissance devenue conscience*]?"

The born epigrammatist, Malraux asks if he can make this startling *pensée* his own.

"It's yours, André."

"Must I cite you?"

"Not at all. What's given is given."

Robert Oppenheimer, Valéry Giscard d'Estaing, Charles Lindbergh, Juan Perón, Brigitte Bardot, Jackie Kennedy—all meet Herzog and fall under the spell of his genius and charm. In a similar vein, Herzog limns his public career as noblesse oblige, rather than political ambition: To serve others was "a sacred duty."

Yet one must conclude that that public career has been a remarkably successful one. Herzog would never be able to climb again after Annapurna—though he hiked up Monte Rosa in 1955 with Lachenal as (some would argue) a publicity stunt. But by the 1990s, the man was firmly lodged in his country's pantheon of heroes of sport and exploration. Herzog's name means to the French-speaking world what Sir Edmund Hillary's does to the English, what Reinhold Messner's does to the German. Meanwhile, by the 1990s, the names of Herzog's Annapurna teammates had slipped into limbo, known well only within the insular circles of serious mountaineers.

So things stood, that is, until 1996. That year, the publication of Ballu's biography of Rébuffat and Guérin's edition of Lachenal's diary exploded like twin bombshells. Annapurna was suddenly back in the news—but as the subject of revisionist revelations. The perfect fairy tale of Herzog's book became a suspect fable. The iconoclasts started throwing stones.

Herzog had told me that the controversy had troubled him not at all: "I have the experience of the truth." Journalists close to the scene knew better. Says *L'Equipe's* Benoît Heimermann, "Herzog was distraught about the controversy. He tried everything he could do to stop it. He tried to use his influence with the press.

"This business has done a fair amount of damage to Herzog's reputation. In Chamonix or Grenoble, people are disappointed. In Paris, I suppose, he's still a great man."

AMONG ALL NINE TEAMMATES on Annapurna, none—not even the liaison officer, Francis de Noyelle—emerges in Herzog's book as more shadowy than Jean Couzy. Indeed, in *Annapurna*, Couzy is almost faceless. The youngest climber at twenty-seven, the one who has the most trouble acclimatizing, the one whom Herzog relegates to organizing load-carries low on the mountain, always (it seems) ill and weak—Couzy stumbles through the expedition like a sleepwalker. He never complains, never enters into the "polemics" that always seem to center on Lachenal, yet he is seldom cited by Herzog as having done much at all to help the team's efforts.

On the basis of his portrait in *Annapurna* alone, it would have made sense had it been Couzy, rather than his close companion, Schatz, who would quit mountaineering within the year following the expedition. Instead, Couzy went on to become a brilliant climber, with, as Terray wrote in *Conquistadors*, "one of the greatest alpine records of all time."

Couzy started climbing on modest routes in the Pyrenees at age fifteen. Meeting Schatz in 1946, he embarked on a career of solid face climbs all over the Alps. Eventually he would knock off many of the most vaunted routes of his day, including the Walker Spur on the Grandes Jorasses and the wildly overhanging north face of the Cima Ovest di Lavaredo in the Dolomites. He also put up new routes stamped with an elegant purity of line, a boldness of conception. Yet he was known to be a very safe climber. He had chosen never to attempt the north face of the Eiger (of which Terray and Lachenal had made the second ascent), because he judged it too dangerous.

Couzy's climbing was carved out of a promising career as an aeronautical engineer. He made an art form of the three-day weekend, borrowing a plane from his flying club to whisk off to whatever part of France had the best weather forecast, where he would storm up some route that would take lesser climbers a week to prepare for.

At the age of twenty-seven, he was thin, lithe, and remarkably handsome, with a penetrating gaze and a strong, thin-lipped mouth. According to Schatz, Couzy "burned with ideas, impassioned alike by jazz and art." He was an omnivorously curious climber who taught himself Italian and relearned German so that he could read the local guidebooks and better commune with the pioneers of the routes he attacked.

In 1948, Couzy married a young woman who promptly went out and climbed many difficult routes with him. After Annapurna, Lise Couzy would give birth to four children, including twins in 1955.

Terray analyzed Couzy's strengths and weaknesses in *Conquistadors:*

> Muscular and with tremendous stamina under his almost frail appearance, he was an accomplished athlete. Unshakeable health and the digestive system of an ostrich were further assets on big climbs. A certain lack of manual dexterity handicapped him, by contrast, in his earlier days; and on mixed ground [i.e., the very terrain that was Terray's forte], where no technique or intelligence can make up for instinctive neatness of gesture, he always remained slow and ill at ease. . . . On rock, in particular, he became a pastmaster.

Other climbers would have been content to specialize in the alpine big-wall routes that quickly became Couzy's specialty. Yet despite his unhappy experience on Annapurna, Couzy returned twice to the Himalaya, in 1954 and 1955. On the reconnaissance of Makalu, the world's fifth-highest mountain, the first year, and on its successful ascent the following, Couzy became the "motor"— the strongest climber, driving his teammates to triumph, even though Terray, by then the finest expeditionary mountaineer in France and maybe the world, was along on both expeditions.

In *Conquistadors*, Terray acknowledged what may have been Couzy's stellar deed in the mountains, the lightning-strike first ascent of Chomolonzo in 1954, after the team had run out of time on Makalu. This subsidiary peak, which stood only 200 meters below the prestigious 8,000-meter line, was a major challenge in its own right.

> Throughout the whole of the previous night we had been battered by the most violent tempest I have ever known in the Himalayas. Our tent seemed likely to rip in two at any moment, and some of the seams did in fact yield under the sledge-hammer blows of the wind. At dawn the temperature was -27° Centigrade inside the tent. . . . [P]ersonally I had no thought but to get down out of it all as quickly as possible. Only Jean's magnetic personality constrained me to follow him like one condemned to the scaffold. There were tears in the Sherpas' eyes when they saw us preparing to set out, so little hope had they of seeing us again!

The following year, Couzy and Terray were the first pair to reach the summit of Makalu, on a French expedition so strong that all nine climbers eventually reached the top. None of the other thirteen 8,000-meter peaks would first succumb to such a clockwork victory.

On November 2, 1958, Couzy was attempting a new route on the Roc des Bergers in the Alps with his friend Jean Puiseux. Couzy was leading. Puiseux heard a noise he knew all too well—that of a rock falling from high above. He yelled, "Watch out!" The stone struck the wall and caromed wildly. Couzy never had time to move. The rock struck him square in the head, killing him at once.

Somehow Puiseux soloed up the rest of the wall, then accomplished an arduous descent. The recovery of Couzy's body took a crack team two days of perilous toil.

Eight men, including Schatz, carried Couzy's bier to his grave near Montmaur, in the Hautes-Alpes. Two years later, a commemorative plaque was mounted on the forest hut where Couzy had bivouacked the night before the fatal climb. Its legend reads:

JEAN COUZY
1923–1958
Alpinist extraordinaire who opened or repeated,
from the Olan to Makalu,
the most beautiful routes in the world.

At the time of his death, at thirty-five, Couzy left children of seven, five, and (his twins) three years of age.

In a moving obituary, Schatz spoke of Couzy's "purity." "That was the secret of his demeanor in the mountains in the face of danger—no physical fear ever bothered him; he acted always as though, with everything carefully weighed, he had decided to act." In *Conquistadors,* Terray wrote, "Jean was not made for the rat-race of this world. He was a sort of saint, an idealist tormented by visions of the absolute."

In Paris in the spring of 1999, I met Lise Couzy. A strikingly handsome, dignified woman, she had never remarried. She recounted the moment forty-one years earlier when she had received the terrible news. Puiseux had telephoned a friend in Lyon, who in turn telephoned Lise's mother, whom Lise was visiting. "When I saw my mother's face, I knew," she told me.

At first, it was more than she could bear to tell her children. "Where's Papa?" asked her son that evening. "Maybe he'll come back later," she prevaricated.

"Jean stayed friends with the other Annapurna climbers," Lise Couzy recalled. "He and Terray were particularly close. And he very much liked Lachenal. He was not at all disappointed in Annapurna, even though for him it was a very hard expedition, a very tough return.

"When he was off on Makalu, I had a lot of fear. But I knew this was his passion. On Makalu, Terray lost six kilograms, but Jean put on six kilos! It was a matter of different metabolisms.

"After his death, everybody spoke so well of Jean, but they didn't really know him. I never thought of marrying again. Jean was my hero. He still is."

GASTON RÉBUFFAT RETURNED from Annapurna deeply disenchanted. According to Françoise, one of the first things he said was, "I don't believe any more in friendship." His long relationship with Terray was irrevocably damaged by the expedition. Says Françoise of the dolorous march out from Annapurna, "After that, Gaston was no longer friends with Lionel, because Lionel had seen the political advantage of taking care of Herzog. Often Lachenal was left alone lying on his stretcher, so Gaston stayed with him."

Rébuffat would never again join an expedition to the far-flung ranges, restricting his climbing instead to the Alps. Yet for the next two years, he pushed the limits of what was humanly possible in his beloved mountains. Only eleven days after getting home from Annapurna, Rébuffat put up an important new route on the Aiguille de Blaitière near Chamonix.

On July 29, 1952, Rébuffat reached the summit of the Eiger, the last of the six great north faces of the Alps, the ensemble of which he was the first man to climb. That ascent through storm, waterfall, avalanche, and falling stones was Rébuffat's most harrowing "epic" in the Alps. Of the nine climbers who found themselves trapped on the Nordwand that July, Rébuffat and the fiercely motivated Austrian Hermann Buhl were the strongest. The ascent verged toward chaos, with ropes entangled, climbers setting loose small avalanches upon one another. Buhl's stubborn refusal to share the lead, even when his lapses of judgment threatened to maroon the whole party, drove the calm and premeditating Rébuffat into a silent fury.

In his account of the Eiger in *Starlight and Storm*, Rébuffat casts no aspersions on the Austrian. Even reading between the lines, the reader would be hard put to discern the sharp interpersonal conflict that unfurled high on the face. "Buhl and Gaston didn't like each other," says Françoise. "Buhl knew that Gaston could outclimb him."

After 1952, Rébuffat lowered his sights slightly, although he continued to make the occasional first ascent, as well as to guide talented clients on routes otherwise reserved for experts. With the success of *Starlight and Storm* in 1954, Rébuffat started to believe that he might pursue a second career as an author.

For almost three decades after 1955, Rébuffat published large-format picture books about his beloved Alps. Some, such as *Mont-Blanc, Jardin Féerique,* were primarily historical; others, including *Entre Terre et Ciel* and *Les Horizons Gagnés,* amounted to lyrical evocations of his "enchanted garden."

It was these books that revolutionized the aesthetic of mountaineering. Virtually never before had a professional guide written about his craft—let alone written at such a high poetic pitch. Nor had any previous photographs captured the grace and elegance of climbing as did the dozens of pictures of Rébuffat, shot by alpine lensmen, that spangled these luxurious volumes. In a typical photo, Rébuffat was seen in profile against a vertical cliff, with a distant glacier providing a backdrop. No apparent struggle breathed in these images: instead, the lanky acrobat calmly clasped the clean granite with his fingers, while his toes adhered to minuscule holds. The rope plunged free in space out of the bottom of the picture, with not a single piton for protection. The patterned pullover sweater that Rébuffat wore in every photo became his signature. (A photo of Rébuffat on the Aiguille de Roc was chosen by NASA as a representation of human life on Earth, to ride aboard Voyager II probing the remote reaches of outer space in search of extraterrestrial intelligence.)

The most revolutionary aspect of Rébuffat's works, however, was his thoroughgoing rejection of the martial metaphors that had dominated mountaineering from Mont Blanc in 1786 on. His own emphasis on a harmonious embrace of the alpine world owed something to Antoine de Saint-Exupéry, one of his favorite authors. But this new philosophy was not one Rébuffat consciously created, in reaction to the militarism of the Herzogs and Devieses; it seems to have been inborn, instinctive.

With the success of *Starlight and Storm*, Rébuffat began touring on the lecture circuit, giving slide shows. He soon gravitated to film. Collaborating with several visionary filmmakers, he produced classics of mountaineering cinema, including *Starlight and Storm* and *Entre Terre et Ciel*, that brought the enchanted garden to vast new audiences. By the late 1960s, Rébuffat was the most famous guide in Europe.

MY OWN ENTHRALLMENT to the Rébuffat aesthetic lasted most of a decade, after I first read *Starlight and Storm* at age sixteen. But in the late 1960s, as climbing itself embraced the counterculture passions that swept America, I found myself drifting away from the lyrical poets of mountaineering and toward its rowdy skeptics.

A turning point for me came in a long discussion in the middle of the night with a Harvard friend, Hank Abrons, as we drove the Alaska Highway toward my first expedition, on Mount McKinley. Twenty years old, I earnestly voiced a cardinal Rébuffat tenet: that in the mountains we seek difficulty, not danger. Could climbing be divorced from danger altogether, it would reach its purest possible expression.

Nonsense, said Hank, who was two years older. Danger was precisely what made our pastime so real, so rewarding. If you could separate danger from difficulty, climbing would become just another sport. We wrangled on, but there, with the dusky tundra plodding by us as we steered north toward the ineluctably dangerous Wickersham Wall, I began to wonder whether Hank didn't have a point. (Today I believe Hank was right, and Rébuffat, seduced by his own idealism, wrong. The sterility of such latter-day developments in the climbing scene as indoor gyms, where risk has truly been divorced from difficulty, furnishes my evidence.)

Climbing in the Shawangunks in New York State, I found the first gang of live climbers (as opposed to eminences, such as Lachenal and Terray, whom I had met only in books) to become my heroes. They were the Vulgarians—a hard-drinking, drug-taking, pretension-pricking band of dropouts and misfits who also happened to be the best climbers in the East.

The Vulgarians' counterparts in the United Kingdom were the iconoclasts of the Creagh Dhu and Rock and Ice, loosely organized clubs of working-class blokes who had replaced the Oxbridge gentlemen of the previous generation to become the finest climbers in Britain. My friends and I listened in awe to the tales of Joe Brown, a plumber from Manchester, and Don Whillans, also a plumber and a high school dropout from a grimy town in the north of England, who might at the moment be the nerviest climbers in the world. Brown was the first man to have solved the fierce and perilous short crack called Cenotaph Corner, in north Wales; but he had dismissed his own first ascent of Kanchenjunga, the world's third-highest mountain (where he was paired with those Oxbridge throwbacks), as "a long slog."

One day in my late twenties I discovered the writing of Tom Patey, a Scottish ice climber and crony of Brown and Whillans, who had perfected a satiric take on our pastime that on first reading won me over utterly. That initial Patey essay, which I came across in 1969, was his quarrel with Rébuffat, titled "Apes or Ballerinas?" published in the splendidly counterculture British journal *Mountain.*

In the piece, Patey launches boldly into an attack on what he called the "stylist" climber.

> The French, as might be expected, are the supreme stylists. If you don't know what I mean, have a look at the illustrations in Rébuffat's book, *On Snow and Rock.* Every picture shows the author examining himself in some graceful and quite unbelievable posture. . . . Even the captions carry a note of smug satisfaction: "Climbing means the pleasure of communicating with the mountain as a craftsman communicates with the wood or the stone or the iron upon which he is working" (portrait of Rébuffat, standing on air, studiously regarding his left forearm, hands caressing smooth granite).

Patey then imagines the climber trying to learn from Rébuffat's injunctions to graceful, effortless movement:

> Stage Two: the left boot is aligned with the right boot by stepping up smoothly and deliberately. Any effort is imperceptible. . . .

Strange! You're lying flat on the ground with a squashed nose. Another attempt; another failure. Time passes, along with your faith in Rébuffat.

Eventually, in Patey's piece, the climber gets up the cliff by ignoring the ballerina of Rébuffat's "stylist" and reverting to the primal ape.

Heave, clutch, thrutch, grunt! Up you go, defying gravity with your own impetus. So what, if it looks ungraceful? Joe Brown doesn't look much like a ballet dancer.

Patey's delicious burlesque swept away what was left of my former adulation. At the time, I was too sociologically naive to realize that there yawned between French and British climbers an unbridgeable gulf of mutual contempt, that on the crags above Chamonix they traded curses in Scots and Savoyard. Out of such animus was born a caricature of "Ghastly Rubberface," as the British wickedly nicknamed Rébuffat.

On reexamination, all those beautiful pictures in Rébuffat's books started to smack of the inauthentic. In *On Snow and Rock* (published in 1959), Rébuffat had been one of the first to realize that to take a picture that truly captured the vertiginous glory of our pastime, you had to set it up. Today, most good climbing pictures are set up beforehand, with photographers resorting to machinations to get in positions that Rébuffat would never have dreamed of. In 1969, however, Patey could imply that the only honest climbing photo was one taken by the belayer as he whipped a Brownie out of his rucksack and snapped, one-handed, a shot of the leader scrabbling above.

All those photos of Rébuffat frozen in sublime equipoise against ethereal granite began to seem an affectation. The insistence on himself as subject, my friends and I took for arrant vanity (as opposed to what I now suspect—that no other climber was good enough to pose on the perches that Rébuffat wished to illuminate). The famous pullover sweater became a standing joke.

Swept up in the iconoclasm of the late 1960s, I could even de-

light in Patey's morbid but clever ballad mocking the legend of Annapurna itself (it mattered little that Patey miscounted the frozen
digits):

Twenty frozen fingers, twenty frozen toes
Two blistered faces, frostbite on the nose
One looks like Herzog, who dropped his gloves on top
And Lachenal tripped and fell, thought he'd never stop.
Bop bop bop bop bop bop bop bop bop.

"Take me down to Oudot" was all that he would say
"He'll know what to do now," said Lionel Terray
"Your blood is like black pudding," said Oudot, with his knife
"It is not too late to amputate if I can save your life."
Chop chop chop chop chop chop chop chop chop.

No tiny fingers, No tiny toes
The memory lingers but the digit goes
In an Eastern Railway carriage, where the River Ganges flows
There are Twenty Tiny Fingers and Twenty Tiny Toes.
Chop chop chop chop chop chop chop chop chop.

Thus I "outgrew" Rébuffat. Had I known, in the late 1960s,
that side by side in the breast of the lyric singer of the brotherhood
of the rope there lurked an iconoclast as fierce as Patey, a debunker
of all things false and sentimental, I would have been astonished.
But Rébuffat guarded that side of himself in hermetic privacy. Only
a decade after his death would that well-hidden critic emerge, in his
hitherto unpublished notes and jottings on the 1950 expedition.
The man whom the crowds at Orly and in the Salle Pleyel wished to
salute as one of the heroes of Annapurna would become instead its
ultimate skeptic.

AFTER THE FIVE-YEAR INTERDICTION against writing about the expedition had expired in 1955, Rébuffat toyed with the idea of publishing his own account of Annapurna. "I talked him out of writing
this," Françoise told me, "because it would be too bitter." She was

guided, as well, by simple pragmatism. The reputation of the man who, by virtue of his poetic celebrations of the mountain world, had become the most famous guide in France would not be well served by a polemic from his hand undercutting the most sacred myth in French mountaineering.

So Rébuffat kept the bitterness to himself. In 1981, Herzog published a book called *Les Grandes Aventures de l'Himalaya*, a collection of accounts of other people's expeditions. One chapter, called "Un Autre Regard" ("Another Look"), serves as Herzog's own meditation on Annapurna, three decades later. More personal than *Annapurna*, the chapter stands as a kind of first draft of the "subjective" account of the famous ascent that Herzog would publish in *L'Autre Annapurna*.

In the seclusion of his study, Rébuffat opened his copy of *Les Grandes Aventures* and scribbled marginal comments throughout the text of "Un Autre Regard." I first saw this remarkable document in Yves Ballu's house near Grenoble in 1999.

Rébuffat is plainly disgusted with Herzog's self-preoccupation. Sometimes he circles key words, then draws lines between them, creating a branching tree of emphasis. In the paragraph beginning, "Yes, there we were on June 3, 1950," Rébuffat has highlighted "we," "my [feet]," "I was [the first]," "Around me," "I spoke to the 8,000-ers" that "surrounded me." He has also circled the words "victory" and "conquered." In the margin he notes simply, "And Lachenal?"

Above another paragraph, Rébuffat scrawls "Blah-blah-blah!" Beside yet another, "This is stupid." Beside another, "A fairy tale."

The annotations add up to an extended rant against the leader to whom, three decades earlier, Rébuffat had been forced to pledge total obedience. Another branching tree, covering more than two pages, links Herzog's professions of fear of death and frozen flesh: "My carcass was transformed into ice," "would cost me my life," "lost consciousness," "die in battle," "capitulate," "out of breath." Beside one section of this text, Rébuffat writes, "*Quel cinéma!* [What a comedian!]"

Sometimes the comments have the taunting yap of an adolescent jeering his rival. When Herzog, narrating the dropped gloves on the descent from the summit, writes, "The incident, however, failed to provoke me to get out of my pack a pair of wool socks I had stuck there for such an emergency," Rébuffat adds, "Wrong. The socks are for the feet, the gloves for the hands."

"Wrong." *"Quel cinéma."* "The cinema continues." *"Le cinéma intime!"* Beside the single word "curiously," when Herzog writes of his strength as he rakes through the snow at the bottom of the crevasse in search of the precious boots as "curiously underestimated during the previous hours," Rébuffat editorializes, "Yes, very curiously, if this isn't cinema." When Herzog, describing Schatz's embrace near Camp IVA, writes, "He gave me a kiss of peace," Rébuffat annotates, "What is he trying to say?" Herzog wonders aloud if he can survive the night in the crevasse, prompting Rébuffat to circle the word "survive" and gibe, "The cheater of death. He's going to die ten times." Later, "Again the cheater of death." Narrating his avalanche fall with the two Sherpas, Herzog reflects on his survival, "Was this not another miracle?" Here Rébuffat jots, "One more time! The everlasting miracle."

Taken in sum, the savage annotations to Herzog's chapter do not begin to add up to a coherent critique. Instead, they bespeak the furious frustration of a man who has had to live all his life in silent acquiescence to a sacred text and a "number one national hero," both of which Rébuffat knows to be profoundly false. In their petulant wit, their exasperated disdain, those jottings are utterly unlike anything Rébuffat published in his lifetime.

In the last years of his life, as Ballu interviewed him for the biography, Rébuffat began to write down his own version of Annapurna. These notes never amounted to more than a series of *aperçus*, discrete sentences and paragraphs that ponder the pivotal events of the 1950 expedition. The tone is almost that of a literary critic, as if Rébuffat had come across some ancient, anonymous saga preserved on vellum and were using all his intuition to probe to the core of the story's meaning. In their lucidity, their epigrammatic perfection, some of these *pensées* promise to stand alone as a kind of last word on the myth of Annapurna, magisterial pronouncements by one who, after all, was there.

A boy who loses his gloves on Mont Blanc is an imbecile. An alpinist who loses his gloves in the Himalaya, we make of him a national hero.

Is the myth of the hero, then, founded on frozen feet and hands?

It seemed to me at that moment [of Lachenal's and Herzog's return from the summit] that Terray and I were charged with a mission that, in my innermost heart, pleased me more than going to the top, because it converged with what I love about my métier as guide: to taste renunciation in the name of friendship and to negotiate with the storm to save my companions.

I have never liked those martial terms so often applied to the mountain: "The Himalayan assault," "the conquest of . . ." Least of all, so often employed, "Victory over Annapurna." I have never considered myself a victor over Annapurna.

Oh, if only Herzog had lost his flags instead of his gloves, how happy I would have been!

RÉBUFFAT CONTINUED to climb into his fifties. In 1975, at the age of fifty-four, he made a remarkable ascent of the Freney Pillar, one of Mont Blanc's hardest and most extended routes.

That same year, he was diagnosed with cancer of the breast. There followed a decade of hope and despair, of radio- and chemotherapy, of brief remissions followed by more serious onsets, as the cancer slowly worked its ravages. By now, Gaston and Françoise had three children. As the children grew Rébuffat had taken them up classic routes in his enchanted garden.

Refusing to give in to his ailment, the tall guide made two more major climbs: the first ascent of the southeast face of the Aiguille du Plan, in 1979, and—by now seriously debilitated—the south face of the Aiguille du Midi in 1983, of which he had made the first ascent twenty-seven years earlier. After the latter climb, Rébuffat jotted a laconic entry in the guide's notebook he had kept all his life: "August 18. South face of Aiguille du Midi. Start at 9:00. Summit 15:00. Great fatigue."

Two years before he died, Rébuffat fulfilled a lifelong dream by rafting the Colorado River with Françoise, signing up for a commercial trip. "He was very tired, just out of chemotherapy," she told me. "There were clients of all ages on the river. They quickly saw that Gaston was very sick. Very discreetly the other clients started to do everything for him. To get in and out of the boat, he needed help. Two young Germans found the best campsites for him."

Did these companions realize who Rébuffat was, I wondered. Did they know what this man had done in the mountains in his prime?

"No," said Françoise. "All they knew was that he was French, and that he was very sick."

A year after Gaston's death, Françoise began to write a memoir about her life with her husband. Still unfinished, never published, it nonetheless contains passages of heartbreaking pathos, as well as bearing witness to a rapport as complete as any married couple may have ever had. By addressing her lost husband as "you," she achieves a kind of hallucinatory intensity.

"June ? 1986," Françoise writes atop the first page. "It is now one year since you left me." The memoir opens with a "radiant memory" of the couple's first meeting at the *salon de thé* in Chamonix, where the young fashion student hoped to encounter a mountain guide. Yet by the second page, she has plunged into the ordeal of Gaston's degeneration.

> Those last four years, we lived thinking only about your survival.
> We existed, but in another identity. The characters left the stage, giving way to others who walked into a new novel that was too short, the ending already written, menacing like a cataclysm that was in the air. . . .
> That last week of May, the issue was there, perceptible. It infested the air, making it hard for us to breathe.
>
> I sensed the time that was inexorably abandoning you, without appeal. Our happiness slipped through our fingers . . . the cancer charged ahead. Silently, from the bottom of my soul, I pleaded with you to live. I could no longer do anything to make you live, the hemorrhaging of your vigor was operating in me also. Yet up until

the last moments, I tried to communicate to you those waves of love that could work miracles, perhaps even help the medicine.

The losses accumulated, one by one. One of the bitterest came the day Rébuffat, after long deliberation, asked the Compagnie des Guides de Chamonix, of which he had been a member since 1942, to take him off the list of active guides. As Françoise understood, that step "already signified death, a first death."

Other losses were more intimate, manifesting themselves in scenes that Françoise later vividly recaptured:

> The last night that we had dinner at our daughter's apartment, at the moment of leaving you didn't have the strength to go home. There was no bed available for me.
>
> No one offered to accompany me home. I left by taxi, alone, in despair. Thus I understood the full horror of what awaited me. The next morning, you told me of your distress at seeing me go away.

The night before you entered the hospital, you were exhausted, there was nothing you desired. You got up in the morning, wracked by the pain in your bones, reeling with weakness, but you wanted to go out all the same. For the first time I had to help you to get dressed. You cried, you held me in your arms and said, "I can't take it any more. I'm holding on only for you."

In the hospital, Françoise discovered her husband on his deathbed:

> I found you alone in a vast, cold, repellent room. I had been authorized only a one-hour visit. How could the medical corps . . . so lack common humanity as to tear one of us away from the other, two beings who were never meant to be separated?
>
> You did not seem to be conscious. You lay there inert. Did you smell my scent? Your lips were slack and loose, as if in a smile. Your pupils were half open, but your sight was gone—it had already left us.
>
> I was petrified.
>
> You were so cold, your body no longer breathed, but in that extreme moment, by a reflex of will, you raised your arm to pass your hand through my hair. From the light touch of your fingers, I

understood that you wanted me to bring my face near to yours and embrace you. That stroke of your hand in contact with my skin, that kiss, that gesture—I keep that as your final gift.

Rébuffat died on June 1, 1985. In the months that followed, Françoise was haunted not so much by his absence as by a feeling that he was still there: "I write to you, as though you were simply away on a voyage. I continue to wait for you." And yet, "The monotony of my days grows heavier and heavier." Still, "In the darkness, our complicity goes on. There is no decision that I make without asking you about it. . . . Love has its excuses, it ought to be unconditional, and sometimes it persists only through an absence of logic.

"In return, I sense that wherever you are, you hear me and pardon me."

Rébuffat lies buried on a hill near the side of the old Chamonix cemetery, surrounded by other guides. For his epitaph, Françoise chose an epigram from Rébuffat's most poetic book, Les Horizons Gagnés, that defines the essence of mountaineering: "Conduire son corps là où un jour ses yeux ont regardé"—"To transport one's body to the place where once the eyes first gazed."

EIGHT

The Silence of Lachenal

UPON HIS RETURN TO FRANCE, Louis Lachenal entered the hospital in Chamonix. Like Herzog, he would undergo painful operations on his feet—sixteen of them over five years—as well as many difficult skin grafts.

For Lachenal, in his anguish, there was no "new life," no mystical discovery of a higher purpose his suffering had revealed. Only one thing mattered: would he be able to climb again? And if so, would he ever again approach the transcendent level at which he had climbed when he and Terray had stormed up the hardest routes in the Alps in the late 1940s?

158

From the moment he had frozen his feet, Lachenal's thoughts had focused on the similar plight of his friend the great Swiss climber Raymond Lambert. After a survival ordeal in winter on the Aiguilles du Diable, Lambert had lost all his toes to frostbite. Yet he had come back to climb at an exceptional level. His triumphant moment was also the sternest test of his rehabilitation, when in 1952 he reached 28,200 feet on the South Col route on Everest, higher than anyone before him had ever climbed. (Lambert, who reached that record height with Tenzing Norgay, missed stealing the next year's first ascent from Sir Edmund Hillary by a mere 800 feet.)

In September 1951, Lambert made a surprise visit to Lachenal in the hospital. Herzog, receiving special treatments in Chamonix, lay in the neighboring bed. In *L'Autre Annapurna*, he recaptures that meeting as a joshing exchange:

"So, Raymond," says Lachenal, "have we joined the club?"

"Wait a minute, you haven't been enthroned yet."

"The proof is here," returns Lachenal, showing Lambert his feet covered with bandages. "Do we have to get down on our knees?"

"No, *en pointe*. Like a dancer."

To the invalids' astonishment, Lambert takes off his shoes and socks and begins to dance on the tips of his amputated stumps. "Listen, Biscante, the day you can do the same, then you join the club. Not before."

The dialogue, as usual, has been invented by Herzog, recalling an episode forty-seven years in the past. But there is no reason to doubt the tenor and substance of that meeting. It would have been very like Lachenal to use black humor as a screen to cover his fears about his future. In any event, Lachenal's son, Jean-Claude, who was eight in 1951, remembers Lambert's visit. "My father was very low at the time," he says. "Lambert came to the foot of the bed and showed him that he could still climb without toes. He was joking, dancing, kicking a soccer ball."

That same month, both Herzog and Lachenal were awarded the Legion of Honor. Terray and Rébuffat were passed over.

For two years after Annapurna, Lachenal was unable to make a single ascent. The Compagnie des Guides, which had received their comrade as a hero, kept him busy with administrative jobs. Meanwhile he undertook his first timid promenades in the foothills with Jean-Claude and with the young daughter of a fellow guide. Alone in his bedroom, he walked barefoot, trying out some of the maneuvers Lambert had showed off in the hospital; but the pain quickly curtailed his experiments. As months passed with little improvement, he lapsed into discouragement.

The testimonies about Lachenal's mental state during these years vary greatly. According to Herzog (In *L'Autre Annapurna*), Lachenal was inconsolable about his loss, and "ceaselessly bewailed" the fact that he might never climb or ski again.

If that testimony is suspect—Herzog would forever portray himself as the uncomplaining survivor, Lachenal as the hypochondriac—so too may be the more sanguine witness of some of Lachenal's closest Chamonix friends, who were at pains to emphasize the positive. Jean-Pierre Payot, fellow guide and climber, remembers that Lachenal "was not so terribly anguished. We laughed all the time together." According to Mauricette Couttet, widow of one of Lachenal's best friends, "He joked a lot about losing his feet." Payot recalls Lachenal returning a pair of special shoes he had commissioned, sneering at the shoemaker, "These are good only for spreading manure." Several friends testify that Lachenal plunged himself into town meetings, conferences, and guides' affairs.

Yet Terray, who knew him as well as anyone, later wrote of these years:

> In the end he recovered sufficiently to work as a mountaineering instructor, but he could never recover his genius. This curtailment profoundly changed his character. Once he had seemed magically immune from the ordinary clumsiness and weight of humankind, and the contrast was like wearing a ball and chain.

Too poor to own a car, Lachenal had never learned to drive. As a surprise present, late in 1950 Adèle bought him a Citroën 2 CV. A shaky driver herself, she taught her husband how to operate an automobile. (On the driver's license Lachenal received in January

1951, an official has written across the top, "Amputation of all the toes of the 2 feet.")

Driving quickly became a consuming passion for Lachenal. Behind the wheel, his lost toes made little difference. Speed on the road took the place of his legendary speed on the cliff. He quickly taught himself all the maneuvers of a driver at Le Mans. Wrote Terray, "I have driven with quite a number of notorious drivers, and if some of them perhaps showed more judgment I have never known one to equal him for daring and natural skill."

There are many stories about Lachenal's wild driving, with enough concurrence among the versions to keep them this side of the apocryphal. Jean-Pierre Payot was riding with his friend once when they came to a hazardous junction. A road sign warned: "Danger. Slow Down." Instead, Lachenal sped up, explaining, "You have to accelerate to avoid the danger here."

On the highway, Lachenal would pass on blind corners, and even cut across fields to get the jump on poky traffic. In one persistent story, as he drove with Adèle, his foot grew weary holding down the pedal, so he insisted she floor the accelerator while he drove. After a stretch of driving thus, he abruptly stopped, got out of the car, and picked up a wayside brick. From then on, the brick held down the accelerator, to be nudged aside only in extremis.

Speed gave Lachenal's life momentary purpose again. He set out to break the unofficial records for long-distance jaunts in France, whittling his Paris–Chamonix time down to six hours and forty minutes. (Today's best time, on the *autoroutes* that have changed the countryside, is still only five and a half hours.)

Lachenal suffered a number of spectacular one-car accidents, rolling his vehicle more than once, yet emerging unscathed. Adèle was terrified of his driving from the start; soon no one else wanted to get in the car with him. Some witnesses insist that Lachenal was utterly scrupulous to avoid involving other vehicles in a crash. Yet another persistent tale has him driving back from Paris with Terray's wife, Marianne, who was a great beauty. Jean-Pierre Payot recalls the aftermath: "Lachenal called me by phone. 'Where are you?' I asked. 'Come to Geneva and pick me up,' he said. 'I missed a corner in Burgundy and the car rolled. I had to take a train to Geneva. As for Marianne—she's had herself done over well.'

"I wondered what he was talking about. When I picked him up, I found out. Marianne had been knocked out or fainted in the crash. He stopped a cattle truck and laid her down in the straw. He took advantage of her state to look at her breasts. Evidently she'd had plastic surgery. In the official version of the story, he only looked at her eyes."

In *Conquistadors,* Terray cogently analyzed the motivation behind Lachenal's wild driving:

> Those who saw in it a taste for exhibitionism were quite mistaken. Lachenal's passion for speed bore no relation to vanity. It was a drug to some imperious inner need of his nature. I have often seen him about to set out in his Dyna, and asked: "Where are you off to?" He would reply: "Nowhere. Just a drive." Nobody ever heard of most of his exploits, which he indulged in for the sheer joy of the thing.

In 1952, Lachenal traveled to the Belgian Congo with Adèle to present a number of slide shows on Annapurna. The heat debilitated him, but while there he seized upon the idea of climbing the highest peak in the snow-capped Ruwenzori—the "Mountains of the Moon." A climbing friend from the Alps happened to be heading for the same range with a small team, so Lachenal joined forces with them. The mountain posed no real technical obstacles, but at 17,100 feet, it stood more than a thousand feet higher than Mont Blanc, and simply to get to the peak required a lengthy journey through forest and foothills.

The climb was exhausting for Lachenal, but to his great joy he and a Swiss alpinist named Coquoz reached the summit. There, he discovered and retrieved an ice axe left by the legendary Duke of the Abruzzi (leader of the second expedition to attempt K2, in 1909), who had made the first ascent of the mountain forty-six years earlier. Lachenal became the first Frenchman to reach the highest point in the Ruwenzori.

In a piece he wrote about the climb for a Lyon newspaper, Lachenal reveals a penchant for hijinks and whimsy of which Herzog gives no hint in *Annapurna*. In the jungle, the team meets a local man reputed to be a cannibal.

> We must not have seemed very appetizing to him. He let us photograph him like a regular chap on salary from the Tourism Office. So I asked him how we could meet tribes of true cannibals. I wanted to see them, to get to know them!
> "They certainly exist," he answered.
> "But where?"
> "We don't know. No one knows. But they're nothing special. Nothing distinguishes them from other blacks."
> "I want to eat a man. I want to know the taste. Oh, just to taste!"

At the foot of the Stanley Glacier, the team approaches a sign. Writes Lachenal:

> The text ought to be pondered in France: "It is forbidden to venture onto the glacier or on the mountain without being accompanied by a guide." Since that was what we were, we continued.

On the mountain, Lachenal savors a unique experience: "Coquoz took the lead on the rope, and I found it marvelous to play for once at being the 'client.' "

By the end of the hike out, Lachenal's feet were in excruciating pain. He had to be helped by the natives to stagger the last few yards to his hotel. Yet the success deeply heartened him: for the first time in two years, he began to think it possible to return to alpinism.

Privately and alone, Lachenal began to hike up to the Col des Montets, where he soloed short cliffs, developing a technique appropriate to his abbreviated feet. Gradually his confidence blossomed. One day, leading a group of students in a beginner's course with his friend André Contamine—one of the best climbers among his fellow Chamonix guides, himself a maverick individualist—Lachenal stunned the group by challenging Contamine to a race up the cliff. Arriving neck and neck at the top, the two guides gasped with the effort and laughed out loud with joy.

Yet on another outing, Lachenal confessed his limitations to Contamine. "The skin grafts won't stand up to a prolonged outing," he said. "On the descent, the ends of my feet bang against the leather. Ah, Conta! Where are the days when we did the Caïman, the Croco, and the Peigne in the same day? Where are those days?"

This vignette appears in the 1956 *Carnets du Vertige*, and it exemplifies an acute biographical problem. The chief source for Lachenal's life after 1950 is that book, which—apart from the heavily censored Annapurna diary—is composed of third-person chapters written by Gérard Herzog. These passages are based on Lachenal's notes, and on further notes composed by a journalist, Philippe Cornuau, whom Lachenal enlisted to help him with his book. For the most part, Gérard Herzog's chapters follow the chief themes of Lachenal's life post-Annapurna, as corroborated by still-living friends. Yet, as in *Annapurna*, the *Carnets* abounds in invented dialogue. And it paints a portrait of Lachenal that blunts his arch-critical candor, his acerbic wit. There is a softening Herzog stamp throughout.

Nowhere is the 1956 *Carnets* more unreliable than in its account of Lachenal's relations with Maurice Herzog after 1950. Thus Gérard has Lachenal hear of Maurice's plans to plunge, despite his amputations, back into alpinism with an ascent of the Matterhorn in 1952. "The obsession with being unequal to his ambitions," writes Gérard, "made [Lachenal] turn down the chance to share this experience, despite Herzog's advances." (Nothing came of Herzog's Matterhorn plans.)

More unctuously, Gérard paints Lachenal responding to a friend's entreaties to take up skiing again on an easy slope. "My feet are messed up," complains Lachenal. "I would make a fool of myself." Then he learns that Herzog is about to try to ski again, and that he hopes Lachenal will join him in the effort. Suddenly Lachenal changes his mind. "Ah! With Maurice," Gérard quotes him, "that would be really great."

Lachenal was devoted to his two sons, and to Adèle, but he may also have been something of a ladies' man. According to Mauricette Couttet, Lachenal found that his crippled state could charm women: "He had a different approach with young ladies [after Annapurna]. He was allowed things afterward that he wasn't before." Says Payot's sister, Elisabeth, "He was a wonderful friend, but an odious husband. He either did all the housework, or emptied all the drawers and said to Adèle, You clean all this up."

By 1953, Lachenal had become ambitious in the mountains. That year, with Rébuffat, Payot, Contamine, and two other friends, he pulled off an extraordinary ascent of the south ridge of the Aiguille Noire de Peuterey, a long and serious route in the same class as the northeast face of the Piz Badile (one of Rébuffat's six great north faces). Though Contamine led most of the pitches on Lachenal's rope, the very fact that Lachenal could complete such a climb was proof that his genius had not altogether left him.

Lachenal threw himself back into the mountains. In 1954, he was involved in a harrowing catastrophe, when a group of beginners he was leading got bombarded with tons of falling rock as they descended the Aiguille Verte. Lachenal's fellow guide, Alexis Simond, was killed beside him, and one of the beginners gravely injured. Yet even this memento mori failed to dampen Lachenal's enthusiasm.

In the summer of 1955, Lachenal agreed to climb Monte Rosa (at 15,217 feet, the second-highest peak in the Alps) with Herzog. In the 1956 *Carnets,* Gérard Herzog claims the idea was Lachenal's:

Already in 1954 Lachenal had wanted to make a good climb with his companion from Annapurna. Then the circumstances had not been right; but now Herzog was in Chamonix, the weather seemed stable and fine, the moment had come. For both of them, this project had a great emotional significance.

Jean-Claude Lachenal remembers the "project" quite differently: "Herzog wanted the press along. My father said no, not with any publicity."

After the climb, Lachenal wrote an account of it. This too was suppressed by Devies and Gérard Herzog in the 1956 *Carnets,* remaining unknown until Michel Guérin rescued it in the 1996 edition.

Lachenal's narrative is full of his characteristic wit and candor.

And it confirms Jean-Claude's memory that the climb may have been concocted as a publicity stunt.

> Thus we wanted to go into the mountains. This became known in Chamonix. Several friends wanted to join us; one of them wanted to make a photographic *reportage*, the proceeds of which he would have donated to mountain rescue groups. Even with that aim, the project hardly pleased us. There was a moment of uncertainty, because it bothered both of us to turn down such good will.

On the typescript of Lachenal's account, a marginal annotation in Maurice Herzog's hand reads, "I propose to suppress"; the circled passage begins with "one of them" and ends with "such good will."

Later, as the pair sets out from the mountain village of Macugnaga, Lachenal writes of the locals,

> They gave us a welcome that I will not soon forget. Herzog and I could not pass through unnoticed, but their welcome was not that of stupid curiosity about pseudo-stars, it was the joy of *montagnards* who love their mountains and are happy because other *montagnards* have come from afar to admire them.

Herzog has circled "about pseudo-stars" and written in the margin, "propose to suppress."

The two reached the summit at 7:00 or 8:00 A.M. on the second day. The moment awakened for Lachenal glimmerings of Annapurna:

> It was perfectly clear, with a little wind. We had all the time in the world to dawdle. It would be difficult to describe our thoughts, except that all the bad memories had been wiped out.

On the typescript another hand, that of Lucien Devies, has circled the second half of the last sentence and written "No."

In the end, not one line of Lachenal's account was published in the 1956 *Carnets*. Instead, Gérard Herzog summarized the climb in two pages, whitewashing it: "The ascent unfurled without the slightest incident." The account ends with a different summit moment:

> As on Annapurna, they said nothing of their buoyant feelings, which forebade the slightest word. Their gazes crossed in a flash. Each one cast a furtive glance at the short little boots of the other. Jubilant, Lachenal smiled.

By 1955, Lachenal was climbing at near his pre-Annapurna level. He was still only thirty-four years old. Terray had started going off every summer on an expedition. In his absence, André Contamine became Lachenal's regular partner.

In the spring of 1955, when the five-year interdiction against publishing any account of Annapurna expired, Lachenal now set out to write a memoir of his climbing life, with his version of Annapurna as the centerpiece. He had guarded his diary, and he appealed to an acquaintance, Philippe Cornuau, who had just come off a landmark first ascent on the Droites and was in need of a spell of recuperation, to help him. Lachenal had never had much confidence in his writing ability, thinking his style too crude and down-to-earth. Cornuau was a professional freelance writer, contributing regularly to *Réalités, L'Express,* and other journals.

"He was in a hurry to get it out," recalls Cornuau. "We didn't have quite the same idea of the book. Lachenal wanted a quick book, I wanted a more ambitious one. I thought, there are very few biographies of climbers. I knew Lachenal's reputation as a breakneck daredevil was inexact. I wanted to produce a personal, psychological account of a climber's life."

By September, the men were working regularly together. Word of the project got out. At one point, Lachenal showed his manuscript to Rébuffat, hoping the stylish writer Gaston had become could help him improve it. According to Françoise, Herzog called Rébuffat: "He was crying on the telephone, for fear Gaston would help the *Carnets* to get published." Indeed, by the autumn of 1955, Lachenal and Cornuau had secured a contract from the Parisian publisher Pierre Horay.

On November 25, 1955, Lachenal prowled the streets of Chamonix looking for a friend to join him on a ski outing. It was his notion to take the *téléphérique* up to the Aiguille du Midi, then ski down the Vallée Blanche all the way to the town of Montenvers. It was a cold, wintry day with a violent wind, but Lachenal had his heart set on his project. His good friend the ski champion James Couttet turned him down, saying, "I have to do some painting on my house." Lachenal sought out Elisabeth Payot, but she had had a recent foot operation. "Call up your brother," said the impatient guide.

So it was Jean-Pierre Payot who accompanied Lachenal up to the cable car station on the Midi. Forty-four years later, Payot remembers that day. "We went down a snowy couloir, chatting easily, to the Vallée Blanche. The wind and cold were pretty bad. Lachenal said, 'It dopes you a bit—gets you going.'

"We arrived at the first seracs. It was blowing in our faces. We had no goggles in those days. We started out skiing, unroped. The last thing Lachenal said was, 'Il y a le pêt.' " The remark, in local patois, means, "The wind's so bad it's dangerous."

"I was only two meters ahead of him," Payot continues. "In the moment it took to turn around, I heard the sound of his aluminum skis clacking against the ice as he went down. That noise stayed in my head for ages."

Lachenal had broken through a snow bridge and fallen into a hidden crevasse. Had the pair been roped, he might have been saved—but the Vallée Blanche was Lachenal's backyard, where he had performed many more dangerous exploits than this swift ski descent.

"I heard him fall. Then there was silence. Later we learned that he had suffered *le coup de lapin*—the way you kill a rabbit. He'd hit the back of his head, breaking his neck. Lachenal was forty-five meters down. I shouted, but there was no answer. I thought, what should I do? In my despair, I thought, maybe I should just jump into another hole, and nobody will ever find us.

"Instead, I climbed back up to the *téléphérique* station." (This ascent, in howling wind, through loose snow, was a superhuman feat.) "The station was closed when I got there, so I traversed a thousand meters to the cosmic ray research hut. The hut keeper was as drunk as a lord. I kept trying to explain, but he understood nothing. I asked to use the telephone. 'No, it's not working,' he said. Finally I got through at 11:00 P.M. Then I went back down to the crevasse to wait. I had taken bearings on the spot, so I wouldn't lose it."

Payot's sister, Elisabeth, details the search effort. "It was minus 20 degrees Centigrade. The guides didn't want to go out, but all of Lachenal's friends went up." Among them was Rébuffat.

Jean-Pierre: "Finally the others started to arrive. We burnt tires at the side of the crevasse, as a beacon. Somebody went down into the crevasse and tied Lachenal onto a rope. Then we pulled him out, put his body on a sledge, and pulled it all the way up to the Aiguille du Midi. We were down to Chamonix by 11:00 A.M.

"Someone went to tell Adèle. She was prepared beforehand. She knew this was part of the mountain life."

LACHENAL WAS BURIED in the Chamonix cemetery, not far from the monument to guides killed in the mountains, which today names eighty-four victims between 1820 and 1995—including Lachenal. His headstone is a slab of brownish gray granite, on which appears a simple inscription, with no mention of Annapurna:

LOUIS LACHENAL

GUIDE

1921–1955

VALLÉE BLANCHE

25-11-1955

From the soil beside the stone sprout lilies and the gray-green plants the French call *corbeille d'argent*.

In the journal *La Montagne et Alpinisme*, Herzog wrote an obituary for Lachenal. Generous and heartfelt, it nonetheless perpetuates the image of his teammate that *Annapurna* had advanced, of a driven genius just this side of madness:

He didn't live, he "burned." Action intoxicated him, and at its approach, his impatience multiplied. . . . All those who knew him well knew his affectation for wishing to believe himself capable, with his appetite for action and enterprise, of pulling off at any given instant whatever piece of folly.

Herzog tips his hat, however, to Lachenal's blunt honesty. "With no evasions or prudence, he expressed the truth, even if that sometimes seemed cruel." And he lavishes an encomium on the *cordée* Lachenal-Terray, "at its time, the strongest in the world." Herzog remembers, "It was at once marvelous and touching to hear Terray affirm that his friend Lachenal was the most gifted alpinist he had ever seen, and to hear Lachenal say that Terray was the strongest alpinist he had ever heard anyone talk about."

Yet the obituary cannot resist advancing the idea that with the reconstituting of their own Annapurna *cordée* on Monte Rosa, Lachenal's comeback reached its culmination:

Together, we produced the proof that the mountains were ours once more. When, five years before, we lay despairing side-by-side in the Chamonix hospital, thinking that never again would we rediscover these great joys of our lives, we could not have imagined so great a happiness, shared with one another.

Six years after Lachenal's death, in *Conquistadors*, Terray offered a more nuanced and wistful encomium for his best friend. "Lachenal was by far the most talented climber I have ever met," Terray wrote, "and I would go so far as to say that at the height of his career his quality amounted to genius."

Yet Terray was not fooled into believing that after his amputations Lachenal could ever fully regain his mastery. "Outside the mountain world he was like an eagle with clipped wings, ill-adapted to the humdrum life of society." The loss of his toes, thought Terray, dictated Lachenal's increasing "eccentricity and bitter wit," and explained his driving:

What he really sought in the intoxication of speed was escape from the human condition which he now felt so heavily. Once he had poised over the fall of cliffs with the lightness of a bird, and it hurt him to be transformed into a blundering animal like the rest of us. Behind the wheel of his car he seemed to recapture those instants of heavenly grace.

Terray set his hopes not on Lachenal's return to alpine mastery, but on his acceptance of his limitations:

Yet wisdom seemed to be coming with the years. Already he was driving less madly, and it had begun to look as though he would soon resign himself to being a man like any other. The affectionate father he had always been was getting the better of the panther of the snows. All the signs pointed to his ending up as a comfortable, well-known local citizen, looked on by all with affection and respect. Fate, however, had decided otherwise.

For Adèle, widowed with two young boys, practicing no profession of her own, the future promised to be hard. It was at this point that Herzog made a consequential intervention. In France, the legally recognized position of *tuteur*—a kind of guardian, godfather, and benefactor rolled into one—had been established to ameliorate the lot of widows such as Adèle. Herzog offered to serve as *tuteur* to the two boys, and she accepted.

Over the coming years, Herzog went for walks in the woods and ski outings with Lachenal's sons. He supervised their uncertain progress through a series of schools. He may well have given the family money.

In *L'Autre Annapurna* Herzog offers several vignettes of "my dear little angels." These emphasize their unruly misbehavior, particularly that of the older son, Jean-Claude: threatening another boy with a razor, swinging a croquet mallet that hits a female TV star guest square in the face. Such delinquency Herzog softens as a boys-will-be-boys penchant for mayhem, but in a subtle way his handling of it extends to the next generation his conceit of Lachenal as an impetuous genius-madman. Herzog in fact quotes a schoolmaster, complaining about Jean-Claude's bullying of classmates, as seeing in the son "the very picture of his father when it comes to character."

There is no evidence that Herzog took on the role of *tuteur* to Lachenal's sons out of any Machiavellian motive. He seems, moreover, to have taken his responsibilities as guardian of those sons seriously. But at the same time as he sprang to the rescue of the family, he took over the preparation of *Carnets du Vertige* for publication.

Philippe Cornuau, Lachenal's collaborator, recalls how this happened. "Not long after Lachenal's death, Herzog told me to give the papers to his brother, Gérard. All of Lachenal's business was taken over by Herzog. At the time, I didn't protest. It seemed logical, for Herzog was the *tuteur*. I couldn't have finished the book alone. At first I helped a bit with the preparation of *Carnets*. And I didn't want to provoke any scandal by resisting—I didn't want people to say, 'Cornuau is making a profit out of Lachenal.'

"Later I realized just how worried Herzog was about what Lachenal might say. One day he said to me, 'People have a great need of dreams, of beautiful stories. It's important not to disappoint them.' I didn't understand him at the time. Later it made sense. Herzog didn't want any of the negative stuff to come out.

"But when I gave all my notes to Gérard Herzog, I had no premonition of what would happen. I was shocked when the book came out."

Cornuau had typed up a copy of Lachenal's diary from Annapurna. On that typescript, Maurice Herzog and Lucien Devies made their marginal comments, for Gérard's guidance in editing it. Thanks to the survival of the typescript, we gain an intimate perspective on the process by which Lachenal's truth was posthumously expurgated.

In a short preamble to the journal that Lachenal wrote in 1955, he ironically quotes part of the next-to-last line of *Annapurna*, which reads, "Annapurna, to which we had gone emptyhanded, was a treasure on which we should live the rest of our days." After "a treasure on which we should live the rest of our days," Lachenal comments, "In any event, it's certainly several hundred thousand copies, and I would love to be able to say as much about my book!" Devies has circled this jape and marked it with the proofreader's squiggle for "delete." In the next paragraph, the word "official" must go, in Lachenal's phrase, "Herzog has written the official book . . ."

The daily entries are likewise combed of imperfections. In Lachenal's mordant record of the April 2 reception at the French ambassador's in Delhi, the judgment "Bored me to tears" wins a "No" from Devies and a delete mark. Herzog too puts his two cents' worth in, though his contribution is less imperious than Devies's, amounting usually to quibbles and corrections. Thus on April 23, when Lachenal writes, "We convinced Momo to head off toward the great glacier on the east face . . ." Herzog changes the phrase to "We headed off toward the great glacier on the east face," clucking in the margin, "A closer fit with reality, but could stay in its present form."

On May 3, "Momo encouraged us again to make a new attempt toward the right. We obeyed." Herzog circles "We obeyed" and jots, "It was not an order." On May 14, after Herzog's "council of war," Lachenal writes, "A long discussion began, at the end of which almost everyone leaned in favor of a departure in the direction of Annapurna." Herzog complains, "There were no objections."

And so on, throughout the diary. But as Lachenal covers the summit dash and the long descent, Herzog and Devies grow more petulant. On the summit, says Lachenal, the pair shot "the several official photographs that we had to take." Herzog: "No one required us to do this." As Lachenal is carried on his stretcher in the lowlands, he unleashes the vitriolic long sentence summing up his miseries (quoted on page 127). Herzog underlines "of being surrounded by no one who is kind to me, of passing whole days alone on my stretcher with at best one Sherpa as companion, with no sahibs, knowing full well that nothing will get done, not even ordinary tasks, without my having to ask many times and then to wait a long, long time." In the margin, he scolds, "Not very nice to his comrades, who were doing their duty. Should we leave this in, as written in the heat of battle?"

For the *Carnets*, Lachenal wrote a 2,000 word "Commentaires" that he intended to append after the last entry in the diary. This cogent summary of Lachenal's feelings five years after Annapurna stirs Herzog and Devies to something like fury. "No," "No," "No," writes Devies again and again; "No, absolutely wrong." With his sly iconoclasm, Lachenal characterizes the dual quest for Dhaulagiri and Annapurna as like "chasing two rabbits at the same time." "Wrong," thunders Devies. "This had nothing to do with chasing two rabbits at the same time, but with choosing between two objectives the one that would be easier."

Lachenal dares to remark that "Herzog was chosen leader by a decision among the powers that be, not for any incontestable alpine supremacy." Devies: "Wrong. Herzog was chosen for a combination of qualities, not for his acrobatics. His quality as a *grand montagnard* was not overlooked."

Everywhere Devies and Herzog go to great pains to correct Lachenal's plainspoken spin on the expedition. The attack on the impossible Northwest Spur was hardly a blunder and a delay; it was in fact, according to Devies, "not an attack but a reconnaissance." Lachenal raises the important question of why the expedition failed to use willow wands—thin bamboo stakes, usually painted green— to mark their route above Camp IVA. Had they used them, the bivouac in the crevasse would have been obviated. "I have been a partisan of willow wands," insists Devies. "But nobody brought them along. . . . Why didn't Lachenal want to bring them?"

Lachenal characterizes the team's descent as a *débandade:* a retreat in complete disorder. "But no!" cries Devies; and Herzog: "Is this the place to say so?!"

The attack on Lachenal's text reaches a frenzy in its last two pages. Scrutinizing the marginal annotations, Gérard Herzog prepared Lachenal's diary for inclusion in the *Carnets.* In the end, he did not so much attempt to restore a Devies-Herzog spin to Lachenal's text as simply to excise anything that contradicted *Annapurna.* Most notably, he suppressed the whole of the "Commentaires."

It is a godsend that Michel Guérin was able to rescue those 2,000 words, for they amount to the most powerful thing Lachenal ever wrote. As a judicious reconsideration of the expedition— which had already, by 1955, passed into the realm of legend—the "Commentaires" represents a tour de force of self-appraisal, pinpointing both the team's errors and its successes. Finally, it casts a light on Annapurna that no one else was capable of shining.

"Oh, yes! The morphine was necessary!" Lachenal begins his "Commentaires." "More than a third of my diary is given over to the return [from Annapurna], and it is nothing more than a long succession of complaints and recriminations."

Stubbornly, Lachenal refuses to see any redeeming value in the suffering he underwent. Not for him, Herzog's transcendent sense of fulfillment:

> The discomfort became intolerable. Fatigue, physical and moral, seized the sahibs. It is this that explains why the attitude of my comrades often justified my reproaches. I could no longer be a cheerful invalid. To discomfort was added suffering. Beforehand, I had been overjoyed at the prospect of sauntering out through this very interesting countryside, which we had dashed through on the approach in order to lose no time. Even this pleasure was denied me.

And, writes Lachenal, to suffering was added anguish. As the porters carried his stretcher through the lowlands, he dwelt on Raymond Lambert, on the question of whether he could climb without toes. "Lambert said that even if [his amputations] were often a disadvantage, on the other hand there were sometimes holds which his shortened feet gripped better than normal."

Perhaps an implicit dig at Herzog, the "amateur," lurks in the next sentence: "For me, the mountains are not a Sunday pastime; they are my life." The anguish over losing that life stirs Lachenal to a lucid bitterness:

> For others, to live is to stoop over books, to paint, or to give orders. This can be done with cut-off feet, with cut-off hands.
>
> For me, to live is to choose a mountain, to find its weakness and feel the wrinkles of granite under the tread of my feet. Each digit cut off took with it some of my hope.

Next, Lachenal asks the cardinal question: "Was Annapurna worth this suffering?" Yet he answers it only indirectly, by emphasizing the strangeness of the Himalaya to his ken.

These were other mountains, and I want to know all the mountains that exist. This said, however, among the ones I know, I have seen nothing comparable to the beauty of the massif of Mont Blanc. The scale is much greater [in the Himalaya], to be sure, but for their proportions, the balance of their panorama, their thrust (look at the Chamonix Aiguilles), I distinctly prefer our own massif.

Lachenal had a vivid memory of being awakened to the alienness of the Himalaya as he and Rébuffat wandered through a maze of giant seracs on the glacier east of Dhaulagiri. In the Alps, seracs tend to be modest-sized and benign; In the Himalaya, thanks to thin air and vertical sun, they grow to massive proportions and teeter menacingly. An inordinate number of good climbers have been killed in the Himalaya when seracs fell on them.

Feeling a kindred malaise to Lachenal's, Rébuffat said, "You know, I promised my wife I wouldn't screw things up here!"

"This day," recorded Lachenal, "I had the feeling of moving through a strange and hostile world; the very idea of wanting to penetrate it was also strange. I thought, 'What the hell are we doing here?'"

By contrast, the Alps were a familiar playground. Yet, paradoxically, that alienness conferred a boon: "The Himalaya gave us a second youth."

Next, Lachenal tried to place the style of the Annapurna expedition in historical context. Later generations would hail the two-week dash up the north face as a brilliant application, ahead of its time, of alpine-style tactics to a Himalayan objective. Yet, never one to pat himself on the back, Lachenal attributed the alpine-style assault to necessity, rather than bold conception: "In fact, the lightness [of the assault] was due more to our poverty than to any tactical conception: since Annapurna, climbers have returned to a heavy style." ("No, absolutely wrong," screamed Devies in the margin: "Lightness was a deliberate tactic.")

On Makalu that summer of 1955, Lachenal pointed out, each climber had been issued a half dozen pairs of boots, including ones specially made of reindeer skin. On Annapurna five years earlier,

"We were happy to have a single pair of ordinary alpine boots each, reinforced with a felt lining."

Lachenal admitted that, lacking Himalayan experience, the team misjudged everything about Annapurna. That accounted for the five-day blunder of attacking the Northwest Spur.

Herzog had a difficult role, conceded Lachenal, revealing that before the expedition, the three Chamonix guides held a low opinion of him as a leader: "We even thought beforehand that he might have been chosen as a kind of arbiter among the three professionals within the team."

Yet Herzog surprised everyone by his performance, and Lachenal was quick to give him his due: "Very soon, we realized there was no difference between him and us in terms of stamina or technique, either on ice or on rock." What Herzog lacked, however, thanks to his inexperience, was the knack "of judging beforehand the best choices among the many possible itineraries." Herzog had, in Lachenal's view, only the most rudimentary grasp of expedition organization. Thus "He very skillfully oriented his role toward what truly suited him, that of an extraordinary amateur."

Herzog's poor organizational skills, in Lachenal's view, were what caused all the floundering in the lowlands during the first six weeks.

> Personally, I have a great need to be animated! These perpetual hesitations during the approach march, these probes with no follow-through, this disorder didn't suit me at all—it depressed me. I began to regret missing a good season in the Alps, where the attack immediately follows the decision, and usually the victory the attack. It was only on the day when Annapurna was declared our objective and an assault in force was launched that I found at last what I had come to look for.

Lachenal's critique offers here an intriguing fun-house mirror image of Herzog's. In *Annapurna*, the Chamonix guide is presented as a man too impatient and impulsive to pay heed to reason or judgment. But from Lachenal's strictures, Herzog emerges as an indecisive ditherer.

Because of the team's shortness of time, Lachenal believed, they had been forced to follow an unjustifiably dangerous route up the north face of Annapurna. The whole basin between Camps II and IV was a gigantic avalanche slope. Only extraordinary good luck had allowed the team to be swept by but a single avalanche— the one that had carried Herzog, Sarki, and Aila 500 feet on the descent. But, "there was no choice: it was either this route or a complete fiasco." To future teams of alpinists, Lachenal recommended a far lengthier route traversing beneath the dangerous basin and climbing the face well to the east. (Subsequent tragedies on the north face have proven Lachenal's advice prophetic.)

In these tempered words, we see a canny and cool-headed mountaineer reassessing the perilous ascent that Herzog had blazoned as sheer glory and triumph. If, at this point, Lachenal has still not answered his own crucial query—was Annapurna worth the cost?—in the last two pages of the "Commentaires" he makes it clear how that question played itself out in the *agon* of June 3, 1950. Those seven concluding paragraphs amount to a testament from beyond the grave, furnishing, in their laconic eloquence, a last word on Annapurna. To the truths they embody, we shall return.

As Jean-Claude Lachenal came of age in Chamonix, reading the *Carnets du Vertige* that Gérard Herzog had thrust into print in 1956, comparing it to the manuscript diary his father had brought home from Annapurna, a quiet rage burned in his heart. Yet he squelched any thought of exposing the gulf between his father's story and that of the brothers Herzog, for he sensed that he owed a certain gratitude to the *tuteur* of his adolescence. Jean-Claude was, moreover, a shy and modest man, with no connections in the world of *belles lettres* or journalism beyond the valley of the Arve. He made a living as a ski instructor, though he never became a serious mountaineer.

After moving to Chamonix in 1994, Michel Guérin—a former book dealer and passionate collector of mountain literature—decided to go into business as a publisher of deluxe reprints of mountaineering classics. By now, the "red books" of Editions Guérin (so named for their uniform covers and bindings in scarlet cloth) have won a cachet as perhaps the most handsome climbing books ever published, but at the outset the whole project was a risky one-man venture. Guérin began with Terray's *Les Conquérants de l'Inutile,* which came out in 1995.

Having befriended Jean-Claude Lachenal, Guérin was enthralled to read his father's original diary. For several years, he tried to persuade Jean-Claude to permit an unexpurgated publication of the diary, embedded in a reprint of *Carnets du Vertige.* Jean-Claude deliberated, then agreed.

As a goodwill gesture, Guérin and Lachenal *fils* invited Herzog to write a preface. Herzog responded with his characteristic courtesy, agreeing to the task. In his letter, he betrayed little of the anxiety he must have felt on learning of Guérin's publishing plans, though he added a few words to remind Guérin of Lachenal's excessive nature, which no doubt spoke in certain ill-considered judgments in the diary. It would be disappointing, Herzog allowed, if the publication backfired, making Lachenal look mean-spirited or jealous of his Annapurna teammates.

In the end, Jean-Claude changed his mind about the preface, realizing that his father's long-dormant witness might only be compromised by one last effort on Herzog's part to put his own spin on the Annapurna story. Herzog was tactfully disinvited.

With the publication of Guérin's new *Carnets,* which coincided nearly to the month with Ballu's biography of Rébuffat, a storm of controversy seized France. Rébuffat's profound disillusionment, as revealed in his letters to Françoise, and his acidic and epigrammatic latter-day *pensées* on Annapurna intersected with the unmistakable evidence of heavy censorship of Lachenal's diary. Journalists cried foul and demanded an accounting. Only a handful came to Herzog's defense.

Some of the new revelations were devastating. According to Claude Francillon, writing in *Le Monde,* in Kathmandu Rébuffat had been bodily searched by Ichac, to make sure the guide wasn't smuggling home any canisters of exposed film he had shot up high on Annapurna. As official photographer, Ichac would control all the images to emerge from the expedition. (In *Annapurna,* the title page indicates "Cartographic and Photographic Documentation by Marcel Ichac," even though all the climbing pictures above Camp II—the highest point Ichac reached—were shot by Rébuffat, while the summit photo was taken by Lachenal.)

Quoting Rébuffat, Yves Ballu told a story about an early attempt by Lachenal to defy his oath-ordained silence. In 1951, he had apparently prepared his own account of Annapurna; knowing Rébuffat had connections at *Le Monde*, he asked his fellow guide for help placing the piece in that prestigious newspaper. Rébuffat asked the editor-in-chief, who said he would welcome it.

Lachenal had made the mistake of talking too freely about his account, and the Himalayan Committee got wind of it. "One of its members," Lachenal told Rébuffat, "came from Paris to see me and say to me, 'Lachenal, do you like your job at the Ecole Nationale de Ski et d'Alpinisme?'

"Of course, what else could I do with my amputated feet?"

"If you want to stay there, it would be preferable if you gave up this intention of publishing your account of Annapurna in *Le Monde*." Lachenal had no choice but to acquiesce.

A younger generation of journalists, long jaundiced by the chauvinism of the de Gaulle era, critical of the neocolonial prejudices that lingered in French culture, was only too delighted to see the sacred cow of the Annapurna myth come under attack. But even in their revisionist glee, these writers saw that the new revelations did not simply undercut the grandeur of the 1950 accomplishment: they raised the contributions of the three Chamonix guides to a new level of respect. By 1996, Rébuffat was far from the most famous guide in Europe; even Terray's reputation had lapsed into obscurity. Reviewing the two new books in *Dimanche 8*, journalist Frédéric Potet wrote:

> It is neither a lie nor an aspersion to say that history has superbly, magnificently, royally forgotten them. Gaston Rébuffat, Lionel Terray, Louis Lachenal: three names that continue to awaken faint memories in certain hearts. Three names that one somehow knows were associated with the grand history of alpinism. But more than that? . . . The whole world remembers Maurice Herzog, the first

biped to have trod, in 1950, atop a mountain of more than 8,000 meters. The others—Rébuffat, Terray, Lachenal? Who were they? Where did they come from? What did they do?

Such mainstream publications as *Le Monde*, *Libération*, and *L'Equipe* weighed in with major pieces on the controversy. The furor crossed international waters, with the British journal *High*, the American magazine *Climbing*, and the *American Alpine Journal* publishing essays sympathetic to the debunkers. Wrote Patrick Barthe in the last publication, reviewing Guérin's *Carnets*, "I am sorry we had to wait so long for the true story. All around us we can see the damage done by false information. We have an obligation to tell our children the truth of our days. We don't have to be afraid of it."

In France, the climbing journals dug deep. *Montagnes* magazine ran a seven-page analysis entitled "Annapurna: The Other Truth." Its writers discovered long-buried details that even Ballu and Guérin had not brought to light. They quoted a letter from one Pierre Chabert to Terray's father, explaining the reason that Terray had been passed over for the Legion of Honor:

> I have received formal confirmation that if your son, who saved the whole Himalayan mission, was not decorated, that was because of the position taken by the president of the CAF [Devies] and by M. Herzog. I swear by this information, but ask you to treat it confidentially.

The editors also discovered an obscure, forgotten article published in the regional newspaper *Dauphiné Libéré* in June 1950, even before the Annapurna team had returned to France. Its author, Phillippe Gaussot, complained that while gossip was rife that several of the Annapurna victors were seriously injured, their wives were given not a shred of information. "They insist they have had no news, but no one can ignore the likelihood that they are kept in absolute darkness by M. Lucien Devies because of the exclusive contract the Fédération Française de la Montagne [FFM] has granted to the newspaper *Le Figaro*."

A few voices spoke out in defense of Devies and Herzog. In *La Montagne et Alpinisme,* Claude Deck pooh-poohed the controversy as a tempest in a teapot. The distinction between professionals and amateurs in climbing was obsolete by 1950, Deck maintained. The contract interdicting publication for five years had been a normal expedition practice for decades. No one had censored Lachenal: rather, Gérard Herzog, at the request of Lachenal, had collaborated in a biography. (This was nonsense, as Philippe Cornuau pointed out in a letter to Deck: "Gérard never had any contact with Lachenal in connection with this book.") There was no evidence, Deck argued, that Lachenal really wanted his diary published.

Deck grew passionate in praise of Devies, who, he acknowledged, had long been editor-in-chief of *La Montagne et Alpinisme:* "It is indecent that anyone should so lightly betray the memory of Lucien Devies. . . . All his authority derived from his intense labor and from a great intellectual rigor." Deck ridiculed the notion of the FFM—"with its two desks and four chairs at the foot of a staircase"—wielding the power to suppress uncomfortable truths.

Inevitably, the journals sought out Herzog for comment, and he was willing to talk. The stance he consistently took was one of earnest puzzlement that any controversy had arisen. He had nothing to hide; *Annapurna* after all told the whole story. Thus, interviewed by *Le Monde,* Herzog baldly stated, "What I wrote in *Annapurna* is the exact truth. I am willing to put myself in the line of fire if anyone says I lied about anything. My writings have never been contradicted."

As for the sharper entries in Lachenal's diary, these Herzog attributed to the passion of the moment, spontaneous outbursts of discontent or disappointment. "One consigns these feelings to the page [of one's diary], and there they stay."

Montagnes asked Herzog about Ballu's story of the Himalayan Committee member threatening Lachenal's job if he tried to publish in 1951. "I find it bewildering to picture Lachenal suppressed like this! Imagine, in that climate of apotheosis—to fire Lachenal from ENSA would have caused a veritable scandal! No minister would have taken the risk."

The so-called censorship of Lachenal's diary? "There was no blocking of information. If none of those passages were published, it's because they didn't interest the editors. Perhaps they were leery of accounts focused on the moods and personal complaints of one member or another."

In his "true novel," Herzog insisted, he had captured an epic adventure. "My greatest pleasure was that my teammates said they recognized themselves in my writing." Had he not, however, embellished reality a bit? "No!" Herzog fired back. "That *was* the reality!"

Five days after *Le Monde* interviewed him, Herzog published a letter in that newspaper. In it, his tone shifts from serene openness to counterattack. Of course, Lachenal wrote some of his "excessive" diary entries in the heat of battle. Minor conflicts were normal on expeditions. "After the event, we ended up laughing."

Lachenal, Herzog insisted, had never been censored, neither in 1951 nor 1955. The revelations of how low an esteem the Chamonix guides initially held for Herzog, how ill-qualified they thought him for leadership, now drove him to sardonic indignation:

> Without wishing to flatter myself, I find it hard to comprehend how an alpinist of such modest achievements could have become president of the Groupe de Haute Montagne, a particularly elitist academy since it brings together the greatest climbers in the world. In the same vein, how could it have been that all the camps, in spite of the greatest difficulties, were established by me, and that, during our final push, I was always in the lead, arriving moreover first on the summit?

The last claim is true only in the most narrow technical sense, and ignores the part played by Herzog's teammates, including the Sherpas. Terray, Herzog, and several Sherpas established Camp II; Terray, Pansy, and Alla were the first to Camp III, failing to "establish" it only because they did not pitch a tent there; Terray and Herzog established Camp IV; Herzog and Lachenal Camp IVA; and Herzog, Lachenal, Ang-Tharkey, and Sarki Camp V.

In his letter, Herzog waxed emotional about his heroism in World War II.

> It fell to me to command a unit of 25 "Joyeux" composed of young soldiers, heads of [communist] cells, veterans of the Spanish civil war, German Jews, absentees from Switzerland, and a number of criminals on probation. . . . To take such a small army into battle in the Tarentaise, always above 3,000 meters altitude, in deplorable conditions, gives one the kind of exceptional experience that I put into the service of our expedition.

Herzog added, "Except for Lionel Terray . . . I don't believe that any of my Annapurna companions took any such part [in the war]."

This backhanded insult roused the ire of Françoise Rébuffat, who responded with haughty dignity in *Le Monde:*

> According to [Herzog], Gaston didn't go to war.
> Nonsense! He was no *planqué* [a man who goes under cover to wait out the war]; that would not have fit his character at all.
> M. Herzog seems to be going to great lengths to minimize the merit of his rope-mates and the valor of their contribution, without whom he would not have returned [from Annapurna] alive.

Rébuffat's widow then backhanded Herzog with her own sharp slap:

> To dare to write that with Terray he alone went to war, while he is perfectly aware of the past lives of his companions, gives precisely the tone in which *Annapurna* was written.

Finally, Françoise laid out the details of the unmistakably heroic campaign of Rébuffat's battalion in liberating the valley of Chamonix from the Nazis.

The end of Herzog's letter to *Le Monde* reaches a pinnacle of proud dudgeon:

> In conclusion, these latter-day and to my mind utterly niggardly rewritings matter very little in the face of our historic victory. The

facts are plain. No one contests them. All that remains of the tragedy that followed are the stigmata on my flesh. No one talks of that, but I will remember it forever.

Here, at last, Herzog's identification with Christ becomes explicit. During much of 1997, as the controversy slowly died down, Herzog was preoccupied with putting the finishing touches on his memoir, *L'Autre Annapurna*. When that book appeared in 1998, however, the passages devoted to the famous expedition—so oddly at variance here and there with Herzog's first telling in *Annapurna*—only stirred the flames anew.

Reaction to the book fell out along political lines. Among major newspapers and magazines, only the right-wing *Le Figaro* gave it a rave review. That newspaper, the same with which Devies and Herzog had negotiated their 1950 exclusive, hailed "this witty and modest account," which was "not a biography; simply a meditation, free of grandiloquence, on an exceptional life." Buttressing the review were two sidebars hailing Herzog himself. One, by Jean D'Ormesson, saluted "our Lindbergh, our Redford, our Senna. Children are avid to see him; men fall at his knees." "He was a hero," D'Ormesson went on. "He was a great man. He was a marvellous friend."

In contrast, the left-wing press had a field day ridiculing the memoir. *Libération* mocked Herzog's name-dropping by simply quoting it. A gossip column in *Le Faucigny* reported the dinner chat of Pierre Mazeaud, one of the great alpinists of Herzog's generation and himself politically minded: "He sent me the book, with a dedication," Mazeaud was quoted. "I succeeded in getting to page 16. But when I saw that he had not a single word for poor Lachenal, I couldn't get any further."

According to Benoît Heimermann of *L'Equipe*, a principal motivation for Herzog in writing his memoir was his desire to enter the Académie Française, that august body of luminaries that elects a new candidate only on the death of a standing member. Recent publication is required for consideration, and indeed, *L'Autre Annapurna* won a prize offered by the Académie. Yet in June 1999, when an election was held, Herzog garnered only three votes, far short of the seventeen that enshrined novelist René de Obaldia.

With the publication of the memoir came a whole new raft of interviews. During the two years he had stewed over the controversy, Herzog, now seventy-nine, had grown petulant toward his detractors. Now he was inclined to see a conspiracy to discredit *Annapurna*. To Jean-Michel Asselin, of *Vertical*, he said, "This ridiculous polemic was set on fire and stirred higher by so-called alpinists who aren't really climbers. It was born of commercial motives. It had to do with selling books that had just appeared."

In his irritation, Herzog now both condescended toward Lachenal, as he always had, and derogated him as he never had before. Explaining the "censorship" of the *Carnets* one more time to Benoît Heimermann, Herzog said, "[Lachenal's] was an excessive temperament, an overflowing imagination. . . . This excessive side of his character, Lucien Devies and I hoped to temper, in saying, 'There, that word is too strong.' We did him a service; there would have been attacks and defamation. It had nothing to do with 'censoring' him. . . . Lucien Devies, especially, but also I, played the role of godfather. We calmed him down a bit."

To the sympathetic interviewer for *Le Figaro*, Herzog contrasted Lachenal and himself on the summit day on Annapurna:

> I thought of the ladder of St. Theresa of Avila, he thought—
> mountain guide that he was—of the dangers we were running. I
> thought of France, of the little flag that we were going to plant on
> the summit. He thought that a mountain course was simply a
> mountain course.

To the same interviewer, Herzog elaborated, "We had been trussed up [in the war], France had suffered. Our exploit ought to be that of the whole nation. We couldn't think just about ourselves; we climbed the icy slopes with thoughts in our hearts of the country and all the youth of France that we represented."

To Jean-Michel Asselin of *Vertical*, Herzog confided, "I believe that Lachenal had a will to make things banal." Startled, Asselin asked him what he meant. "I don't know," Herzog answered.

"Maybe he thought, 'There's a leader, I must follow him, but if I follow him, in a sense I'm doing something banal.' "

By 1998, Herzog was still adopting the stance that the controversy was beneath him, too trivial to disturb him. Yet the full vexation of the reexamination of Annapurna burst out in a tirade at the end of his interview with Benoît Heimermann, where the conspiracy theory emerged full-blown.

Asked about Jean-Claude Lachenal, Herzog answered, "It's not that he wasn't intelligent [as a boy], but that he was a little crazy. . . . He was the one who was at the bottom of this 'affair.' He thought that the diary of his father had some huge value, to the point where he transported it to Switzerland. We're not talking about a work of art.

"What's more, Lachenal had no pretensions in this area. He knew well that he was incapable of writing. He asked I don't know how many people to help him write a book. Finally, it was my brother who wrote up *Carnets du Vertige* for him. He was very happy with the result.

"Afterwards, it was his son who invented this story of manipulation, because he desperately wanted to place his father as Number One. The problem is that Louis Lachenal wasn't Number One. After that, Michel Guérin published this story, appending the diary itself. . . . It didn't work.

"So Jean-Claude arranged with Claude Francillon of *Le Monde* to launch this 'affair.' I don't know why, but Francillon seems to have been taken in by Jean-Claude."

In 1998, Foutharkey, one of the few surviving Sherpas from the 1950 expedition, came to Paris. With press in attendance, Herzog briefly greeted the man, whom he had not seen in forty-eight years. Just afterward, Bernard George, filming a documentary about Annapurna, interviewed the Sherpa. Through an interpreter, the soft-spoken Foutharkey contrasted his people's views of Herzog and of Sir Edmund Hillary, who had devoted his post-Everest life to building schools and hospitals for the Sherpas. "Hillary is a hero in Nepal, but Herzog, I don't think so. . . . I carried this man on my back until I could taste the blood in my mouth, and today he has only five minutes for me. It's too bad for him."

• • •

IN MAY 1997, I WENT TO CHAMONIX to begin my investigation of the complex and ambiguous story Annapurna had recently become. The first day, I walked through the cemetery. Finding Lachenal's plain granite headstone with its taciturn inscription, I stood there for long moments.

Thirty-four years earlier, after reading *Conquistadors of the Useless*, I had chosen the man who lay buried at my feet not simply as my hero, but as the climber with whom, in my shared fantasy with Don Jensen, I utterly identified. With five others the previous summer, Don and I had climbed a dangerous new route on Mount McKinley's north face. The next summer we would attempt a fiendish unclimbed ridge on Mount Deborah, just the two of us, hiking in and out from the Denali Highway, failing at last 2,000 feet below the summit.

In the course of that year, caught up in our hero worship, Don had merged with Terray, I with Lachenal. Shouting with sheer high spirits on some windswept crag, I would call out to "Lionel," and he would answer with "Louis." Like Terray and Lachenal, we climbed better together than either us did with others. In the heady flush of youth, we started to think we were invincible.

After several days in Chamonix, I was invited by Michel Guérin to an informal dinner at the house of Jean-Claude Lachenal. A shy, portly man of fifty-four, Jean-Claude looked nothing like his father. Michel had wisely divined that a social occasion with friends would make a better ice-breaker than an office interview. Various friends arrived; Jean-Claude broke out a local red wine; and his wife, Arlette, laid out a hearty spread of sausage from the Grisons, ham, cheese, goose pâté, bread, and homemade cornichons. Later, as Jean-Claude served champagne, the group waxed reminiscent.

I asked Jean-Claude why he thought Herzog had received such disproportionate credit for Annapurna, at the expense of his father's. He cocked a jaundiced eye, then recited an answer that I guessed he had used before: "It was easier to find Maurice Herzog in the salons of Paris than Louis Lachenal in the mountains of Chamonix."

After dinner I toured the comfortable chalet, which Lachenal *père* had built with his own hands, employing a beautiful dark varnished wood, on a sunny hillside directly opposite the great north face of the Dru. Every detail bespoke loving craft. The central roof beam was inscribed in Latin:

EDIFICATA ANNO DOMINI 1949
SIT NOMEN DOMINI BENEDICTUM
ADELE ET LOUIS LACHENAL

Jean-Claude opened for me a cunning attic door disguised as a fold-up staircase. I poked my head into the dark annex. "We slept up there when we were little kids," he said.

The walls were hung with memorabilia: framed drawings of the great Swiss guide Lochmatter and of the British pioneers Mummery and Whymper; photos of the Eiger and Annapurna with the routes inked in; Lachenal's diplomas as ski instructor and mountain guide.

I asked about Lachenal's bond with Terray. "There aren't any *cordées* like that any more," said Jean-Claude. "Nowadays everybody climbs with one partner, then with another."

Jean-Claude made much of the Paris-Chamonix axis among the Annapurna team. "It was necessary for France to have a great achievement," he said. "Paris needed it, but it couldn't be done without the three Chamonix guides. At all costs, Herzog wanted to prevent Lachenal and Terray from going to the top together. Paris had to be at the summit—not two Chamoniards."

I asked Jean-Claude what Herzog had done for him as a youth, in his service as the boy's *tuteur*. His answer was measured: "He consoled my mother. We skied together. Later, he opened some doors for me."

Two years later, on a return to Chamonix, I would meet Jean-Claude in a bar. In the Interim, *L'Autre Annapurna* had been published, with its vignettes of Jean-Claude as a delinquent rascal whom Herzog had barely kept out of legal trouble. I happened to have a copy of the book lying on the table as Jean-Claude walked in. "Why you buy this piece of shit!" he railed in English, pounding the paperback with his fist. "He writes about me," Jean-Claude brooded, "only to say that I inherited the craziness of my father." A few minutes later, he pounded the book again. "This man trashed my father!" he raged.

In Jean-Claude and Arlette's chalet that evening in 1997, the mood had been nostalgic rather than angry. As we grew tipsy, Jean-Claude brought out some keepsakes. A faded box of Lucky Strike matches held a pressed edelweiss, accompanied by a note indicating that Lachenal, then fifteen years old, had found the flower, together with a piece of the French flag, atop a peak near Annecy in 1936.

Jean-Claude handed me a long, rusty soft-iron spike. "This was a piton Andreas Heckmair drove into the Eiger on the first ascent in 1938. My father brought it back from the second ascent, with Terray, in 1947." I turned the piton, with its bent tip, over and over in my hands. Heckmair, I knew, was still alive at ninety-one. "In 1987," added Jean-Claude, "someone showed this piton to Heckmair at a film festival. He said he remembered making it in his forge in Munich."

Next Jean-Claude handed me the head of an antique ice axe. To my surprise, I realized that it was the axe that the Duke of the Abruzzi had left on the highest point of the Ruwenzori Mountains in Africa in 1906, which Lachenal had retrieved in 1952.

Awed by these talismans, I was unprepared to hold the next relic thrust into my hands. It was a sort of homemade book, bound between heavy pieces of cardboard. I opened the cover, and stared in shock at what I realized was Lachenal's Annapurna diary. In a tiny hand, in spidery blue ink, Lachenal had covered every square inch of paper with his meticulous jottings.

I turned to June 3 and read the passage I already knew by heart. As I did so, my mind drifted back to my old fantasy that Don Jensen and I were Terray and Lachenal.

I had long since given up that daydream. By now, I knew much more about Lachenal than I had at age twenty. He was no longer the simple romantic embodiment of grace, speed, impetuous drive. He had grown in my consciousness to become a rounded character, flawed by his shortcomings—his contempt for those who disagreed with him, his ingratitude to some who went out of their way to be helpful. There was little, in Lachenal's writings, of the deep emotional loyalty to Terray that Terray expressed for him on page after page of *Conquistadors.*

Yet for all that, as I stared at the cramped blue paragraphs in that spidery hand, I admired Lachenal as much as ever—for his candor and honesty, for his intolerance of pretension, and ultimately, for his lucidity in extremis.

Hero worship, I reflected, was appropriate for twenty-year-olds. Respect and admiration were harder-won. Lachenal had been dead for almost forty-two years that day in May when I held his handwritten testament in my hands. For forty-two years, his truth had been lost in the shadow of Herzog's blazing myth. It deserved the chance to emerge once more into the light.

NINE

The
Passion
of
Terray

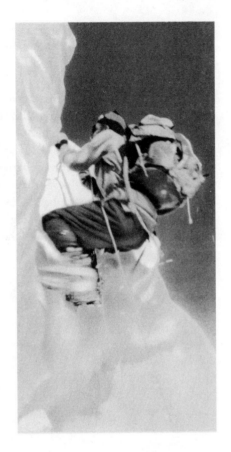

EVEN TERRAY, whose account of Annapurna in *Conquistadors* for the most part agrees with Herzog's, was irked at the public response to the expedition:

> Deliberately ignoring anything so difficult to understand as teamwork, the papers proceeded to transform Herzog into a national hero, concentrating all their attention on him as a kind of fabulous Big White Chief. The rest of the expedition, including Lachenal, were relegated to the position of mere accessories.

Terray ended his account of the climb with the avalanche that nearly swept Herzog, Pansy, and Aila to their deaths. Only a single sentence—one that commentators have long puzzled over, trying to read between the lines—covers the month-long retreat from the mountain: "And so, as the dream faded, we returned to earth in a fearful mix-up of pain and joy, heroism and cowardice, grandeur and meanness."

Unscathed by his ordeal on Annapurna, Terray flung himself back into mountaineering. Herzog, Rébuffat, Lachenal, and Schatz would never go on another expedition. Couzy's zeal for the far-flung ranges, which flowered in his stellar performances on the two Makalu expeditions, would be cut short by his untimely death. Terray, however, used Annapurna (and the coffers of the FFM, swollen by the sales of *Annapurna*) as a stepping-stone to launch a decade and a half of expeditionary mountaineering the equal of which perhaps no other climber has ever enjoyed.

Before he could head off again to remote mountains, however, he suffered one of the tragedies of his life on a climb near Chamonix. As he would throughout the rest of his career, Terray had taken a gifted protégé under his wing. Francis Aubert had taught skiing with Terray in Canada the winter before Annapurna, and he had showed immense promise on hard rock and ice. Now, with Lachenal *hors de combat*, it seemed natural for Terray to recruit Aubert for the ambitious projects that were never far from his heart.

In September 1950, only two months after his return from Annapurna, Terray set out with his protégé to tackle the unclimbed and very difficult west face of the Aiguille Noire de Peuterey. The pair never got to the foot of the wall. Descending a slope on the approach in the half-light of dawn, on terrain Terray judged not sufficiently difficult to warrant roping up, Aubert got slightly off route. Terray paused, then coached his partner back toward the proper line. Just as Aubert was about to reach safe ground, a large block of granite that he had clasped with his hands came loose on top of him. There was an agonizing, endless moment as Aubert tried to throw the block away from him and regain his balance, but it was too much to ask. As Terray watched, his young friend fell 300 feet to his death.

In *Conquistadors*, Terray does not address the guilt he must have felt for not roping up. He does not wonder whether he had dragged his protégé in over his head. But a few sentences register the impact of this accident:

> Crazed with grief I called and called to my friend. There came no answer but the sound of the wind.
> This experience left me badly shaken for several months, and for the first time I began to doubt. Were the mountains worth such sacrifices? Was my ideal no more than a madman's dream?

Nonetheless, by 1952, Terray was off on another expedition. This time the objective was Fitzroy, a magnificent spear of granite and ice in the heart of storm-lashed Patagonia. Though only 11,319 feet high, Fitzroy was technically more difficult by a whole order of magnitude than any remote mountain yet climbed in the world. Several previous attempts had accomplished nothing more than reaching the base of the 2,500-foot-high pyramid where the climbing began in earnest.

Fitzroy too would be marred by tragedy on the approach, when one of France's most talented young climbers, Jacques Poincenot, drowned in a botched river crossing, as the rope he had hoped to use for safety jammed, holding him instead pinned and helpless under water. His teammates pondered abandoning the expedition, but in the end pushed on. (The Aiguille Poincenot, one of Fitzroy's handsomest satellites, commemorates the lost climber.)

After three weeks of effort getting into position, with the team hunkering down in 125-mile-an-hour winds, Terray and Guido Magnone tackled the 2,500-foot pyramid. They succeeded only after both men led pitches of a higher grade of difficulty than had yet been solved in the expeditionary ranges. On the final headwall below the summit—after that revelatory outburst "Guido, the sardine tin!"—Terray pounded in the pair's last piton, then pulled himself up the cliff. A tentless bivouac ensued before the exhausted duo got off the last rappel and joined their jubilant teammates.

In a journal article the next year, Terray wrote, "Of all the climbs I have done, the Fitzroy was the one on which I most nearly approached my physical and moral limits." Nine years later, in *Conquistadors*, he saw no reason to revise that judgment.

Throughout the decade of the 1950s, Terray's appetite for what he called "mountain ranging" was astounding. Back from Fitzroy, he stayed briefly in Chamonix before heading off again to Peru, lured by the invitation of a pair of well-off and talented Dutch clients he had guided in the Alps. In the prime of life, brimming with confidence despite the deaths that had clouded his joy in the mountains, Terray now demonstrated his strength by knocking off the highest unclimbed peak in the central Andes, 20,981-foot Huantsan, with clients rather than colleagues as his ropemates.

For Terray, further expeditionary triumphs followed at the average rate of one a year. During the 1950s, no one else in the world was spearheading such bold deeds in the remote ranges at even half Terray's pace. There was the Makalu reconnaissance, culminating in the bagging of Chomolonzo with Couzy in 1954, then Makalu itself with Couzy the following year. Although Annapurna had cost its victors all but their lives, Makalu was such a smooth success that Terray confessed to a feeling of anticlimax, even of disappointment, on the summit. In a characteristically passionate flight, he later scolded his own hubris:

> Was I completely stupid, to be feeling like this? Madman, for whom there is no happiness but in desire, rejoice for once in reality, exult in this moment when, half borne up by the wind, you stand over the world. Drink deep of infinity: below your feet, hardly emerging from the sea of cloud that stretches away to the horizon, armies of mountains raise their lances toward you.

Never again would Terray undergo the experience he had freely chosen on Annapurna, where he gave up his summit chances first to haul loads to Camp IV, then to save Herzog and Lachenal. If Terray's team made a first ascent, Terray reached the summit himself. More often than not, he led the hardest pitches and was in the first pair to arrive on top.

Terray's choice of objectives after 1950 bore the stamp of his passion. The mountains that he sought out—usually not only unclimbed, but previously unattempted—were not necessarily the highest in their ranges; instead, they were the most beautiful and the most difficult. In Peru in 1956, Terray had an *annus mirabilis:* as warm-up for his team's principal objective, he made the first ascents of two difficult mountains in the Cordillera Blanca, Veronica and Soray. Then the party turned its sights toward 20,046-foot Chacraraju in the Cordillera Vilcabamba, possibly the hardest mountain in the Peruvian Andes, declared impossible by both Austrians and Americans who had reconnoitered it.

Eschewing tented camps on the route, prepared instead to bivouac in the open, Terray led the ascent, as he had on Fitzroy, in brilliant lightweight style. The party arrived on top at 5:00 P.M. and descended *en rappel* by headlamp in the dark. Most expeditions would have turned toward home after Chacraraju, but Terray snagged the highly technical Taulliraju almost as an afterthought. In little more than two months, his team had claimed four of the finest unclimbed peaks in the Peruvian Andes, including its cynosure, Chacraraju.

One of Terray's paramount achievements was the first ascent of Jannu in 1962. This 25,295-foot Himalayan mountain, near Kanchenjunga in far eastern Nepal, was not the highest summit in the world still untrodden, but a group of French experts had deemed it, in Terray's words, "the most spectacular of all the unclimbed peaks . . . the most impregnable of nature's remaining fortresses." Fiendishly complex, with no weaknesses, Jannu defeated the best French climbers in 1959, to Terray's vexation. Stopped by an unclimbable crag 900 feet below the summit, the team, led by Terray, had to admit "that our ambition exceeded our abilities." Yet three years later, Terray led another attempt, solving the hardest pitches himself, paving the way by which the whole team eventually reached the top. In the same year, Terray climbed Chacraraju East in Peru (fully as hard as the mountain's main peak) and the Nilgiris, near Annapurna. From the latter summit, he gazed across at the north face of the mountain that had cost him and his comrades so much agony twelve years before.

Terray had never deceived himself about the risks of climbing. He had seen Francis Aubert and Jacques Poincenot killed before his eyes, and had grieved the loss of his two closest Annapurna teammates, Lachenal and Couzy. It was remarkable that in all his big-range mountaineering, Terray had never suffered a serious accident.

Yet in 1959, tragedy struck him again in the Alps of his backyard. On a routine traverse of the Fresnay Glacier, as Terray moved with a roped client in tow, a jumble of seracs collapsed above and avalanched over the two men. The client was instantly killed. Terray came to rest under fifteen feet of debris in the bottom of a crevasse, with a huge block of ice directly over him. In his glacial prison, he could barely twitch, let alone move.

Terray's escape is virtually without parallel in alpine annals:

> I managed by a series of contortions to reach a knife which I had by sheer chance left in my pocket. With its aid I was able to reach a cavity in the debris which, once again, had formed close to me by the merest luck. With an ice piton and my peg hammer I then carved out a gallery toward the light. Five hours later I reached the fresh air. This stay in the antechambers of death, where yet another companion was lost at my side, ripened me more than ten years of successful adventures.

As he turned forty in July 1961, Terray wrote the last pages of his autobiography, which Gallimard published within the year as *Les Conquérants de l'Inutile*. The book was immediately popular, for Terray was riding the crest of his fame as France's greatest active mountaineer. Two years later, the book was translated into English.

Conquistadors of the Useless (to use its English title) has its faults. From the outset, Terray set too leisurely a pace, so that halfway through the book he was only on the north face of the Eiger in 1947, with all his greatest climbs ahead. Recognizing this too late, he crammed his astounding decade of expeditionary triumphs after Annapurna into a mere forty-one pages. His early success with Rébuffat on the Col du Caïman thus occupies eleven pages, Chacraraju only a page and a half.

Terray's style can be plain and even clumsy. And his penchant for idealizing his comrades can get in the way of our seeing them as fully rounded characters.

Yet from humdrum paragraphs of route description or logistical summary, he bursts again and again into sudden passages of startling eloquence. All in all, there is so much that is vivid, true, and deeply pondered in *Conquistadors* that more than a few aficionados of mountain literature regard it as the finest climbing autobiography ever written.

As he neared the last pages of his book, Terray lapsed into a valedictory mood. Turning forty, he sensed that his best years lay behind him. He prepared to pass the baton to younger "tigers," and looked forward to the settled, self-accepting maturity he had vainly hoped Lachenal might find. *Conquistadors* ends with a paragraph as memorable and perfect as the closing lines of *Annapurna:*

> My own scope must now go back down the scale. My strength and my courage will not cease to diminish. It will not be long before the Alps once again become the terrible mountains of my youth, and if truly no stone, no tower of ice, no crevasse lies somewhere in wait for me, the day will come when, old and tired, I find peace among the animals and flowers. The wheel will have turned full circle: I will be at last the simple peasant that once, as a child, I dreamed of becoming.

Contrary, however, to his own valedictory prescription, Terray charged ahead in his early forties into expeditionary adventures every bit as grueling as Fitzroy and Makalu. In 1962 alone came the stunning trilogy of Jannu, Chacraraju East, and the Nilgiris. And in 1964, for the first time, Terray went to Alaska.

Very few Europeans had yet ventured into the subarctic mountains of "Seward's Icebox." The Duke of the Abruzzi, who seemed to have gone everywhere, had pulled off a dazzling first ascent of Mount Saint Elias way back in 1897, approaching North America's third-highest mountain from the seacoast. Heinrich Harrer, the veteran of the Eiger Nordwand, had enjoyed a single brilliant summer in 1954, when with the American legend Fred Beckey, he had claimed the first ascents of Mounts Hunter and Deborah. In 1961, Ricardo Cassin (the great Italian pioneer of the Walker Spur and the Piz Badile, whom a youthful Terray and

Lachenal had despaired of emulating), now fifty-two years old, crafted the first ascent of a rib in the center of the south face of McKinley, then the mountain's hardest route. Cassin's party had badly underestimated Alaskan cold, and several members incurred serious frostbite on the route.

By 1964, however, unlike the Andes, Alaska remained all but terra incognita to the top European climbers. Terray had first cast his eye on some of the territory's finest unclimbed mountains in 1955, but year after year, other expeditions had claimed his attention. During those years, he had corresponded often with Bradford Washburn, Alaska's finest mountaineer of the previous generation—the first man to climb McKinley three times and the author of a dozen first ascents of lower mountains. Washburn had tempted Terray with some of the breathtaking large-format aerial photos he had taken of Alaska's unclimbed prizes.

In 1964, Terray came to Alaska to try Mount Huntington, about ten miles south of McKinley. Though only 12,240 feet high, it was Alaska's Fitzroy. Many regarded it as the most beautiful mountain in the Alaska Range, and it promised to be the hardest climb in the McKinley massif.

Yet just like Cassin, Terray underestimated Alaskan conditions. With a very strong cohort of seven younger French alpinists, Terray landed on the Ruth Glacier in early May, planning to knock off Huntington and then move on to another objective, perhaps a new route on McKinley. Huntington, however, gave the team all they had bargained for.

The high winds and interminable storms reminded Terray of Fitzroy, but the severe cold surpassed that of Patagonia. None of the climbers had previously encountered the quality of ice and snow they ran into on Huntington, from rock-hard black ice to unconsolidated froth as airy as Styrofoam. Inching their way up the lacy, spectacularly corniced northwest ridge, the team made pitifully slow progress. After two weeks, they were nowhere near the final obstacles.

Meanwhile Terray had suffered the worst accident of his big-range career. Descending from a new high point, he felt a snow ridge crumble underfoot. To avoid falling into a crevasse, he made a small jump—a maneuver he had often performed in the Alps. But the ice was so hard his crampons skittered off: suddenly he was plummeting toward the void. Terray's partner, unprepared, hadn't bothered to belay, but stood tightening a crampon strap. Only a fluke kept both men from being snatched off the mountain to their deaths, when a thin fixed rope Terray had been trailing, anchored to a snow picket by the second team only moments before, brought him to a wrenching halt.

Terray had severely sprained his right elbow. There was no choice but to descend to Base Camp. Several days later, his right arm useless, Terray watched his teammates head back up the mountain. For the first time ever, he faced the prospect of lingering impotent in the rear, while his companions completed a first ascent. As he later wrote in the *American Alpine Journal*:

> All morning, sick at heart, I watch my friends climb. Rarely in my entire life have I felt so lonely and so miserable. I have not even the will to prepare lunch. During the night I can scarcely sleep, but by morning I have made up my mind.

Terray's resolve was to climb the mountain one-handed. Pulling on his ascending device with his good left hand, he hauled himself brutally up the fixed ropes to Camp I to join his comrades.

On May 25, Jacques Batkin and Sylvain Sarthou stood on top of Huntington. The next day, the other six members followed their track to the summit. As on Makalu, the whole team had collaborated in a first ascent that saw every member top out.

Terray felt a sense of despondency as he headed down. "On this proud and beautiful mountain," he later wrote, "we have lived hours of fraternal, warm and exalting nobility. Here for a few days we have ceased to be slaves and really been men. It is hard to return to servitude."

By 1965, DON JENSEN AND I had begun to think of ourselves as Alaska veterans, even though we were only twenty-two. Despite our failure on the east ridge of Mount Deborah the previous summer, we set our sights on an equally difficult objective for our third expedition. Bradford Washburn had become our mentor. In the inner sanctum of his office atop the Boston Museum of Science (which Washburn had founded), I spent long hours leafing through his thirty years' worth of aerial photos of Alaskan mountains.

By February, Don and I had settled on Mount Huntington as our challenge. Terray's team had beaten us to the first ascent, but in Washburn's pictures we had found a plausible route on the mountain's west face. It would require landing on the Tokositna Glacier, where no one had ever been, and it looked harder than anything yet climbed in Alaska, but we were at the apogee of youthful ambition.

In bad French, I wrote to Jacques Soubis, the author of the article on Huntington's first ascent that had appeared in *La Montagne et Alpinisme*. He was generous with advice and encouragement, informing us that Terray's team had considered only the northwest and east ridges as likely routes on Huntington, but that he would hesitate to call the west face—however grim it looked—impossible.

On Deborah, Don and I had realized that a two-man party was stretching the odds too thin in Alaska. For Huntington, we recruited a pair of younger Harvard climbers, Matt Hale and Ed Bernd. Relatively inexperienced, they seemed daunted by Don's and my ambition, but they could hardly say no to so heady an invitation.

By that year, Don's and my identification with Terray and Lachenal had become full-blown. On Huntington, however, it was Terray who seemed an almost tangible presence. We had all but memorized his article in the *American Alpine Journal*. Over and over again, Don would quote his favorite line from that account: "It is not the goal of *grand alpinisme* to face peril, but it is one of the tests one must undergo to deserve the joy of rising for an instant above the state of crawling grubs." Like the French, we built a snow cave for our Base Camp. As the bad weather raged outside, I would cite another of Terray's lines: "I have read somewhere that in this range the big storms can last for eight or ten consecutive days." (On Deborah and McKinley, we had sat out several interminable tempests.)

There was a kind of adolescent hubris in comparing ourselves to Terray. We knew in our hearts that, as alpinists, we weren't in the same league with the French master. None of us, in fact, would ever climb in the Himalaya or the Andes. But in this one part of the world we had chosen as our specialty—the Alaska Range—we dared to believe that at the height of our twenty-two-year-old powers we might match the recent deed of a forty-three-year-old veteran who had confessed in his autobiography, "My own scope must now go back down the scale."

After a month of discouragements and setbacks, we climbed the west face, arriving all four on top at 3:30 A.M. on July 29. Our triumph was short-lived: only twenty hours later, as Ed and I descended in the dark, a rappel anchor failed. Without uttering a sound, Ed fell 4,000 feet to the lower Tokositna Glacier, to a basin so inaccessible we never had a chance to search for his body.

News of our ascent reached France, where it caught Terray's ear. Having never heard of these four young upstarts from Harvard, Terray was incredulous that little-known Americans might have succeeded on a route harder than his northwest ridge. He wrote Washburn inquiring whether or not we might have lied about the climb. Washburn wrote back, vouching for our ascent, and he told us about Terray's doubt-filled missive.

It was of course disappointing to have our hero wonder whether we were liars. Yet at the same time, for Don and me, it was the giddiest imaginable gratification to know that we had crossed the radar screen of his consciousness. Once Washburn had convinced Terray that we were telling the truth, perhaps we might even correspond with our hero, swapping details of our respective battles on Mount Huntington. Perhaps in the future we might even meet.

Having turned forty-four that summer, Terray was far from ready to see his scope go down the scale. He had, in fact, begun to experience a rejuvenation. Even as he had become the finest expeditionary mountaineer of his time, Terray had seen his skill as a rock climber deteriorate to the point where, on a local crag with youthful companions in top-notch shape, he felt embarrassed by his ineptitude. Such a progression is normal for aging mountaineers. As Terray's generation was the first to discover, climbing was becoming so specialized a business that no single practitioner could excel in both big-range mountaineering and pure rock gymnastics. Other veterans accepted that fact, and contented themselves with leading expeditions. For Terray, to climb anywhere at less than an Olympian level was intolerable.

He set out, then, to teach himself all over again how to rock-climb. At Fontainebleau, the forest full of giant boulders south of Paris, he devised for himself a training program rigorous enough to challenge a hungry twenty-two-year-old. And he deliberately chose ropemates in their twenties for rock climbs that might test his refurbished mettle.

One of his favorite partners was his Huntington teammate, Marc Martinetti, who was only twenty-five years old. A native of Chamonix, boyishly good-looking, he had already been elected, despite his tender age, to the elite Compagnie des Guides. Martinetti had notched his belt with some of the finest faces in the Alps, including the Walker Spur on the Grandes Jorasses and the north face of the Dru (two of Rébuffat's six great north faces). Optimistic, a great joker, fiercely independent, he had recently married a young local beauty.

On September 19, 1965, Terray and Martinetti set out for a long but moderate rock-climb in Terray's beloved Vercors, the *préalpes* south of Grenoble where Terray had first learned to climb three decades earlier. When the pair had not returned by dark, a search party set off to look for them. At the foot of the wall, they found the bodies of Terray and Martinetti, still roped together. From the damage the men had undergone (their helmets were smashed to pieces), the searchers concluded that they must have fallen as far as a thousand feet. At the top of the route, easy but steep grassy slopes are interspersed with short sections of cliff. It would have been normal for Terray and Martinetti to stay roped here, but to place only the occasional piton. No doubt one man had slipped, pulling off the other. Or perhaps one had seized a loose block and lost his balance, like Francis Aubert on the approach to the Aiguille Noire de Peuterey.

In France, Terray's death was the occasion for national mourning. In my first year of graduate school in Denver, I bought the latest issue of *Paris-Match*, with Terray's rugged portrait on the cover, above a blurb reading "*Mort pour la Montagne.*" Staring at the photos that highlighted Terray's extraordinary career, I mourned, for my own selfish reasons, the near miss of our intersection in life.

Terray had died, I knew, before he could have received and read Washburn's letter. Every young climber's dream is to win the notice of his heroes. I had done that, across two decades and the Atlantic Ocean, only to have Terray die wondering whether some American college kids had faked the second ascent of Mount Huntington.

ONE APRIL DAY IN 1999, Michel Guérin and I decided to hike up to the base of the climb on which Terray had been killed thirty-four years before. Michel himself had done the climb at age twenty. "It was not a pilgrimage for me then," he told me. "When you're young, you don't care about death."

We drove route N75 south out of Grenoble, then left the highway to climb past farmsheds on a country road. It was a damp day, and the long limestone wall of the Vercors lay mostly hidden in mist to the east. The snows of a record winter had been slow to melt: above 4,000 feet, the forest still lay blanketed in wet drifts. Slushy streams coursed everywhere through drab fields.

In the square at the center of the sleepy perched village of Prélenfrey, Michel spotted an inconspicuous plaque affixed to a limestone boulder. We got out to read it.

To Lionel TERRAY
Dead on the mountain, with
Marc Martinetti, 25 years ago.
His comrades in the S.E.S., of the
Compagnie STEPHANE (1/15th BCA)
19 September 1990

The S.E.S., Michel explained, was the Section des Eclaireurs et Skieurs—the Section of Scouts and Skiers; the BCA was the Bataillon de Chasseurs Alpins—the Battallion of Alpine Soldiers. Thus, on the twenty-fifth anniversary of his death, the survivors of Terray's doughty Compagnie Stéphane, with whom he had played his absurd and perilous games in World War II, had assembled in this obscure plaza to commemorate their comrade's passing. I wondered how often even the stray hiker came across this quiet memorial, or paused as we did to ponder it.

Where the dirt road plunged into snowdrift, we parked, got out, and started hiking up the slope. Mats of soggy dead leaves lay in the patches of clearing; birches leaned toward the higher drifts. Soon our feet were completely soaked. In the crisp air, there was only the faintest hint of a late spring.

The route we sought was in the center of a long wall called the Gerbier; its name was the Fissure en Arc de Cercle. With fog covering the upper two thirds of the cliff, I could see only a gray, featureless precipice; but Michel had soon picked out the route. Pointing, he indicated landmarks he remembered from his own youthful ascent.

"The route was put up by Serge Coupé, who was on Makalu with Terray in 1955," said Michel. "Coupé did a lot of new routes in the Vercors and the Chartreuse. Everywhere you go around here, there's a *voie Coupé*."

We stopped to gaze at what we could see of the route. "You go up six or seven pitches there," said Michel, suddenly animated, waving his hands in the eternal pantomime of climbers recalling routes, "then there's a big traverse, then five more pitches. On the top, there are these razor-thin arêtes you have to traverse. Maybe that's why they didn't unrope." Later I read a route description of the fissure. In the accompanying diagram, the top of the cliff was reduced to a pair of stylized horizontal lines, marked "terraces— very easy."

Michel stared at the cliff, as fog drifted in and out, and speculated out loud: "Possibly the accident was due to a competition between the young, very good climber running ahead, with the older, heavier climber still trying to prove he could keep up. Or maybe it was the younger one who was overimpressed. The guiding season was just over. Normally, a guide is exhausted in September." We realized, as is so often the case in fatal climbing accidents, that we would never know what had happened that long-ago day. All the searchers had had to judge by was the rope still linking the dead bodies, with no piton attached.

I was filled with a heavy sense of gloom. No one else was about in this still-wintry landscape. Below us, a deer bounded noiselessly through the trees. I heard the unmistakable sound of rocks plunging down the cliff above. I looked up, but could not find the falling stones against the gray smear of the cliff. Michel had hoped the weather would be good enough for us to climb the route. In that despondent moment, I was glad it was not.

NOT EVERYONE IN FRANCE thought Lionel Terray a hero. Loyal to her husband's estrangement from Terray after Annapurna, Françoise Rébuffat took the man to task for his servility to Herzog. "Terray was a *lèche-bottes*," she told me bluntly, "a *béni-oui-oui*" (a bootlicker; a yes man).

During that interview with Françoise, less than a week before, I had been devastated to learn that Terray had not in fact written *Conquistadors of the Useless*. "It was ghostwritten for him by Roger Nimier, an academician," she said. "Terray was a bit of a country bumpkin. His writing, even in letters, was only semiliterate." Later Yves Ballu independently told me the same thing, naming Nimier, and other journalists confirmed the claim. Michel knew Nimier's name as Terray's original editor at Gallimard, but it came as a shock to him also to be told that Nimier was ghostwriter as well as editor. The consensus was that Terray could never have written a book by himself, let alone so good a one as *Conquistadors*.

A day or two after our hike in the Vercors, Michel took me to visit Terray's childhood home in Grenoble. The château, he had been told, had fallen into disrepair. The ground floor had been rented out to a writer, but the rest of the house had been locked up and left to its decay. The building still belonged to Terray's widow, Marianne, but she never visited the place.

In the course of reprinting *Les Conquérants de l'Inutile*, Michel had befriended Marianne, and he had gotten to know other relatives over the years. From one of them, he secured a key to the Grenoble château.

Terray, Michel knew, had spent weeks in Grenoble as he gathered his materials for his autobiography. We parked nearby, then walked the narrow streets of this oldest sector of the ancient town. On the Rue St. Laurent, we paused to read a plaque affixed high on the building's facade:

Here was born on the 25th of July 1921
LIONEL TERRAY
CONQUÉRANT DE L'INUTILE
From here he set out the 19th of September 1965
For his last climb in the Vercors

We ducked through a gate and started hiking up a steep stone staircase set into the hill that backs Grenoble. The grassy terraces were overgrown with dandelions and irises, and the moldering château was covered with violet wisteria. Old vines crawled helter-skelter across the walls backing each terrace step, and the woods loomed upward beyond. This "perfect world in which to realize the dreams of a child possessed with freedom and the wonders of nature," as Terray had called his backyard in *Conquistadors*, came alive for me now. I could picture Lionel as a boy trapping rats, shooting birds, and playing cowboys and Indians in this diminutive wilderness. No road had ever allowed vehicles to approach the château; instead, as we learned in a brief chat with the writer holed up on the ground floor, a donkey had hauled baggage up a steep track to the front door.

The key Michel had been lent opened a creaky door on the third floor. Inside, we stumbled in the dim light through an immense clutter of old furniture and junk. Everything was covered with dust; the wallpaper hung peeling from the walls; old mirrors had grown cloudy and speckled. The disarray of the rooms testified to a ménage in which no one seemed to have taken any pride. The third floor was like a multiroom attic full of stuff its owner had not had the heart to throw out.

We tiptoed among the bric-a-brac: a bust of Beethoven, an old, broken stereopticon, dusty books in dark bindings lying everywhere. In a closet, we found a heap of old photos, themselves coated with dust. Several images of a pretty woman on horseback evidently captured Terray's youthful mother in Brazil. A sheaf of newspaper clippings about Terray, we realized, represented a collection his father had put together. Despite his sire's disdain for mountain climbing, despite his nearly having disowned Lionel after he was kicked out of school, the old man had evidently taken pride in Terray's mature celebrity.

Michel had been given carte blanche by Marianne to look for old letters to or from Terray. There were piles and piles of dusty papers on tabletops, in closets, inside desk and bureau drawers, but an inordinate proportion of them seemed to be Terray's father's professional correspondence. Old bills, paid or unpaid, lurked everywhere, like reminders of mortality.

There was something claustrophobic and oppressive about the place. It was easy to picture the erstwhile grandeur of these upper-class rooms, and their decay was all the more wistful for that. It was hard to imagine the blithe mountaineer living even temporarily in such squalor.

We were about to go, when Michel, poking through another closet, came across a bulging green cardboard folder. A piece of adhesive tape had been stuck to it, on which, in blue ink, someone had written:

COURSES EXPLOR
BRESIL   ATEURS
DRAME Mt BLANC

"That's Terray's handwriting," said Michel, as he opened the folder. I peered over his shoulder, as he leafed through page after page of carefully scrawled manuscript. "And that's his handwriting too," Michel murmured.

A moment later, he let out a curse under his breath. "It's the manuscript of *Les Conquérants*," he said softly.

Later, back in Chamonix, we studied this lost relic carefully. I went through page after page of the published *Conquérants*, collating it with the handwritten manuscript. With growing elation, I said to Michel, "Hardly a word has been changed. It's word for word what Gallimard published. So much for Roger Nimier!"

Michel ultimately returned the manuscript to Marianne, who was delighted to have it. And we too were delighted. In a moment's accidental discovery, defying his detractors, we had restored the authorship of the book we both regarded as the finest climbing autobiography ever written to the man who not only had performed all those great deeds in the mountains, but had found, with no help from another, the right words to memorialize them.

TWO YEARS BEFORE, on my first visit to Chamonix, I had sought out Terray's grave in the cemetery. I found it just inside the gates, marked by an unshaped slab of brownish granite with a wooden plaque bolted to the stone. The inscription was even more laconic than Lachenal's, declaring only

LIONEL TERRAY

1921 + 1965

Above the name dangled a tiny bronze Christ. The earth covering Terray's coffin ran riot with pansies and forget-me-nots.

Michel Guérin arranged for me to meet Marianne Terray for tea in the chalet Terray had built in 1947. Cozy, full of sun, skillfully crafted out of a pale varnished wood, Terray's house, like Lachenal's, stands proud on a south-facing hillside, looking out not at the Dru but at the Aiguille du Midi.

At eighty-five, Madame Terray was active but hard of hearing. She found my French incomprehensible, so Michel served as interpreter. "Now you mustn't wear me out," she scolded at the outset. But then she became talkative. "Maurice Herzog was not a very well organized leader," she recalled. "He was full of disorder. But physically and morally he was full of courage.

"Because of his success, he became a bit vain and troubled. He loves the glory. And he is very seductive with the ladies. But after the death of Lionel, he did everything he could for me and the children."

"Marianne goes three times a week to Lionel's tomb," Michel had told me before our visit. "She talks to him, asks his advice. If she finds her lost eyeglasses, it's thanks to Lionel."

Now Marianne concurred. "He is always present. For me, he isn't dead. For the children also. I don't believe in death. He's somewhere else. I don't know where. He's just gone somewhere."

Despite their falling out, Rébuffat had asked Marianne's permission to help carry Terray's coffin in his funeral. The request had deeply moved her.

The chalet had the feeling of being still inhabited by Terray. Given free rein of the house since he had worked on his reprint of *Conquistadors*, Michel took me on a tour. The study was like an accidental museum. There, on a shelf, stood a picture of Francis Aubert, Terray's young companion killed on the approach to the Aiguille Noire—impossibly handsome, his face full of guileless ebullience. On one wall a picture of the Eiger; on another, a familiar photo of Terray surmounting an overhang with metal stirrups, and a photo of Terray the father carrying his son on his shoulders.

Yet another wall bore Terray's framed marriage announcement. Nearby were a photo of Lachenal and a drawing of Couzy.

Mounted on a wall in the antechamber to the study I found Terray's belated Legion of Honor medal, awarded in later years for his alpinism, not for Annapurna. There was also a framed commendation for his heroism in the war. I read a personal letter to Marianne from de Gaulle himself, mourning the death of Lionel, "who carried so high the worldwide reputation of French alpinism."

Michel started going through drawers. I saw a chaos of loose slides, letters, old mountain journals. We found, still rolled in the mailing tube, four large-format Washburn photos of Huntington, with a 1965 interoffice memo attached: "Un petit souvenir d'Alaska—Brad."

Marianne invited Michel to look inside a high cupboard. On tiptoe, he pulled open the door, reached inside, and retrieved an old, scarred rope and a beat-up rucksack. "I've never seen this before,"

Michel mused. The pack had holes torn in it. Michel opened it. Inside, we saw a smashed headlamp, stirrups, broken carabiners.

It hit us both at the same moment. This was the rope and pack and hardware Terray had been carrying on his fatal climb in the Vercors in 1965. Never before had Marianne chosen to show these relics to Michel.

I looked at my friend. Stricken—for Terray had been the hero of his youth too—he turned away. Tears choked the back of my throat.

In the silence, I took one of Terray's broken carabiners in my hands, and turned it this way and that. It was as close as I could come to meeting the man.

TEN

Une Affaire de Cordée

BEFORE THE SUN ROSE THAT MORNING of June 3, 1950, Louis Lachenal and Maurice Herzog struggled to get dressed in their camp at 24,600 feet. "We could not light the stove," Lachenal later wrote in his diary, without offering an explanation. "It was very cold."

Without the stove to melt snow, the men had had nothing to drink since a few cups of tea the evening before. They had slept not at all, as the violent wind in the night threatened to rip the tent from its platform, despite the pitons that anchored its uphill pull-outs. It took a concerted effort for both men to force their feet into their frozen leather boots. Lachenal was unable to fasten his gaiters over his ankles, so he left them in the tent. Both men strapped their crampons onto their boots. Because the snowfield stretching above them looked easy, they did not bother to rope up. The pair were off by 6:00 A.M.

Soon, as the sun crept over the skyline to their left, the men emerged from the icy shadow of Annapurna's east ridge into flooding sunlight. Already, however, Lachenal's feet were numb. He stopped to take off his boots and rub some feeling into his feet—as virtually all the team members had done even below Camp V. "This didn't help much," Lachenal later wrote, "because there was a fairly cold wind." As he sat there chafing his stockinged feet, "Momo told me that in the war he had often felt as cold as this and that his feet had always come back to life." With difficulty, Lachenal got his boots back on, and the men continued, plodding slowly upward and toward the right across the interminable snowfield.

"For my part," Lachenal wrote in his diary, "I moved slowly but without too much difficulty." Herzog, however, was beginning to lapse into a trance. Of this silent trudge in the cold, he later wrote, "Each of us lived in a closed and private world of his own. . . . Lachenal appeared to me as a sort of specter." Once more, according to Herzog, Lachenal voiced his fear of frostbite: "We're in danger of having frozen feet. Do you think it's worth it?" Herzog's own feet had gone dead, but he wiggled his toes and climbed on, convinced this was simply another passing numbness such as he had often undergone in the mountains.

Curiously, Lachenal never mentions in his diary the pivotal event of the day—although he acknowledges it in the "Commentaires" he wrote five years later. This was the exchange in which Lachenal suggested turning back, giving up all chances for the summit. For forty-five years, the only rendering of that critical moment available to the public was Herzog's. *Annapurna* fails to make clear at what point in the day the exchange took place, although a few sentences before, Herzog notes, "We still had a long way to go to cross [the summit snowfield], and then there was that rock band—would we find a gap in it?"

Here, then, is the version of that brief exchange that *Annapurna* presents, stripped of Herzog's internal commentary. Lachenal suddenly grabs his partner and says, "If I go back, what will you do?"

"I should go on by myself."

"Then I'll follow you."

In the next paragraph, Herzog feels all the weight of ambiguity and indecision lifted from his shoulders:

> The die was cast. I was no longer anxious. Nothing could stop us now from getting to the top. The psychological atmosphere changed with these few words, and we went forward now as brothers.

Every reader of *Annapurna* has thus understood the crucial exchange as a simple case of Lachenal's faint heart given fresh courage by Herzog's stiff resolve.

By now, Herzog's trance has taken hold of him:

> I had the strangest and most vivid impressions, such as I had never before known in the mountains. There was something unnatural in the way I saw Lachenal and everything around us. . . . [A]ll sense of exertion was gone, as though there were no longer any gravity. This diaphanous landscape, this quintessence of purity—these were not the mountains I knew: they were the mountains of my dreams.

Lachenal, on the other hand, records the hours following the turnaround exchange in the plain, pragmatic terms of a climber seeking the route:

> After the traverse, a few rocks, neither difficult nor particularly congenial to climbing, then a couloir led us toward something that, from where we stood, looked like the summit. We climbed up to it. The top of the couloir was merely a kind of saddle from which

stretched, to the left, a sort of arête that once more seemed to lead to the summit. Oh, it was long!

For Herzog, to reach the summit was to clasp the top rung of the ladder of St. Theresa of Avila, the image that danced in his mind at the time. The climax of *Annapurna* comes in the ecstatic transport of that moment:

> Yes! A fierce and savage wind tore at us.
> We were on top of Annapurna! 8,075 meters . . .
> Our hearts overflowed with an unspeakable happiness.
> "If only the others could know . . ."
> If only everyone could know!

"How wonderful life would now become," Herzog rhapsodizes on the summit. Already, it would seem, he had stepped through the door of that "new life" that Annapurna would bestow on him, despite all his sufferings.

It could scarcely have been more opposite for Lachenal, whose diary notes the end of the quest in the flattest, most prosaic of language: "Finally we are there. An arête of snow festooned with cornices, with three summits, one higher than the others. It is the summit of Annapurna."

According to Terray, in his account in *Conquistadors*, by that evening, after his terrible fall past Camp V at dusk, Lachenal remembered nothing of the descent. But of the summit, he told his best friend (in Terray's paraphrase), "Those moments when one had expected a fugitive and piercing happiness had in fact brought only a painful sense of emptiness."

Only Herzog narrates the long spell while he lingered on top, staring at the horizon, savoring his ecstasy, posing for the camera with his three flags, changing from black-and-white to color film, while an increasingly wrought-up Lachenal urged immediate descent, finally exploding: "Are you mad? We haven't a minute to lose: we must go down at once." Only Herzog indicates that in the end Lachenal took off before him, almost running down the couloir that had led to the final ridge.

Of this summit performance, Lachenal's diary records only

the photo-taking. And rather than hinting at his own mounting anxiety over Herzog's delay, he states merely, "Without lingering any longer, we started down."

EVER SINCE 1950, THERE HAS BEEN a small cadre of skeptics within the mountaineering community who doubted that Herzog and Lachenal reached the summit on June 3. The doubts spring in part from the celebrated summit photo, in which Herzog holds aloft the Tricolor tied to his ice axe. Beyond the triumphant climber, a snow slope seems to angle toward higher ground. Frankly speaking, the summit photo does not look as though it had been taken on a summit.

In 1957, *Berge der Welt*, the official journal of the Swiss Alpine Club, posthumously published an interview with Lachenal; Swiss commentators then appended the judgment that Lachenal's memories of the summit were "insufficient." Two years later another Swiss, Marcel Kurz, wrote, "Lachenal told us that he had lost all memory of that summit day."

To put the Swiss canards in perspective, it helps to remember that before the war it was the British, the Germans, and the Swiss who had led the way in the Himalaya. The French had only their 1936 attempt on Gasherbrum I to their credit. That the first 8,000-meter summit would be bagged by a French team might stick in the craws of some of their rivals.

Yet as I traveled in France in 1999, I found that skepticism alive and flourishing among certain French journalists. Charlie Buffet, of *Libération*, told me, "Almost everyone who gets involved in this controversy thinks they didn't make the summit." Buffet pointed out that Herzog had described "a fierce and savage wind" stinging the pair's faces on top; yet in the famous photo, Herzog seems to be holding the flag taut as if to simulate a wind-blown banner on an all but windless day. (It is possible that Herzog is instead holding the flag to keep it from flapping in the wind.)

Buffet had asked Herzog point-blank if he had made the summit. "He answered, 'There is a polemic of doubt about the 1960

Chinese expedition to the north side of Everest. They can produce no evidence they reached the summit. People come to me and ask me if it was true that we made the summit. My answer is, "If one climber says he made the summit, you have to believe him." ' "

Buffet paused, then said, "I thought this was a strange answer.

"Some people in Chamonix," Buffet went on, "tell a story of meeting Lachenal one day in 1954 or '55, when he was very drunk, and he admitted he hadn't been to the summit."

Buffet went so far as to play out a purely speculative scenario for me, which he said certain observers had toyed with: "Lachenal wants to turn around, Herzog does not. At last Herzog agrees to turn around, if Lachenal will agree to say they'd been to the summit."

Jean-Michel Asselin, editor of *Vertical*, had interviewed Rébuffat extensively during the 1980s. Asselin told me, "When Rébuffat spoke of the summit, he didn't say that Lachenal and Herzog hadn't made the top. But when he talked about it, he had a certain irony about his look."

Françoise Rébuffat, on the other hand, insisted that Gaston had never doubted that his friends had reached the summit. And Yves Ballu countered Asselin by saying, "Rébuffat gave me no reason to doubt the summit. This is too serious a question to base the answer on a grimace."

In the 1996 controversy provoked by the publication of Ballu's biography of Rébuffat and Guérin's edition of Lachenal's diary, the question of the summit burst to the fore. Herzog countered with an air of patient exasperation. To *Le Monde*'s query about the summit photo, he answered, "Because of the perspective, the photo gives the impression that above us there was a snow arête. In fact, that 'arête' only reached to my waist. We could not climb to the very crest of that ridge, which was in truth a cornice. But we were indubitably on the summit."

To cast light on the question, *Montagnes* published for the first time all five black-and-white photos purportedly taken on the summit. By themselves, they are inconclusive. Yet they raise other interesting points of debate. Four of the photos were taken of Herzog by Lachenal, using Herzog's Foca camera. Two (including the famous image) show Herzog hoisting the French flag; one, the CAF flag; and the fourth, the banner of Kléber-Colombes. The fifth photo Herzog took of Lachenal. It is badly out of focus, but in it Lachenal sits slumped against a rock in a decidedly unvictorious posture.

In Chamonix, Elisabeth Payot told me, "What's incredible is that Herzog kept this photo hidden until the death of Lachenal." Certainly Lachenal had seen the photo. As they worked together preparing the text of Carnets du Vertige, Lachenal told Philippe Cornuau, "I took a photo of Herzog that was clear. He took one of me that was fuzzy. And I'm the one who was supposed to be out of my mind." Cornuau also told me, "Lachenal was deeply shocked that Herzog would raise the banner of Kléber-Colombes—that a man would hold up the flag of the company that employed him."

There is perhaps a simple explanation of the odd perspective in the summit photos, which commentators have overlooked. Lachenal's diary for June 3 says,

> A little below [the top] on the north face a rock bench received us, so that we could take the several official photographs that we had to take. CAF, French flag, black [and white], color. I didn't take my own camera out of my pack, but used Momo's Foca.

From a ledge a bit below the summit, of course, the "summit photo" would appear to be taken somewhere short of the top.

It is possible that Herzog and Lachenal, hypoxic and exhausted, could have confused a bump on the ridge for the summit. It is even possible to entertain suspicions of a hoax. But I am inclined to second the characteristically gnomic remark Michel Guérin offered Le Monde: "If Lachenal had wanted to avoid writing that he was on the summit, he would not have worded it otherwise."

Whatever his faults, Lachenal had a bedrock integrity. His diary is full of blunt truths that more squeamish expeditioneers (including Herzog) preferred to veil. Had Lachenal chosen to fake the summit, would he have described to Terray that very evening his emptiness on top? Would he not have concocted an imagined transport more akin to Herzog's? For me, the plain statement in Lachenal's diary settles the case: "It is the summit of Annapurna."

IN JANUARY 2000, thinking I had learned virtually all I could know about Annapurna 1950, I visited Chamonix once more, only to be startled out of my complacency by an extraordinary encounter with a man named Leonce Fourès. Just a few weeks before, Fourès had first met Michel Guérin, from whom he had learned about my researches.

Over dinner, Fourès unveiled his revelations. A mathematician in his seventies from the south of France, he had been a climber of modest abilities but a very close friend of Rébuffat and Lachenal, as well as a classmate of Couzy. (Both Françoise Rébuffat and Jean-Claude Lachenal later verified the depth of those associations.)

Fourès seconded Philippe Cornuau's suggestion that, when Herzog had pulled out his Kléber-Colombes flag on the summit, Lachenal had been shocked and disgusted. But Fourès went on to say that Lachenal had later told him that when Herzog had changed the film in his camera to color, he had handed the black-and-white cartridge to Lachenal, who had kept it on his person. Some forty hours later, as the four men shivered through their bivouac in the providential crevasse, Lachenal, unable to find his boots among the drifts of fine snow the pre-dawn avalanche had dumped into the crevasse, had despaired of getting off the mountain alive. He had then, Fourès claimed, given the black-and-white cartridge to Rébuffat, making his friend promise that he would never let Herzog get his hands on the Kléber-Colombes photo.

Rébuffat had smuggled the roll of film back to France, Fourès went on, developed it, and returned all the photos to Ichac except the picture of Herzog hoisting the flag of his tire company, which he had jealously guarded until his death in 1985. As punishment for his subversion, Rébuffat was never invited on another FFM-financed expedition. I had assumed—as both Yves Ballu and Françoise Rébuffat had told me—that after Annapurna, Rébuffat had simply chosen never again to climb in the remote ranges. But

Fourès insisted that Rébuffat had told him he would have dearly loved to accompany Terray on such South American jaunts as his Fitzroy or Chacraraju expeditions. It was this sacrifice that Rébuffat alluded to in telling Fourès, "I have paid a heavy price."

On first hearing this outlandish story, both Michel and I were inclined to skepticism. The Annapurna controversy, as Michel pointed out, had brought the fantasists out of the woodwork. Had such a covert exchange taken place in the crevasse, why hadn't Lachenal written about it in his *Carnets*? Why had Françoise Rébuffat never breathed a hint of it? (Later Françoise confirmed that among Gaston's papers, she had found three or four contact prints of the Kléber-Colombes photo.)

Yet in person Fourès seemed a modest and intelligent man, with no particular axe to grind. And the more we mulled over what the man had told us, the more both Michel and I realized that the bizarre story tied up all kinds of loose ends. It might explain why Ichac had searched Rébuffat for hidden film cartridges in Kathmandu. It could very well explain why the Kléber-Colombes photo was not published until 1996 (by *Montagnes* magazine). The tire company had made the single largest donation to the expedition budget; Fourès set the figure at 500,000 francs. Had Herzog returned with a photo of the company's banner hoisted on the summit of Annapurna, what better advertising coup could Kléber-Colombes possibly have devised? If the firm had the photo in their possession, what earthly reason could prevent them from using it? Finally, Fourès's story might help explain Rébuffat's bitterness over Annapurna in later life.

By the end of the evening in Chamonix, I was awash in a mixture of confusion and fascination. The full ambiguity of what had happened on that distant mountain almost fifty years ago came home with a vengeance, and I realized that no single person could ever grasp the whole truth of Annapurna 1950.

BROODING IN LATER YEARS about the expedition, heeding his wife's admonitions not to make a public fuss about his doubts and disappointments, Rébuffat pondered the theatricality of Herzog's sum-

mit performance. In the most trenchant of the aphoristic notes he
jotted down about Annapurna in the 1980s, Rébuffat distilled his
misgivings into the single pithiest commentary on the summit day
ever penned:

> After the sequence of the flags, this jingoistic and supremely
> pragmatic moment, Maurice organized his ecstasy. Losing, if not his
> reason, at least his sense of reality, he began complacently to soar,
> plunged into a kind of happiness, a beatitude of the moment when a
> sense of the real ought to have been primordial. . . . Lachenal was
> aware: what good does it do to reach a summit if it means losing
> one's feet? His repeated entreaties had no effect, so he began
> the descent in order that Maurice would come to his senses and
> follow him.

Yet the last word on Annapurna deserves to be Lachenal's.
Bernard George, assembling his 1999 documentary on the legendary expedition, viewed all the period newsreel and feature
footage he could find. "In the hospital [in Chamonix]," George told
me, "not a word comes out of Lachenal's mouth. In all these old
films, I heard the voices of Terray, Rébuffat, and of course Herzog.
But I could find not a trace of Lachenal's voice."

Only in those last seven paragraphs of his 1955 "Commentaires"—suppressed entirely by Gérard Herzog—does Lachenal at
last speak. As he begins to discuss the summit day, he warns his
readers that they should not expect from him any absolute truths.

> That my memories sometimes differ from those of Maurice Herzog
> is a very normal business, when one thinks of the tension under
> which we attempted the summit and of the retreat in complete
> disorder (I measure my words) that immediately followed our
> success. . . . There was a divergence [in our memories], that
> is all.

Yet in the next breath, Lachenal takes issue with his portrait in
Annapurna. For five years, he knew, he had been "consistently de-
picted as badly affected by the altitude, by the final struggle, and especially by the fall that I took in the vicinity of Camp V." Herzog,

Lachenal complains, had implied "that I no longer knew what I was doing." Yet his cries for help, which Terray heard and which guided him to his fallen friend's side, and before that his instinct to plunge his gloveless hands into his pack to save them, were both, Lachenal insists, the reflexes of a sane man doing what he had to do to survive—not the hysterical responses of a climber driven half mad by his ordeal. As for Herzog's vignette of Lachenal trying to seize Terray's axe to descend alone to Camp II—Lachenal denies this ever took place.

Yet none of these discrepancies matter, continues Lachenal, because the descent became a multiplying sequence of errors and desperate acts. As the four men had stumbled lost through the fog late on the afternoon of June 4, Herzog saw Lachenal's behavior as proof of his dementia: "Perhaps he was not quite in his right mind. He said it was no use going on; we must dig a hole in the snow and wait for fine weather. He swore at Terray." Now Lachenal reclaims his exhortation at that grim moment as "not the counsel of an unbalanced man, but of a sane one."

> We were all sorely tried by the altitude—as I said, this was normal. Herzog noted as much about himself. Beyond that, however, he was illuminated. Marching toward the summit, he had the sense of fulfilling a mission, and I truly believe he thought of St. Theresa of Avila on the summit. As for me, I wanted above all else to go down, and that is exactly why I believe I kept my head on my shoulders.

At last, Lachenal turns to the pivot point below the summit, when he had raised the possibility of descending rather than pushing on toward the top. It is worth putting that decision in historical perspective.

Three years after Annapurna, the talented and driven Austrian climber Hermann Buhl would reach the summit of Nanga Parbat alone. On the only 8,000-meter peak whose first ascent was a solo achievement, Buhl won his lasting glory and fame, at the cost, like Herzog and Lachenal, of losing all his toes to frostbite.

In the decades since that Golden Age of Himalayan mountaineering, however, some of the strongest climbers in the world have perished as they pushed beyond their limits trying to reach 8,000-meter summits. Along the way, an inordinate number have lapsed into trance states not unlike Herzog's. In 1996, for instance, during the memorable Everest disaster, both immensely experienced chief guides, Scott Fischer and Rob Hall, drifted into apathetic stupors from which even the frantic entreaties of their teammates (in Hall's case, over the radio) could not in the end budge them. The pull of the summit, intersecting with the fog of hypoxic trance, cost them their lives.

In this context, mountaineers have learned to reserve their highest praise for peers who have had the guts to turn back even as close as a hundred yards below the summit. Reinhold Messner, the finest high-altitude mountaineer of all time, the first man to climb all fourteen 8,000-meter peaks, survived this most dangerous game by more than once heeding the mountain's warning and turning back.

It was in such a state that Lachenal alone, on June 3, 1950, recognized the consequences of his pivotal decision. In his "Commentaires," he writes plainly, "I knew that my feet were freezing, that the summit would cost me them." (In the margin of the typescript, Devies ranted, "Between simply feeling cold and freezing, there is a difference. Lachenal never told me this story.")

In the last analysis, at this critical juncture, it was Herzog who miscalculated. It was he who mistakenly thought his feet would "come back" from temporary numbness, he who loitered in bliss on the summit when every minute squandered narrowed the two men's margin of safety, he who dropped his gloves on the descent. Though Himalayan history would have been radically altered, though there would have been no *Annapurna*, had Lachenal's canny judgment prevailed at the moment he proposed giving up the summit, the French team would have probably returned from the mountain intact and safe, after another gallant failure in the quest to reach the summit of the first 8,000-meter peak. Lachenal's instinct to turn around, with the summit tantalizingly close, was the right one.

"For me," continues Lachenal in his "Commentaires," "this climb was only a climb like others, higher than in the Alps but no more important. If I was going to lose my feet, I didn't give a damn about Annapurna. I didn't owe my feet to the Youth of France." And so, why continue toward the summit?

Thus I wanted to go down. I posed the question to Maurice to find out what he would do in that case. He told me he would keep going. I didn't need to judge his reasons: alpinism is too personal a business. But I guessed that if he continued alone, he would not return. It was for him and for him alone that I did not turn around.

Reading this passage in the typescript of the *Carnets*, Herzog was given pause. Instead of annotating the remark with the kind of marginal criticism he had indulged in on page after preceding page, he wrote poignantly, "I didn't sense this. Perhaps after all I was unfair." But Lucien Devies was unimpressed, scribbling, "C'est entièrement à revoir"—"This must all be rewritten." In the end, of course, Gérard Herzog suppressed the "Commentaires" altogether.

NO ONE EVER QUESTIONED Herzog's courage or perseverance. On Annapurna, whatever his faults, he never led from the rear. Without his ultimate effort, no one would have reached the summit in 1950. Nor does anyone doubt that *Annapurna* is a stirring, even a sublime narrative of bravery, endurance, and teamwork.

That Herzog's tale turns out not to be the whole truth of Annapurna in no way undercuts the fundamental heroism of its protagonists. The more we learn, from all the warring viewpoints, about what happened on that brilliant and tragic expedition, the more the loyalty and self-sacrifice of Terray and Rébuffat shine forth. Terray, in particular, played an extraordinary role: the strongest climber, he twice gave up his chance for the summit, and after only a brief hesitation he traded boots with Lachenal, risking frostbite to enable his best friend to stagger down the mountain.

When all is said and done, moreover, is there any deed in all of mountaineering history more noble than Lachenal's? For as he pushed on toward the elusive summit that bitter day in June, he knew quite clearly that he was sacrificing his feet to save his comrade's life.

With all the laconic eloquence of his writing at its best, he closes his "Commentaires" with a condensed statement of his truth. If there can never be a definitive last word on the complex and ambiguous saga that was Annapurna 1950, still, Lachenal's two sentences stand as its epigraph: "That march to the summit was not a matter of national glory. It was *une affaire de cordée.*"

Note on Sources and Acknowledgments

THE BEST-SELLING mountaineering book of all time, Maurice Herzog's *Annapurna* was first published in France by Editions Arthaud in 1951, in the United States by E. P. Dutton & Co. the year after. It is currently in print in the U.S. in a Lyons Press edition. Herzog's 1998 memoir, *L'Autre Annapurna* (Editions Robert Laffont), has not yet appeared in English.

Louis Lachenal's heavily expurgated *Carnets du Vertige* was first published in 1956 by Pierre Horay. The 1996 publication in a deluxe edition by Editions Guérin restores all the suppressed passages. The book has never been published in English.

Lionel Terray's admirable autobiography, *Les Conquérants de l'Inutile,* was first published by Editions Gallimard in 1961, then republished, also in a deluxe edition, by Editions Guérin in 1995. Translated into English as *Conquistadors of the Useless*, the book appeared in the United Kingdom in 1963 (Victor Gollancz, Ltd.) but is now out of print. A new English-language edition, however, is being jointly planned by Chessler Books in the U.S. and Baton Wicks Publications in the U.K. Terray's account of his 1964 first ascent of Mount Huntington in Alaska appeared in *The American Alpine Journal* for 1965.

Yves Ballu's biography, *Gaston Rébuffat: Une Vie pour la Montagne,* was published in 1996 by Editions Hoëbeke. It has not appeared in English. Rébuffat's masterly *Etoiles et Tempêtes* was published by Editions Arthaud in 1954, and in English, as *Starlight and Storm,* in 1957 (E. P. Dutton & Co.). Though that edition is now out of print, the book was republished in 1999 by The Modern Library.

Tom Patey's hilarious essay critiquing Rébuffat ("Apes or Ballerinas?") and his wicked ballad, "Annapurna," both appear in *One Man's Mountains* (Victor Gollancz, Ltd., 1973), currently in print in the U.S. in an edition by The Mountaineers Books. The Bernard George film on Annapurna, titled *Annapurna: L'Histoire d'une Legende,* aired in 1999 and is available in France on cassette.

The most important articles that appeared during and after the 1996 controversy were "Annapurna: L'Autre Verité," by Christophe Raylat, in *Montagnes* (December 1996); "La Conquête de l'Annapurna 'retouchée' par les guides Lachenal et Rébuffat," by Claude Francillon, in *Le Monde* (November 8, 1996); "Annapurna Premier 8,000," by Claude Deck, in *La Montagne et Alpinisme* (January 1997); "Sous le chapiteau vertical des guides de haute montagne," by Frédéric Potet, in *Dimanche 8* (December 9, 1996); "Annapurna, premier 8000 et sommet de désinformation," by Charlie Buffet, in *Libération* (November 25, 1996); "Le temps de la pose," by Jean-Michel Asselin, in *Vertical* (May 1998); and "Herzog: 80 ans et mille questions," by Benoît Heimermann, in *L'Equipe* (January 16, 1999). Herzog's letter to *Le Monde* appeared on November 13, 1996; Françoise Rébuffat's rejoinder on November 27.

I was disappointed, at the last minute, to be denied permission by Editions Robert Laffont to quote from *L'Autre Annapurna* at greater length than is covered by fair use, and to be denied, by the estate of Marcel Ichac, the chance to reproduce any of his photos from the expedition. In addition, Maurice Herzog refused to respond to my request for permission to reprint his summit photo of Lachenal.

MY PRIMARY DEBT in writing this book is to my French publisher, Michel Guérin, who not only rescued Lachenal's diary from oblivion but who first whispered in my ear that Annapurna 1950 was not exactly what Herzog had written. In the course of my researches, Michel became a fellow sleuth. He also opened doors for me all over France. In almost forty years of climbing, I have never met an alpinist with a surer grasp of the history and culture of our pastime than Michel, nor a cannier analyst of its ambiguities. By publishing my book in France, Michel puts himself in the potentially awkward situation of becoming a character in a book that appears under his imprint. I hope he can rest easy in that spot, for this is how it must be—there would have been no book without him.

Second only to Michel in the roster of my gratitude is Linda Dubosson, *le bon soldat*. Thoroughly bilingual, a keen student of language in all its nuances, she helped me through a number of interviews with sources whose spoken French, for one reason or another, veered into arcane pathways where I found myself completely lost. In the writing, Linda saved me from many a translating blunder. And her year-long enthusiasm for the project, her willingness to drop everything to answer my latest anxious query, served me immensely.

All the staff at Editions Guérin, and in particular Sylvie Monfleur and Catherine Cuenot, have been unfailingly helpful to me, as has Michel's wife, Marie-Christine, my sage and genial hostess on three happy trips to Chamonix. In Paris, my longtime friend Marie-France Moisi solved many knotty puzzles of language and meaning, and transcribed Françoise Rébuffat's reading of crucial passages of her late husband's otherwise indecipherable handwriting.

Many people in France who had various links to the Annapurna principals gave generously of their time, their memories, and their opinions. Particularly valuable were the testimonies of Jean-Claude Lachenal, Marianne Terray, Françoise Rébuffat, and Maurice Herzog. Also greatly useful were the reflections of Jean-Pierre Payot, Elisabeth Payot, Leonce Fourès, Philippe Cornuau, Lise Couzy, Mauricette Couttet, Antoine Terray, Jean-Claude Ichac, Michel Chevalier, Bernard George, Deborah Ford, Charlie Buffet, Benoît Heimermann, Yves Ballu, and Jean-Michel Asselin.

In the United States, the great mountaineer Tom Hornbein advised me on high-altitude physiology. I am grateful also to Duane Raleigh and the editors of *Climbing*, who published my initial article about the Annapurna controversy, and to Tom McCarthy, an editor at International Marine and Ragged Mountain Press (a division of McGraw-Hill), who first urged me to write a book about it.

As I wrote, several friends read and critiqued my chapters: they include Sharon Roberts, Matt Hale, Marie-France Moisi, Kim Millett, Susan Robertson, and Jon Krakauer. Jon was a fierce advocate of the project from the start, and an invaluable advisor along my path.

At Simon & Schuster—for whom this is my fifth book—I owe a huge debt to David Rosenthal for his belief in the book; to Fred Chase and Gypsy da Silva for their brilliant copyediting; and to Johanna Li, for her calm and ingenious resolution of a hundred irksome snags. Finally, to Bob Bender, the best friend I've made in book publishing and the best book editor I've ever worked with, I offer the weary gratitude of a long-distance runner whom his coach, with many a useful shout and prod, has once again guided to the finish line.

Index

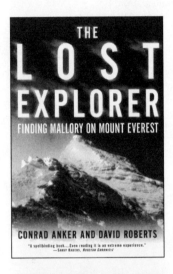

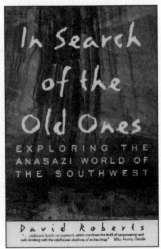